21世纪高等学校工程管理系列规划教材

工程管理专业英语

Specialty English for Project Management

主　编　孟宪强　王凯英
副主编　高　爽　王　淋
参　编　彭自强　史　巍　李晓琳
主　审　廖明军

机械工业出版社

本书以培养和提高读者阅读和笔译工程管理专业英语文献资料的能力为目标，增加了工程英语对话，具有一定的实用性。

本书素材选自近年来国内外工程管理各领域的经典教材、专著、论文，内容涉及工程管理各领域当前的状况和最新进展。本书主要内容包括项目管理体系、工程管理专业概论、工程项目前期策划、工程项目投标和招标管理、工程合同管理、工程成本管理、工程进度管理、工程施工现场管理、工程质量与安全、工程信息管理、工程风险管理、工程索赔、争端和仲裁、国际工程商务谈判。本书内容新颖、覆盖面广、系统性强、可读性好，是学习工程管理专业英语的实用教材。

本书既可供高等院校的工程管理专业和土木工程相关专业师生使用，也可作为工程管理专业人员及其他有兴趣人员的学习参考书。

图书在版编目（CIP）数据

工程管理专业英语/孟宪强，王凯英主编．—北京：机械工业出版社，2018.8（2022.9重印）

21世纪高等学校工程管理系列规划教材

ISBN 978-7-111-60554-6

Ⅰ．①工… Ⅱ．①孟… ②王… Ⅲ．①工程管理－英语－高等学校－教材　Ⅳ．①F40

中国版本图书馆CIP数据核字（2018）第167739号

机械工业出版社（北京市百万庄大街22号　邮政编码100037）
策划编辑：马军平　责任编辑：马军平　李　帅
责任校对：马军平　封面设计：张　静
责任印制：刘　媛
涿州市般润文化传播有限公司印刷
2022年9月第1版第3次印刷
184mm×260mm · 13.25印张 · 363千字
标准书号：ISBN 978-7-111-60554-6
定价：33.00元

凡购本书，如有缺页、倒页、脱页，由本社发行部调换

电话服务　　　　　　　　　　网络服务
服务咨询热线：010-88379833　机工官网：www.cmpbook.com
读者购书热线：010-88379649　机工官博：weibo.com/cmp1952
　　　　　　　　　　　　　　　教育服务网：www.cmpedu.com
封面无防伪标均为盗版　　　　金书网：www.golden-book.com

前　言

随着世界经济全球化的深入发展，工程项目管理国际化水平不断提高，努力学习和借鉴国际上先进的工程项目管理经验，在学习中借鉴、研究，不断提高工程管理水平，需要工程管理专业学生及工程管理从业人员有效阅读国外相关工程资料，掌握与国际工程项目相关的法规、条例及专业知识，能够与他人进行有效沟通。

本书分为15个单元，包括项目管理体系、工程管理专业概论、工程项目前期策划、工程项目投标和招标管理、工程合同管理、工程成本管理、工程进度管理、工程施工现场管理、工程质量与安全、工程信息管理、工程风险管理、工程索赔、争端和仲裁、国际工程商务谈判。

本书每单元的构成体现了循序渐进的学习原则。各单元的结构基本相同，每单元包括以下两部分内容：

Part I　Reading and Translating（阅读与翻译）

Professional Knowledge Guidance（专业知识导读）：本部分有别于其他书籍，是学习前的热身，加入部分中文专业知识点，目的是使学生回忆学过的专业知识内容，帮助学生对所学习的单元内容有总体的把握。

Text（课文）：每课课文与主题对应，篇幅完整。主要目的是帮助读者学习专业知识和专业词汇，掌握阅读技巧，能理解并正确通顺地翻译。本部分包括 **New Words and Phrases**（生词及短语）、**Notes**（注释）、**Exercises**（练习）。**New Words and Phrases** 为课文所涉及的专业、半专业词汇及相关短语。**Notes** 给出重点例句的参考译文，旨在帮助读者通过阅读课文深刻理解专业知识内涵，并掌握英汉互译的表达方式。**Exercises** 分为专业短语汉译英，及重点长难句英译汉，旨在帮助读者进一步通过练习掌握短语表达，以及长难句翻译技巧和方法，并进一步理解专业知识的中英文表达。

Passage A、**Passage B** 为补充课文内容，提供了两篇课外阅读材料，并给出生词及短语，目的是保持专业知识的完整性以及扩充学生的词汇量。教师可根据情况决定是否课堂讲授。

Part II　Speaking（工程英语实用对话）

本书工程英语实用对话部分，以FIDIC条款为依据，表达方式通俗易懂；模拟对话场景，极具实用性；覆盖了一般工程管理活动中的主要环节。

本书由北华大学孟宪强、盐城工学院王凯英任主编，北华大学高爽、王淋任副主编。具体的编写分工为：孟宪强编写 Unit 1、Unit 3、Unit 13，王凯英编写 Unit 2、Unit 6、Unit

15，武汉理工大学彭自强编写 Unit 4、Unit 7，王琳编写 Unit 5、Unit 11，高爽编写 Unit 10、Unit 12，黑龙江工程学院李晓琳编写 Unit 8、Unit 9 单元，东北电力大学史巍编写 Unit 14。

  本书参考了许多行业相关技术规范以及国内外大量的著作、教材、论文及其他研究成果，在此，对这些作者表示感谢！由于作者水平有限，书中难免有诸多不足，敬请各位读者批评指正。

编 者

目 录

前 言

Unit 1　Management System 1
 Part I　Reading and Translating 1
  Professional Knowledge Guidance 1
  Text　Introduction to Project Management 1
  Passage A　The Project Life Cycle 5
  Passage B　Selection of Professional Services 7
 Part II　Speaking 11
  Company Presentation 11

Unit 2　Project Management 12
 Part I　Reading and Translating 12
  Professional Knowledge Guidance 12
  Text　Project Management for Construction 12
  Passage A　Project Management and Construction Project 17
  Passage B　The Changing Environment of the Construction Industry 21
 Part II　Speaking 24
  Discussion of a Project at a Preliminary Phase 24

Unit 3　Construction Project of Planning and Decision 26
 Part I　Reading and Translating 26
  Professional Knowledge Guidance 26
  Text　Strategic Planning and Project Programming 26
  Passage A　Project Life Cycle and Economic Feasibility 30
  Passage B　Basic Concepts of Economic Evaluation 31
 Part II　Speaking 35
  Talks Between the Owner and the Program Manager 35

Unit 4　Bidding and Tendering of Construction Projects 37
 Part I　Reading and Translating 37
  Professional Knowledge Guidance 37
  Text　Standard Bidding/Tendering Documents 37
  Passage A　The Bidding /Tendering Process 44
  Passage B　Bidding Procedure of Construction Projects 47
 Part II　Speaking 52

  Collecting Tender Document ·· 52

Unit 5 Contract Management of Construction Projects ···················· 54
 Part I Reading and Translating ··· 54
  Professional Knowledge Guidance ·· 54
  Text Project Contract Management ·· 54
  Passage A Types of Contracts ·· 61
  Passage B Contract Provisions for Risk Allocation ································· 64
 Part II Speaking ·· 67
  The Owner Hands Over the Site Late ·· 67

Unit 6 Management of Engineering Cost ··· 69
 Part I Reading and Translating ··· 69
  Professional Knowledge Guidance ·· 69
  Text Project Cost Estimate and Cost Control ·· 69
  Passage A Cost Estimate ·· 75
  Passage B The Construction Project Budget ·· 78
 Part II Speaking ·· 81
  Project Estimating ·· 81

Unit 7 Project Planning and Scheduling ·· 83
 Part I Reading and Translating ··· 83
  Professional Knowledge Guidance ·· 83
  Text Construction Planing ··· 83
  Passage A Defining Work Tasks ·· 86
  Passage B Work Plan ·· 90
 Part II Speaking ·· 93
  Project Programming ·· 93

Unit 8 Construction Site Management ··· 95
 Part I Reading and Translating ··· 95
  Professional Knowledge Guidance ·· 95
  Text Factors Affecting Job-Site Productivity ·· 95
  Passage A Choice of Equipment and Standard Production Rates ············ 99
  Passage B Material Procurement and Delivery ······································· 101
 Part II Speaking ··· 104
  Field Management ·· 104

Unit 9 Quality Control and Safety During Construction ···················· 106
 Part I Reading and Translating ··· 106
  Professional Knowledge Guidance ·· 106
  Text Construction Quality Control and Management ································ 106
  Passage A Quality Control by Statistical Methods ································· 112
  Passage B Quality Control And Quality Assurance ······························· 113
 Part II Speaking ··· 115
  Site Inspection ··· 115

Unit 10　Model Interoperability in Building Information（BIM） …… 117
Part I　Reading and Translating …… 117
Professional Knowledge Guidance …… 117
Text　Engineering Innovation—Building Information Modeling …… 117
Passage A　Introduction about BIM …… 124
Passage B　BIM：A Primer …… 126
Part II　Speaking …… 129
Subletting the Construction Camp …… 129

Unit 11　Risk Management of Construction Projects …… 131
Part I　Reading and Translating …… 131
Professional Knowledge Guidance …… 131
Text　Construction Risk Management …… 131
Passage A　Construction Risks and Insurance …… 137
Passage B　Basics of Managing Risks …… 145
Part II　Speaking …… 147
Completion and Handing-Over …… 147

Unit 12　Construction Claims …… 149
Part I　Reading and Translating …… 149
Professional Knowledge Guidance …… 149
Text　Construction Claims …… 149
Passage A　Claims …… 156
Passage B　Contractor's Claims …… 161
Part II　Speaking …… 162
Claiming …… 162

Unit 13　Contract Disputes and Arbitration …… 164
Part I　Reading and Translating …… 164
Professional Knowledge Guidance …… 164
Text　Contract Disputes and Arbitration …… 164
Passage A　Resolution of Contract Disputes …… 168
Passage B　Construction and Engineering Consultancy …… 170
Part II　Speaking …… 173
Claim in Request of Flood …… 173

Unit 14　Project Financing …… 175
Part I　Reading and Translating …… 175
Professional Knowledge Guidance …… 175
Text　Facility Financing …… 175
Passage A　Project versus Corporate Finance …… 180
Passage B　Shifting Financial Burdens …… 182
Part II　Speaking …… 184
Pre-Qualification …… 184

Unit 15　International Business Negotiations ················· 185
Part I　Reading and Translating ················· 185
Professional Knowledge Guidance ················· 185
Text　Negotiation ················· 186
Passage A　Construction Negotiation Strategies and Skills ················· 191
Passage B　Negotiation Simulation：An Example ················· 196
Part II　Speaking ················· 199
Negotiation on a Joint Venture Agreement ················· 199
参考文献 ················· 202

Unit 1
Management System

Part I Reading and Translating

Professional Knowledge Guidance

1. 项目管理知识体系：是由美国项目管理学会（Project Management Institute，PMI）在 1987 年首先提出，PMI 公布了第一个项目管理知识体系（Project Management Body of Knowledge, PMBOK），于 1996 年推出第 1 版，2017 年修订为第 6 版。在这个知识体系中，把项目管理的知识划分为 9 个领域，分别是项目集成管理（Project Integration Management）、项目范围管理（Project Scope Management）、项目时间管理（Project Time Management）、项目费用管理（Project Cost Management）、项目质量管理（Project Quality Management）、项目人力资源管理（Project Human Resource）、项目沟通管理（Project Communication Management）、项目风险管理（Project Risk Management）和项目采购管理（Project Procurement Management）。

2. 中国项目管理知识体系：2001 年 7 月推出了第 1 版，2006 年 10 月推出第 2 版，中国项目管理知识体系文件——《中国项目管理知识体系》（Chinese Project Management Body of Knowledge，C-PMBOK）。

Introduction to Project Management

Need for Project Management

In most construction contracts, the contractor is given only one opportunity to set its price (the bid). From that point on, profits are determined by the project manager's ability to save money through better planning of daily operations and the skill to make good decisions. If a project is to be constructed within its established budget and time schedule, close management control of field operations is a necessity. Project conditions such as technical complexity, importance of timely completion, resource limitations, and substantial costs put great emphasis on the planning, scheduling, and control of construction operations. Unfortunately, the construction process, once set into motion, is not a **self-regulating mechanism** and requires expert guidance if events are to conform to plans.

It must be remembered that projects are one-time and largely unique efforts of limited time duration that involve work of a non-standardized and variable nature. Field construction work can be affected profoundly by events that are difficult, if not impossible, to anticipate. Under such uncertain and shifting conditions, field construction costs and time requirements are changing constantly and can seriously **deteriorate** with little or no advance warning. The presence of uncertainty in construction does not suggest that planning is impossible but rather that it will assume a **monumental** role in the success or failure of the project. The greater the level of uncertainty in the project, the greater the need for exhaustive project planning and skilled and unremitting management effort.

Under most competitively bid, fixed-sum contracts calling for construction services only, the general contractor exercises management control over construction operations. Self-interest is the essential motivation in such cases, the contractor being obligated by contract to meet a prescribed completion date and to finish the project for a **stipulated** sum. The surest way for the contractor to achieve its own objectives, and those of the owner in the bargain, is by applying some system of project management.

Serving the best interests of the owner is the primary emphasis of project control under other forms of contracts. Field management under design-construct, construction management, and many cost-plus contracts is directed principally toward providing the owner with professional advisory and management services to best achieve the owner's objectives. [1]

Project Management Characteristics

In its most common context, the term "management" relates to the planning, organizing, directing, and controlling of a business enterprise. Business management is essentially a continuing and internal activity involving that company's own personnel, finances, property, and other resources. Construction project management, however, applies to a given project, the various phases of which usually are accomplished by different organizations. Therefore, the management of a construction project is not so much a process of managing the internal affairs of a single company as it is one of coordinating and regulating all of the elements needed to accomplish the job at hand. [2] Thus, the typical project manager must work extensively with organizations other than his own. In such circumstances, much of his authority is conferred by contractual terms or power of agency and is therefore less direct than that of the usual business manager. Project management is accomplished largely through the personnel of different employers working closely together.

Discussion Viewpoint

As mentioned previously, the responsibility for field construction management rests with different parties, depending on owner preference and the nature of the contracting procedure. Whether the owner, architect engineer, general contractor, or a construction manager performs such duties is very much a matter of context. The basics of the pertinent management procedures are essentially the same, however, regardless of the implementing party. Nevertheless, to show detailed workings and examples of such management methods, it is necessary to present the material from the specific viewpoint of one of these parties. Thus, where the nature of the discussion requires such designation, the treatment of management methods herein will be from the particular viewpoint of the general contractor.

Management Procedures

Field construction has little in common with the assembly-line production of standardized products. Standard costs, time-and-motion studies, process flowcharts, and line-of-balance techniques—all traditional management devices used by the manufacturing industries—have not lent themselves well to general construction applications. [3] Historically, construction project management has been a **rudimentary** and largely **intuitive** process, aided by the useful but inadequate bar chart.

Over the years, however, new scientific management concepts have been developed and applied. Application of these principles to construction has resulted in the development of techniques for the management control of construction cost, time, resources, and project finance, treating the entire construction process as a unified system. Comprehensive management control is applied from inception to completion of construction operations.

Field project management starts with the onset of construction, at which point a comprehensive construction budget and detailed time schedule of operations are prepared. These constitute the accepted cost and time goals used as a blueprint for the actual construction process. After the project has begun, monitoring systems are established to measure the actual costs and progress of the work at periodic intervals. The reporting system provides progress information that is measured against the programmed targets. Comparison of field expense and progress with the established plan quickly detects exceptions that must receive prompt management attention. Data from the system can be used to make corrected forecasts of costs and time to complete the work.

The process just described is often called a management-by-exception procedure. When applied to a given project, it emphasizes the prompt and explicit identification of deviations from an established plan or norm. Reports that highlight exceptions from the standard enable the manager to recognize quickly those project areas requiring attention. As long as an item of work is progressing in accordance with the plan, no action is needed, but there are always plenty of problem areas that do require attention.

In addition to cost and time, the field management system is necessarily concerned with the management of job resources and with project financial control. Resources in this context refer to materials, labor, construction equipment, and subcontractors. Resource management is primarily a process of the advance recognition of project needs, scheduling and expediting of the resources required, and adjusting the demands where necessary. [4] Project financial control involves the responsibility of the project manager for the total cash flow generated by the construction work and the terms of the contract.

As indicated by the preceding discussion, there are several different aspects of a project control system. It must be recognized, however, that these aspects are highly interrelated segments of a total project management process.

New Words and Phrases

deteriorate　恶化，变坏；磨损；解体
monumental　非常的；不朽的
stipulated　规定的；约定的
rudimentary　基本的；初步的；退化的；残遗的
intuitive　直觉的；凭直觉获得的
self-regulating mechanism　自我约束机制

Notes

[1] Field management under design-construct, construction management, and many cost-plus contracts is directed principally toward providing the owner with professional advisory and management services to best achieve the owner's objectives.

设计—施工、项目管理及大量成本补偿合同下的项目现场管理主要是针对业主的，为其提供专业咨询及管理服务，以最大程度实现其目标。

[2] Therefore, the management of a construction project is not so much a process of managing the internal affairs of a single company as it is one of coordinating and regulating all of the elements needed to accomplish the job at hand.

因此，建设项目管理不仅仅是管理单一公司内部事务的过程，也是协调和规范与即将完成的该项工作的所有相关事项的过程。

[3] Standard costs, time-and-motion studies, process flowcharts, and line-of-balance techniques—all traditional management devices used by the manufacturing industries—have not lent themselves well to general construction applications.

标准成本、时间和作业效率研究、流程图以及平衡线法等所有制造业运用的传统管理方法，还没有很好地应用到一般的建筑管理上。

[4] Resources in this context refer to materials, labor, construction equipment, and subcontractors. Resource management is primarily a process of the advance recognition of project needs, scheduling and expediting of the resources required, and adjusting the demands where necessary.

本文中提到的资源是指材料、劳力、建筑设备及分包商。资源管理主要是提前识别项目需求、必需资源的计划和支出、必要时的需求调整等流程或活动。

Exercises

I. Translate the following phrases into English.

1. 项目管理知识体系
2. 项目阶段
3. 项目收益管理计划
4. 项目与开发生命周期
5. 工程项目质量管理

II. Translate the following sentences into Chinese.

1. If a project is to be constructed within its established budget and time schedule, close management control of field operations is a necessity.

2. In its most common context, the term "management" relates to the planning, organizing, directing, and controlling of a business enterprise.

3. As mentioned previously, the responsibility for field construction management rests with different parties, depending on owner preference and the nature of the contracting procedure.

4. In addition to cost and time, the field management system is necessarily concerned with the management of job resources and with project financial control.

5. Project financial control involves the responsibility of the project manager for the total cash flow generated by the construction work and the terms of the contract.

The Project Life Cycle

The acquisition of a constructed **facility** usually represents a major capital investment, whether its owner happens to be an individual, a private corporation or a public agency. Since the commitment of resources for such an investment is motivated by **market demands** or perceived needs, the facility is expected to satisfy certain objectives within the constraints specified by the owner and relevant regulations. With the exception of **the speculative housing market**, where the residential units may be sold as built by **the real estate developer**, most constructed facilities are custom made in consultation with the owners. A real estate developer may be regarded as the sponsor of building projects, as much as a **government agency** may be the sponsor of a **public project** and turns it over to another government unit upon its completion. From the viewpoint of **project management**, the terms "owner" and "sponsor" are synonymous because both have the ultimate authority to make all important decisions. Since an owner is essentially acquiring a facility on a promise in some form of agreement, it will be wise for any owner to have a clear understanding of the acquisition process in order to maintain firm control of the quality, timeliness and cost of the completed facility.

From the perspective of an owner, the project life cycle for a constructed facility may be illustrated schematically in Figure 1-1. Essentially, a project is conceived to meet market demands or needs in a timely fashion. Various possibilities may be considered in **the conceptual planning stage**, and the technological and economic **feasibility** of each alternative will be assessed and compared in order to select the best possible project. The financing schemes for the proposed alternatives must also be examined, and the project will be programmed with respect to the timing for its completion and for available cash flows. After the scope of the project is clearly defined, detailed engineering design will provide the blueprint for construction, and the definitive cost estimate will serve as the baseline for cost control. In the procurement and construction stage, the delivery of materials and the erection of the project on site must be carefully planned and controlled. After the construction is completed, there is usually a brief period of start-up or shake-down of the constructed facility when it is first occupied. Finally, the management of the facility is turned over to the owner for full occupancy until the facility lives out its useful life and is designated for demolition or conversion.

Of course, the stages of development in Figure 1-1 may not be strictly sequential. Some of the stages require iteration, and others may be carried out in parallel or with overlapping time frames, depending on

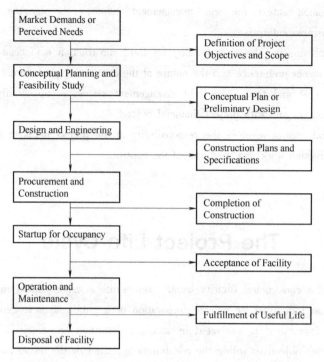

Figure 1-1 The Project Life Cycle for a Constructed Facility

the nature, size and urgency of the project. Furthermore, an owner may have **in-house** capacities to handle the work in every stage of the entire process, or it may seek professional advice and services for the work in all stages. Understandably, most owners choose to handle some of the work in-house and to contract outside professional services for other components of the work as needed. By examining **the project life cycle** from an owner's perspective we can focus on the proper roles of various activities and participants in all stages regardless of the contractual arrangements for different types of work.

In the United States, for example, the U. S. Army Corps of Engineers has in-house capabilities to deal with planning, budgeting, design, construction and operation of waterway and flood control structures. Other public agencies, such as state transportation departments, are also deeply involved in all phases of a construction project. In the private sector, many large firms such as DuPont, Exxon, and IBM are adequately staffed to carry out most activities for plant expansion. All these owners, both public and private, use outside agents to a greater or lesser degree when it becomes more advantageous to do so.

The project life cycle may be viewed as a process through which a project is implemented **from cradle to grave**. This process is often very complex; however, it can be decomposed into several stages as indicated by the general outline in Figure 1-1. The solutions at various stages are then integrated to obtain the final outcome. Although each stage requires different expertise, it usually includes both technical and managerial activities in the **knowledge domain** of the specialist. The owner may choose to decompose the entire process into more or less stages based on the size and nature of the project, and thus obtain the most efficient result in implementation. Very often, the owner retains direct control of work in the planning and programming stages, but increasingly outside planners and financial experts are used as consultants because of the complexities of projects. Since operation and maintenance of a facility will go on long after the completion and acceptance of a project, it is usually treated as a separate problem except in the consideration of the life cycle cost of a facility. All stages may be broadly lumped together and referred to as the Design/Construct process, while the procurement and construction alone are traditionally regarded as the province of the construction industry.

Owners must recognize that there is no single best approach in organizing project management throughout a project's life cycle. All organizational approaches have advantages and disadvantages, depending on the knowledge of the owner in construction management as well as the type, size and location of the project. It is important for the owner to be aware of the approach which is most appropriate and beneficial for a particular project. In making choices, owners should be concerned with the life cycle costs of constructed facilities rather than simply the initial construction costs. Saving small amounts of money during construction may not be worthwhile if the result is much larger operating costs or not meeting the functional requirements for the new facility satisfactorily. Thus, owners must be very concerned with the quality of the finished product as well as the cost of construction itself. Since facility operation and maintenance is a part of the project life cycle, the owners' expectation to satisfy investment objectives during the project life cycle will require consideration of the cost of operation and maintenance. Therefore, the facility's operating management should also be considered as early as possible, just as the construction process should be kept in mind at the early stages of planning and programming.

New Words and Phrases

facility   设施，设备；容易，简易；灵巧，敏捷
feasibility   可行性；可能性
in-house   内部的，内业的
market demands   市场需求
the speculative housing market   投机性住宅市场
the real estate developer   房地产开发商
government agency   政府机构
public project   公共项目
project management   项目管理
the conceptual planning stage   概念规划阶段
the project life cycle   项目生命周期
from cradle to grave   从开始到结束
knowledge domain   知识领域

Selection of Professional Services

When an owner decides to seek professional services for the design and construction of a facility, he is confronted with a broad variety of choices. The type of services selected depends to a large degree on the type of construction and the experience of the owner in dealing with various professionals in the previous projects undertaken by the firm. Generally, several common types of professional services may be engaged either separately or in some combination by the owners.

Financial Planning Consultants

At the early stage of strategic planning for a capital project, an owner often seeks the services of financial planning consultants such as certified public accounting (CPA) firms to evaluate the economic and financial feasibility of the constructed facility, particularly with respect to various provisions of federal, state and local tax laws which may affect the investment decision. Investment banks may also be consulted on various options for financing the facility in order to analyze their long-term effects on the financial health of the owner organization.

Architectural and Engineering Firms

Traditionally, the owner engages an architectural and engineering (A/E) firm or consortium as technical consultant in developing a preliminary design. After the engineering design and financing arrangements for the project are completed, the owner will enter into a construction contract with a general contractor either through competitive bidding or negotiation. The general contractor will act as a constructor and/or a coordinator of a large number of subcontractors who perform various specialties for the completion of the project. The A/E firm completes the design and may also provide on site quality inspection during construction. Thus, the A/E firm acts as the prime professional on behalf of the owner and supervises the construction to insure satisfactory results. This practice is most common in building construction.

In the past two decades, this traditional approach has become less popular for a number of reasons, particularly for large scale projects. The A/E firms, which are engaged by the owner as the prime professionals for design and inspection, have become more isolated from the construction process. This has occurred because of pressures to reduce fees to A/E firms, the threat of litigation regarding construction defects, and lack of knowledge of new construction techniques on the part of architect and engineering professionals. Instead of preparing a construction plan along with the design, many A/E firms are no longer responsible for the details of construction nor do they provide periodic field inspection in many cases. As a matter of fact, such firms will place a prominent disclaimer of responsibilities on any shop drawings they may check, and they will often regard their representatives in the field as observers instead of inspectors. Thus, the A/E firm and the general contractor on a project often become antagonists who are looking after their own competing interests. As a result, even the **constructability** of some engineering designs may become an issue of contention. To carry this protective attitude to the extreme, the specifications prepared by an A/E firm for the general contractor often protects the interest of the A/E firm at the expense of the interests of the owner and the contractor.

In order to reduce the cost of construction, some owners introduce value engineering, which seeks to reduce the cost of construction by **soliciting** a second design that might cost less than the original design produced by the A/E firm. In practice, the second design is submitted by the contractor after receiving a construction contract at a stipulated sum, and the saving in cost resulting from the redesign is shared by the contractor and the owner. The contractor is able to absorb the cost of redesign from the profit in construction or to reduce the construction cost as a result of the redesign. If the owner had been willing to pay a higher fee to the A/E firm or to better direct the design process, the A/E firm might have produced an improved design which would cost less in the first place. Regardless of the merit of value engineering, this practice has undermined the role of the A/E firm as the prime professional acting on behalf of the owner to supervise the contractor.

Design/Construct Firms

A common trend in industrial construction, particularly for large projects, is to engage the services of a design/construct firm. By integrating design and construction management in a single organization, many of the conflicts between designers and constructors might be avoided. In particular, designs will be closely **scrutinized** for theirconstructability. However, an owner engaging a design/construct firm must insure that the quality of the constructed facility is not sacrificed by the desire to reduce the time or the cost for completing the project. Also, it is difficult to make use of competitive bidding in this type of design/construct process. As a result, owners must be relatively sophisticated in negotiating realistic and cost-effective construction contracts.

One of the most obvious advantages of the integrated design/construct process is the use of phased construction for a large project. In this process, the project is divided up into several phases, each of which can be designed and constructed in a staggered manner. After the completion of the design of the first phase, construction can begin without waiting for the completion of the design of the second phase, etc. If proper coordination is exercised, the total project duration can be greatly reduced. Another advantage is to exploit the possibility of using the turnkey approach whereby an owner can delegate all responsibility to the design/construct firm which will deliver to the owner a completed facility that meets the performance specifications at the specified price.

Professional Construction Managers

In recent years, a new breed of construction managers (CM) offers professional services from the inception to the completion of a construction project. These construction managers mostly come from the ranks of A/E firms or general contractors who may or may not retain dual roles in the service of the owners. In any case, the owner can rely on the service of a single prime professional to manage the entire process of a construction project. However, like the A/E firms of several decades ago, the construction managers are appreciated by some owners but not by others. Before long, some owners find that the construction managers too may try to protect their own interest instead of that of the owners when the stakes are high.

It should be obvious to all involved in the construction process that the party which is required to take higher risk demands larger rewards. If an owner wants to engage an A/E firm on the basis of low fees instead of established qualifications, it often gets what it deserves; or if the owner wants the general contractor to bear the cost of uncertainties in construction such as foundation conditions, the contract price will be higher even if competitive bidding is used in reaching a contractual agreement. Without mutual respect and trust, an owner cannot expect that construction managers can produce better results than other professionals. Hence, an owner must understand its own responsibility and the risk it wishes to assign to itself and to other participants in the process.

Operation and Maintenance Managers

Although many owners keep a permanent staff for the operation and maintenance of constructed facilities, others may prefer to contract such tasks to professional managers. Understandably, it is common to find in-house staff for operation and maintenance in specialized industrial plants and infrastructure facilities, and the use of outside managers under contracts for the operation and maintenance of rental properties such as apartments and office buildings. However, there are exceptions to these common practices. For example, maintenance of public roadways can be contracted to private firms. In any case, managers can provide a spectrum of operation and maintenance services for a specified time period in accordance to the terms of contractual agreements. Thus, the owners can be spared the provision of in-house expertise to operate and maintain the facilities.

Facilities Management

As a logical extension for obtaining the best services throughout the project life cycle of a constructed facility, some owners and developers are receptive to adding strategic planning at the beginning and facility maintenance as a follow-up to reduce space-related costs in their real estate holdings. Consequently, some architectural/engineering firms and construction management firms with computer-based expertise, together with interior design firms, are offering such front-end and follow-up services in addition to the more traditional services in design and construction. This spectrum of services is described in Engineering News-Record (now ENR) as follows:

Facilities management is the discipline of planning, designing, constructing and managing space—in every type of structure from office buildings to process plants. It involves developing corporate facilities policy, long-range forecasts, real estate, space inventories, projects (through design, construction and renovation), building operation and maintenance plans and furniture and equipment inventories.

A common denominator of all firms entering into these new services is that they all have strong computer capabilities and heavy computer investments. In addition to the use of computers for aiding design and monitoring construction, the service includes the compilation of a computer record of building plans that can be turned over at the end of construction to the facilities management group of the owner. A computer data base of facilities information makes it possible for planners in the owner's organization to obtain overview information for long range space forecasts, while the line managers can use as-built information such as lease/tenant records, utility costs, etc. for day-to-day operations.

New Words and Phrases

constructability 可施工性；施工能力；可施工度
solicit 征求；恳求
scrutinize 仔细检查
financial planning consultants 财务规划咨询
architectural and engineering firms 建筑与工程公司
design/construct firms 设计/施工公司

professional construction managers 建设项目经理
operation and maintenance managers 运营和维护经理
facilities management 设施管理

Part II Speaking

Company Presentation

A: How do you do?
B: How do you do?
A: I am Huang Jianhua, **marketing engineer** of China Construction Group. Here is my card.
B: Thanks. Here is mine.
A: Please allow me to give you a brief introduction to our group.
B: Sure.
A: Okay, this is our **brochure**.
B: The pictures are beautiful.
A: Thank you. Our company has built many significant projects, the brochure presents some of them.
B: I saw quite a lot of projects in the city with the same logo as yours.
A: Yes, the logo of our mother corporation is CSCEC (China State Construction Engineering Corporation). Our group is one of the **subsidiaries** of CSCEC, and was established in 1953.
B: So your corporation has been in operation for many years.
A: Yes, we have a splendid **job reference** covering the last 65 years, including the First Automobile Factory, Daqing Petroleum Refinery, China World Trade Centre and the office building of China Industrial &Commercial Bank.
B: Is your group focusing solely on the building industry?
A: Though we are better known for our building works, we are also involved in civil works such as highways, bridges and utilities; and we are now looking for more involvement in environmental protection projects.
B: Do you have any experience working abroad or in connection with international contractors?
A: Yes, our group was involved in construction projects in the Mid-east, the Pacific islands and in South-east Asia. We also had very smooth cooperation with contractors from France, Germany, Japan and other countries.
B: What about your recent annual **turnover**?
A: Our group had a turnover level between 6.5 billion and 7 billion RMB annually in recent years.
B: That is an impressive amount.

New Words and Phrases

brochure （宣传）小册子
subsidiary 下属公司
turnover 营业额
marketing engineer 市场营销工程师
job reference 业绩

Unit 2
Project Management

Part I Reading and Translating

Professional Knowledge Guidance

1. 建设工程管理（Professional Management in Construction）
决策阶段的管理：项目前期开发管理 DM——Development Management.
实施阶段的管理：项目管理 PM——Project Management.
使用阶段的管理：设施管理 FM——Facility Management.
2. 建设工程项目管理：自项目开始至项目完成，通过项目策划（Project Planning）和项目控制（Project Control），以使项目的费用目标、进度目标和质量目标得以实现。
1)"自项目开始至项目完成"指的是项目的实施阶段。
2)"项目策划"指的是目标控制前的一系列筹划和准备工作。
3)"费用目标"对业主而言是投资目标，对施工方而言是成本目标。

Text

Project Management for Construction

Definition of Project Management

Term of Project Management

The term project management is defined:
- By PMBOK (Project Management Body of Knowledge) as "The application of knowledge, skills, tools, and techniques to project activities in order to meet or exceed stakeholder needs and expectations from a project."[1]
- By PRINCE2 (Projects in Controlled Environments) as "The planning, monitoring and control of all

aspects of the project and the motivation of all those involved in it to achieve the project objectives on time and to the specified cost, quality and performance."

Project Management Processes

Project management processes can be organized into five groups of one or more processes:

- Initiating processes: recognizing that a project or phase should begin and committing to do so.
- Planning processes: devising and maintaining **a workable scheme** to accomplish the business need that the project was undertaken to address.
- Executing processes: coordinating people and other resources to carry out the plan.
- Controlling processes: ensuring that project objectives are met by monitoring and measuring progress and taking corrective action when necessary.
- Closing processes: formalizing acceptance of the project or phase and bringing it to an orderly end.

Project Management for Construction

The construction industry is a **conglomeration** of diverse fields and participants that have been loosely **lumped together** as a sector of the economy. The **construction industry** plays a central role in **national welfare**, including the development of **residential housing, office buildings** and **industrial plants**, and the restoration of the **nation's infrastructure** and other **public facilities**.

The management of construction projects requires knowledge of modern management as well as an understanding of the **design and construction process**. Construction projects have **a specific set of objectives and constraints** such as a required time frame for completion. While the relevant technology, institutional arrangements or processes will differ, the management of such projects has much in common with the management of similar types of projects in other specialty or technology domains such as **underground tunnel**, chemical and energy developments.

Generally, project management **is distinguished from** the general management of corporations by the mission-oriented nature of a project. A project organization will generally be terminated when the mission is accomplished. Project management is the art of directing and coordinating human and material resources throughout the life of a project by using modern management techniques to achieve **predetermined objectives** of scope, cost, time, quality and participation satisfaction.[2]

Specifically, project management in construction encompasses a set of objectives which may be accomplished by implementing a series of operations subject to **resource constraints**. There are potential conflicts between the stated objectives with regard to scope, cost, time and quality, and the constraints imposed on human, material and financial resources. These conflicts should be resolved at the onset of a project by making the necessary **tradeoffs** or creating new alternatives. Subsequently, the functions of project management for construction generally include the following:

- Specification of project objectives and plans including **delineation** of scope, budgeting, scheduling, setting performance requirements, and selecting project participants.
- Maximization of efficient resource utilization through **procurement** of labor, materials and equipment according to the prescribed schedule and plan.
- Implementation of various operations through proper coordination and control of planning, design, estimating, contracting and construction in the entire process.

• **Development of effective communications** and **mechanisms for resolving conflicts** among the various participants.

Construction Management Approach

Construction management is the coordinated effort of all parties involved in providing the employer with a successful project. The objectives of construction project management are to complete a project within the plans and specifications provided in accordance with the contract requirement. Moreover, the employer may, in time, continue the **facility life cycle** through the process of renovation or alteration to accommodate new requirements. With the complexity of the construction process increasing, employers demand **accountability** and accurate guidance during the entire planning and construction process. In recent years construction practices have changed dramatically, since technology, materials, **financing**, design and engineering have all advanced fast.

Traditional Construction Management

The traditional construction management is usually for ordinary projects of moderate size and complexity, and employer often employs a designer (an architectural/engineering firm) which prepares the detailed plans and specifications for the constructor (a main/**general contractor**). The designer also acts on behalf of the employer to **oversee** the **project implementation** during construction. From the viewpoint of project management, the terms "employer" or "client" or "owner" are **synonymous** because they have the ultimate authority to make all important decisions. The contractor is responsible for the construction itself even though the work may actually be undertaken by a number of **specialty subcontractors**.

The employer may select a constructor either through competitive bidding or through negotiation. Public agencies are usually required to use the **competitive bidding mode**, while private organizations may choose either mode of operation. In using competitive bidding, the employer is forced to use the designer-constructor sequence since detailed plans and specifications must be ready before inviting **bidders** to submit their bids. If the employer chooses use a **negotiated contract**, it is free to use phased construction if it so desires.

The general contractor may choose to perform all or part of the construction work, or act only as a manager by subcontracting all the construction to subcontractors. The general contractor may also select the subcontractors through competitive bidding or negotiated contracts. The general contractor may ask a number of subcontractors to quote prices for the subcontracts before submitting its bid to the employer.

Although the designer-constructor sequence is still widely used because of the public perception of fairness in competitive bidding, many private employers/owners recognize the disadvantages of using this approach when the project is large and complex and when market pressures require a shorter project duration than that which can be accomplished by using this traditional method.[3]

Professional Construction Management

Professional construction management refers to a project management team consisting of a professional construction manager and other participants who will carry out the tasks of project planning, design and construction in an integrated manner. Contractual relationships among members of the team are intended to minimize **adversarial** relationships and contribute to greater response within the management group. A professional construction company is a firm specialized in the practice of professional construction management which includes:

• Work with employer/owner and the architectural/engineering firms from the beginning and make

recommendations on **design improvements**, **construction technology**, **schedules** and construction economy.
- Propose design and construction alternatives if appropriate, and analyze the effects of the alternatives on the project cost and schedule.
- Monitor subsequent development of the project in order that these targets are not exceeded without the knowledge of the employer/owner.
- Coordinate procurement of material and equipment and the work of all construction contractors, and monthly payments to contractors, changes, **claims** and inspection for conforming design requirements.
- Perform other project-related services as required by the employer.

Professional construction management is usually used when a project is very large or complex.

Organization of Project Participants

There are two basic approaches to organize for project implementation, even though many variations may exist as a result of different **contractual relationships** adopted by the employer and builder. These basic approaches are divided along the following lines:
- Separation of organizations. Numerous organizations serve as consultants or contractors to the owner, with different organizations handling design and construction functions. Typical examples which involve different degrees of separation are traditional sequence of design and construction; and Professional construction management.
- Integration of organizations. A single or joint venture consisting of a number of organizations with a single command undertakes both design and construction functions. Two extremes may be cited as examples: owner-builder operation in which all work will be handled internally by force account; turkey operation in which all work is contracted to a **vendor** which is responsible for delivering the completed project.

Since construction projects may be managed by a spectrum of participants in a variety of combinations, the organization for the management of such projects may vary from case to case. There are many variations of management manners between these two extremes, depending on the objectives of the organization and the nature of the construction project. For example, a large chemical company with internal staff for planning, design and construction of facilities for new product lines will naturally adopt the **matrix organization**. On the other hand, a construction company whose existence depends entirely on the management of certain types of construction projects may find the project-oriented organization particularly attractive. While organizations may differ, the same basic principles of management structure are applicable to most situations.

New Words and Phrases

conglomeration 兼并，重组
tradeoff 折中，权衡；交易
delineation 描述，画轮廓
procurement 采购，购买
accountability 有义务，有责任；可说明性
financing 融资
oversee 监督，审查；偷看到，无意中看到
synonymous 同义的，同义词的；同义突变的
bidder 投标人；对手的，敌手的

adversarial 对抗的，对手的
schedule 时间表
claim 索赔
vendor 供应商
project management for construction 施工项目管理
PMBOK (Project Management Body of Knowledge) 项目管理知识体系
project management processes 项目管理流程
a workable scheme 切实可行的方案
lumped together 聚集，合成
construction industry 建筑行业
national welfare 国家福利
residential housing 住宅
office buildings 写字楼
industrial plants 工业厂房
nation's infrastructure 国家的基础设施
public facilities 公共设施
design and construction process 设计与施工过程
a specific set of objectives and constraints 一系列具体的目标和约束
underground tunnel 地下隧道
be distinguished from 有别于……；不同于……
predetermined objectives 预定目标
resource constraints 资源约束
development of effective communications 有效沟通的开展
mechanisms for resolving conflicts 解决冲突的机制
facility life cycle 设备生命周期
general contractor 总承包
project implementation 项目实施
specialty subcontractors 专业分包商
competitive bidding mode 招标/竞价模式
negotiated contract 协商合同
design improvements 设计改进
construction technology 施工工艺
contractual relationships 契约关系
matrix organization 矩阵组织

Notes

[1] The term project management is defined:

• By PMBOK (Project Management Body of Knowledge) as "The application of knowledge, skills, tools, and techniques to project activities in order to meet or exceed stakeholder needs and expectations from a project."

项目管理定义：

- PMBOK（《项目管理知识体系》）定义为"在项目活动中运用各种知识、技能、工具和技术，以满足和超过项目业主对项目的需求和期望"。

[2] Project management is the art of directing and coordinating human and material resources throughout the life of a project by using modern management techniques to achieve predetermined objectives of scope, cost, time, quality and participation satisfaction.

项目管理是在项目的整个周期内，用现代管理技术指挥和协调人力和物质资源，实现范围、成本、工期、质量和参与者满意等预期目标的一门艺术。

[3] Although the designer-constructor sequence is still widely used because of the public perception of fairness in competitive bidding, many private employers/owners recognize the disadvantages of using this approach when the project is large and complex and when market pressures require a shorter project duration than that which can be accomplished by using this traditional method.

尽管设计师—施工方顺序因为在竞争性招标中的公共公平观念仍然被广泛使用，但是，当项目很大、很复杂或者市场压力要求一个比采用传统方式可以实现更短的项目工期的时候，许多私人业主也承认使用这种方式的缺陷。

Exercises

I. Translate the following phrases into English.

1. 项目管理知识体系
2. 拥有至高无上的权力
3. 项目管理解决冲突的机制
4. 工程后续维护
5. 管理矩阵组织结构

II. Translate the following sentences into Chinese.

1. By PRINCE2 (Projects In Controlled Environments) as "The planning, monitoring and control of all aspects of the project and the motivation of all those involved in it to achieve the project objectives on time and to the specified cost, quality and performance".

2. Closing processes: formalizing acceptance of the project or phase and bringing it to an orderly end.

3. While the relevant technology, institutional management or processes will differ, the management of such projects has much in common with the management of similar types of projects in other specialty or technology domains such as underground tunnel, chemical and energy developments.

4. Since construction projects may be managed by a spectrum of participants in a variety of combinations, the organization for the management of such projects may vary from case to case.

5. In using competitive bidding, the employer is forced to use the designer-constructor sequence since detailed plans and specifications must be ready before inviting bidders to submit their bids.

Project Management and Construction Project

What is project management and how is it accomplished? Let's try to answer these questions. Project management is the application of knowledge, skills, tools and techniques to project activities to meet project requirements. Project management is accomplished through the application and integration of the project management processes of initiating, planning, executing, monitoring, controlling, and closing. The project manager is the person responsible for accomplishing the project objectives.

Managing a project includes identifying requirements; establishing clear and achievable objectives; balancing the competing demands for quality, scope, time and cost; adapting the specifications, plans, and approach to the different concerns and expectations of the various stakeholders.

The core factors of managing a project is called "triple constraint" —project scope, time and cost—in managing competing project requirements. Project quality is affected by these three factors. High quality projects deliver the required product, service or result within scope, on time, and within budget. The relationship between these factors is such that if any one of the three factors changes, at least one of the other two factors is likely to be affected. Project managers also manage projects in response to uncertainty. Project risk is an uncertain event or condition that, once occurs, has a positive or negative effect on at least one project objective.

By contrast, the general management of business and industrial corporations assumes a broader outlook with greater continuity of operations. Nevertheless, there are sufficient similarities as well as differences between the two so that modern management techniques developed for general management may be adapted for project management.

The basic ingredients for a project management framework may be represented schematically in Figure 2-1. A working knowledge of general management and familiarity with the special knowledge domain related to the project are indispensable. Supporting disciplines such as computer science and decision science may also play an important role. In fact, modern management practices and various special knowledge domains have absorbed various techniques or tools which were once identified only with the supporting disciplines. For example, computer-based information systems and **decision supporting systems** are now commonplace tools for general management. Similarly, many operations research techniques such as **linear programming** and **network analysis** are now widely used in many knowledge or application domains. Hence, the representation in Figure 2-1 reflects only the sources from which the project management framework evolves.

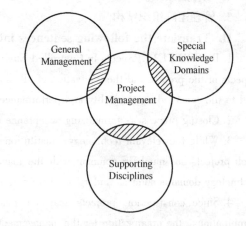

Figure 2-1 Basic Ingredients in Project Management

The Project Management Institute focuses on nine distinct areas requiring project managers' knowledge and attention:

• **Project integration management** to ensure that the various project elements are effectively coordinated.

• **Project scope management** to ensure that all the work required (and only the required work) is included.

• **Project time management** to provide an effective project schedule.

- **Project cost management** to identify needed resources and maintain budget control.
- **Project quality management** to ensure functional requirements are met.
- **Project human resource management** to develop and effectively employ project personnel.
- **Project communications management** to ensure effective internal and external communications.
- **Project risk management** to analyze and mitigate potential risks.
- **Project procurement management** to obtain necessary resources from external sources.

These nine areas form the basis of the Project Management Institute's certification program for project managers in any industry.

Construction Project

Construction projects are intricate, time-consuming undertakings. The total development of a project normally consists of several phases requiring a diverse range of specialized services. In progressing from initial planning to project completion, the typical job passes through successive and distinct stages that demand input from such disparate areas as financial organizations, governmental agencies, engineers, architects, lawyers, insurance and surety companies, contractors, material manufacturers and suppliers, and building tradesmen.

During the construction process itself, even a structure of modest proportions involves many skills, materials, and literally hundreds of different operations. The assembly process must follow a natural order of events that constitutes a complicated pattern of individual time requirements and restrictive sequential relationships among the structure's many segments. To some degree each construction project is unique—no two jobs are ever exactly the same. In its specifics, each structure is **tailored** to suit its environment, arranged to perform its own particular function, and designed to reflect personal tastes and preferences. The **vagaries** of the construction site and the possibilities for creative and utilitarian variation of even the most standardized building product combine to make each construction project a new and different experience. The contractor sets up its "factory" on the site and, to a large extent, custom builds each structure.

The construction process is subject to the influence of highly variable and sometimes unpredictable factors. The construction team, which includes architects, engineers, building tradesmen, subcontractors, material dealers, and others, changes from one job to the next. All the complexities inherent in different construction sites—such as subsoil conditions, surface, topography, weather, transportation, material supply, utilities and services, local subcontractors, labor conditions, and available technologies—are animate part of construction.

Consequently, construction projects are typified by their complexity and diversity and by the non-standardized nature of their production. The use of factory-made modular units may diminish this individuality somewhat, but it is unlikely that field construction will ever be able to adapt completely to the standardized methods and product uniformity of assembly line production. On the contrary, many manufacturing processes are moving toward "one-off" production and adopting many of the project management tools originated in the construction industry.

Project Stages

• **Planning and definition.** A construction project proceeds in a rather definite order; the stages of development that follow are typical. Once an owner has identified the need for a new facility, he or she must define the requirements and delineate the budgetary constraints. Project definition involves establishing broad project characteristics, such as location, performance criteria, size, configuration, layout, equipment, services, and other owner requirements needed to establish the general aspects of the project. Conceptual planning stops short of detailed design, although a considerable amount of preliminary architectural or engineering work may be required. The definition of the work is basically the responsibility of the owner, although a design professional may be called in to provide technical assistance and advice.

• **Design.** The design phase involves the architectural and engineering design of the entire project. It culminates in the preparation of final working drawings and specifications for the total construction program. In practice, design, procurement, and construction often overlap, with procurement and construction beginning on certain segments as soon as the design is completed and drawings and specifications become available.

• **Procurement and construction.** "Procurement" refers to the ordering, expediting, and delivering of key project equipment and materials, especially those that may involve long delivery periods. This function may or may not be handled separately from the construction process itself. "Construction" is, of course, the process of physically erecting the project and putting the materials and equipment into place, and this involves providing the manpower, construction equipment, materials, supplies, supervision, and management necessary to accomplish the work.

New Words and Phrases

tailored   定做的
vagary   异常行为；变幻莫测；反复无常；妄想
the Project Management Institute   （美国）项目管理学会
decision supporting system   决策支持系统
linear programming   线性规划
network analysis   网络分析
project integration management   项目综合管理
project scope management   项目范围管理
project time management   项目时间管理
project cost management   项目成本管理
project quality management   项目质量管理
project human resource management   项目人力资源管理
project communications management   项目沟通管理
project risk management   项目风险管理
project procurement management   项目采购管理

The Changing Environment of the Construction Industry

The construction industry is a **conglomeration** of diverse fields and participants that have been loosely lumped together as a sector of the economy. The construction industry plays a central role in national welfare, including the development of residential housing, office buildings and industrial plants, and the restoration of the nation's infrastructure and other public facilities. The importance of the construction industry lies in the function of its products which provide the foundation for industrial production, and its impacts on the national economy cannot be measured by the value of its output or the number of persons employed in its activities alone.

To be more specific, construction refers to all types of activities usually associated with the erection and repair of immobile facilities. Contract construction consists of a large number of firms that perform construction work for others, and is estimated to be approximately 85% of all construction activities. The remaining 15% of construction is performed by owners of the facilities, and is referred to as force-account construction. Although the number of contractors in the United States exceeds a million, over 60% of all contractor construction is performed by the top 400 contractors. The value of new construction in the United States (expressed in constant dollars) and the value of construction as a percentage of the gross national products from 1950 to 1985. It can be seen that construction is a significant factor in the Gross National Product although its importance has been declining in recent years. Not to be ignored is the fact that as the nation's constructed facilities become older, the total expenditure on rehabilitation and maintenance may increase relative to the value of new construction.

Owners who pay close attention to the **peculiar** characteristics of the construction industry and its changing operating environment will be able to take advantage of the favorable conditions and to avoid the **pitfalls**. Several factors are particularly **noteworthy** because of their significant impacts on the quality, cost and time of construction.

New Technologies

In recent years, technological innovation in design, materials and construction methods have resulted in significant changes in construction costs. Computer-aids have improved capabilities for generating quality designs as well as reducing the time required to produce alternative designs. New materials not only have enhanced the quality of construction but also have shortened the time for shop fabrication and field erection. Construction methods have gone through various stages of mechanization and automation, including the latest development of construction robotics.

The most dramatic new technology applied to construction has been the Internet and its private, corporate Intranet versions. The Internet is widely used as a means to foster **collaboration** among professionals on a project, to communicate for bids and results, and to procure necessary goods and services. Real time video from specific construction sites is widely used to illustrate construction progress to interested parties.

The result has been more effective collaboration, communication and procurement.

The effects of many new technologies on construction costs have been mixed because of the high development costs for new technologies. However, it is unmistakable that design professionals and construction contractors who have not adapted to changing technologies have been forced out of the mainstream of design and construction activities. Ultimately, construction quality and cost can be improved with the adoption of new technologies which are proved to be efficient from both the viewpoints of performance and economy.

Labor Productivity

The term productivity is generally defined as a ratio of the production output volume to the input volume of resources. Since both output and input can be quantified in a number of ways, there is no single measure of productivity that is universally applicable, particularly in the construction industry where the products are often unique and there is no standard for specifying the levels for aggregation of data. However, since labor constitutes a large part of the cost of construction, labor productivity in terms of output volume (constant dollar value or functional units) per person-hour is a useful measure. Labor productivity measured in this way does not necessarily indicate the efficiency of labor alone but rather measures the combined effects of labor, equipment and other factors contributing to the output.

While aggregate construction industry productivity is important as a measure of national economy, owners are more concerned about the labor productivity of basic units of work produced by various crafts on site. Thus, an owner can compare the labor performance at different geographic locations, under different working conditions, and for different types and sizes of projects.

Construction costs usually run parallel to material prices and labor wages. Actually, over the years, labor productivity has increased in some traditional types of construction and thus provides a leveling or compensating effect when hourly rates for labor increase faster than other costs in construction. However, labor productivity has been **stagnant** or even declined in unconventional or large scale projects.

Public Scrutiny

Under the present litigious climate in the United States, the public is increasingly vocal in the **scrutiny** of construction project activities. Sometimes it may result in considerable difficulty in siting new facilities as well as additional expenses during the construction process itself. Owners must be prepared to manage such crises before they get out of control.

Public attitudes towards the siting of new facilities, it represents the cumulative percentage of individuals who would be willing to accept a new industrial facility at various distances from their homes. For example, over fifty percent of the people surveyed would accept a ten-story office building within five miles of their home, but only twenty-five percent would accept a large factory or coal fired power plant at a similar distance. An even lower percentage would accept a hazardous waste disposal site or a nuclear power plant. Even at a distance of one hundred miles, a significant fraction of the public would be unwilling to accept hazardous waste facilities or nuclear power plants.

This objection to new facilities is a widespread public attitude, representing considerable **skepticism** about the external benefits and costs which new facilities will impose. It is this public attitude which is likely to make public scrutiny and regulation a continuing concern for the construction industry.

International Competition

A final trend which deserves note is the increasing level of international competition in the construction industry. Owners are likely to find non-traditional firms bidding for construction work, particularly on large projects. Separate bids from numerous European, North American, and Asian construction firms are not unusual. In the United States, overseas firms are becoming increasingly visible and important. In this environment of **heightened** competition, good project management and improved productivity are more and more important.

A bidding competition for a major new offshore drilling platform illustrates the competitive environment in construction. As described in the Wall Street Journal:

Through most of the postwar years, the nation's biggest builders of offshore oil platforms enjoyed an unusually cozy relationship with the Big Oil Companies they served. Their top officials developed personal friendships with oil executives, entertained them at opulent hunting camps and won contracts to build nearly every major offshore oil platform in the world. . . . But this summer, the good-old boy network fell apart. Shell Oil Co. awarded the main contract for a new platform-taller than Chicago's Sears Tower, four times heavier than the Brooklyn Bridge to a tiny upstart.

The winning bidder arranged overseas fabrication of the rig, kept overhead costs low, and proposed a novel assembly procedure by which construction equipment was mounted on completed sections of the platform in order to speed the completion of the entire structure. The result was lower costs than those estimated and bid by traditional firms.

Of course, U.S. firms including A/E firms, contractors and construction managers are also competing in foreign countries. Their success or failure in the international arena may also affect their capacities and vitalities to provide services in the domestic U.S. market.

Contractor Financed Projects

Increasingly, some owners look to contractors or joint ventures as a resource to design, to build and to finance a constructed facility. For example, a utility company may seek a **consortium** consisting of a design/construct firm and a financial investment firm to assume total liability during construction and thereby eliminate the risks of cost escalation to ratepayers, stockholders and the management. On the other hand, a local **sanitation** district may seek such a consortium to provide private ownership for a proposed new **sewage** treatment plant. In the former case, the owner may take over the completed facility and service the debt on construction through long-term financing arrangements; in the latter case, the private owner may operate the completed facility and recover its investment through user fees. The activities of joint ventures among design, construction and investment firms are sometimes referred to as financial engineering.

This type of joint venture has become more important in the international construction market where aggressive contractors often win contracts by offering a more attractive financing package rather than superior technology. With a deepening shadow of international debts in recent years, many developing countries are not in a position to undertake any new project without contractor-backed financing. Thus, the contractors or joint ventures in overseas projects are forced into very risky positions if they intend to stay in the competition.

New Words and Phrases

conglomeration　混合物，团聚
peculiar　特权的
pitfall　陷阱
noteworthy　显著的，值得注意的
collaboration　合作
stagnant　停滞的，不景气的，污浊的，迟钝的
scrutiny　详细审查，监视，细看，选票复查
skepticism　怀疑论，怀疑的态度
heighten　提高，加强，使更显著
consortium　财团，合伙
sanitation　下水道设施，卫生设施
sewage　污水，下水道
labor productivity　劳动生产率
public scrutiny　公众安全
contractor financed projects　承包商融资项目

Part II　Speaking

Discussion of a Project at a Preliminary Phase

Dialogue 1

Robert: Now, let's get started. About the **location** of the project, what do you think, Mr. Smith?
Smith: Our plan is to establish a **petrochemical plant**. So when we talk about its location, several factors should be taken into consideration.
Robert: Right. The plant will need a large number of skilled and productive workers, and it should be located in a place with a large labor force.
Smith: Also, there is the problem of transportation. We must have an easy **access** to raw materials and to the market.
Robert: I agree with you. We intend to locate the plant in Jia Yi town, about 30 km east of the city.
Smith: 30 km away from the city sounds good.
Robert: We'll go to the spot for a further **feasibility study** tomorrow if you don't mind.
Smith: Good, that's just what we need.

Dialogue 2

Robert: What's your design requirement for the plant office, Mr. Smith?

Smith: It should be a **high-rise** building.
Robert: How many stories should it be?
Smith: Seven stories.
Robert: And what is the **spacing** of each storey?
Smith: About 3 meters. As for the **general layout** of the service and **occupied spaces**, we have some detailed descriptions here in this document.
Robert: How about the structure? A **bolted structural-steel frame** or a **reinforced-concrete structure**?
Smith: A reinforced-concrete structure.
Robert: All right, we'll study your document carefully before we begin with the design. We'll try to meet your requirement.

New Words and Phrases

location 地址；厂址
access 手段；通道；进入
high-rise 高层的（建筑）
spacing 净空
preliminary phase 初步设计阶段
petrochemical plant 石油化工厂
feasibility study 可行性研究
general layout 总体布局，总平面图
occupied space 结构面积
bolted structural-steel frame structure 钢架结构
reinforced-concrete structure 钢筋混凝土结构

Unit 3
Construction Project of Planning and Decision

Part I Reading and Translating

Professional Knowledge Guidance

1. 项目决策：是指从项目投资主体的目标出发，根据客观条件和投资项目的特点，在掌握大量有关信息的基础上，运用科学的决策理论和方法，按一定的程序和标准对各种可供实施的方案进行分析、评价和优选，并对投资项目做出选择或决定的过程。

2. 项目经济评价：是指在对影响项目的各项技术经济因素预测、分析和计算的基础上，评价投资项目的直接经济效益和间接经济效益，为投资决策提供依据的活动。

项目经济评价指标分类：
1）时间性指标：兼顾经济性与风险性，主要由静态投资回收期与动态投资回收期。
2）价值性指标：如净现值、净年值、费用现值、费用年值等。
3）效率性指标：资源利用效率指标，如总投资收益率、净现值指数、内部收益率等。

Text

Strategic Planning and Project Programming

The programming of capital projects is shaped by the strategic plan of an organization, which is influenced by market demands and resources constraints. The programming process associated with **planning and feasibility studies** sets the priorities and timing for initiating various projects to meet the overall objectives of the organizations. However, once this decision is made to initiate a project, market pressure may dictate early and timely completion of the facility.

Among various types of construction, the influence of market pressure on the timing of initiating a facility is most obvious in industrial construction. [1] Demand for an industrial product may be short-lived, and if a company does not hit the market first, there may not be demand for its product later. With intensive competition for national and international markets, the trend of industrial construction moves toward shorter project life cycles, particularly in **technology intensive industries**.

In order to gain time, some owners are willing to **forego** thorough planning and feasibility study so as to proceed on a project with inadequate definition of the project scope. Invariably, subsequent changes in project scope will increase **construction costs**; however, profits derived from earlier facility operation often justify the increase in construction costs. Generally, if the owner can derive reasonable profits from the operation of a completed facility, the project is considered a success even if construction costs far exceed the estimate based on an inadequate scope definition. [2] This attitude may be attributed in large part to the uncertainties inherent in construction projects. It is difficult to argue that profits might be even higher if construction costs could be reduced without increasing the project duration. However, some projects, notably some nuclear power plants, are clearly unsuccessful and abandoned before completion, and their demise must be attributed at least in part to inadequate planning and poor feasibility studies.

The owner or facility sponsor holds the key to influence the construction costs of a project because any decision made at the beginning stage of a project life cycle has far greater influence than those made at later stages. [3] Therefore, an owner should obtain the expertise of professionals to provide adequate planning and feasibility studies. Many owners do not maintain an in-house engineering and construction management capability, and they should consider the establishment of an ongoing relationship with outside consultants in order to respond quickly to requests. Even among those owners who maintain engineering and construction divisions, many treat these divisions as **reimbursable**, independent organizations. Such an arrangement should not discourage their **legitimate** use as false economies in reimbursable costs from such divisions can indeed be very costly to the overall organization.

Finally, the initiation and execution of capital projects places demands on the resources of the owner and the professionals and contractors to be engaged by the owner. For very large projects, it may bid up the price of engineering services as well as the costs of materials and equipment and the contract prices of all types. [4] Consequently, such factors should be taken into consideration in determining the timing of a project.

Example 3-1: Setting priorities for projects

A department store planned to expand its operation by acquiring 20 acres of land in the southeast of a metropolitan area which consists of well established suburbs for middle income families. An architectural/engineering (A/E) firm was engaged to design a shopping center on the 20-acre plot with the department store as its flagship plus a large number of storefronts for tenants. One year later, the department store owner purchased 2,000 acres of farm land in the northwest outskirts of the same metropolitan area and designated 20 acres of this land for a shopping center. The A/E firm was again engaged to design a shopping center at this new location.

The A/E firm was kept completely in the dark while the assemblage of the 2,000 acres of land in the northwest quietly took place. When the plans and specifications for the southeast shopping center were completed, the owner informed the A/E firm that it would not proceed with the construction of the southeast shopping center for the time being. Instead, the owner urged the A/E firm to produce a new set of similar plans and specifications for the northwest shopping center as soon as possible, even at the **sacrifice** of cost saving measures. When the plans and specifications for the northwest shopping center were ready, the owner immediately authorized its construction. However, it took another three years before the southeast shopping center was finally built.

The reason behind the change of plan was that the owner discovered the availability of the farm land in the northwest which could be developed into residential real estate properties for upper middle income families. The immediate construction of the northwest shopping center would make the land development parcels more attractive to home buyers. Thus, the owner was able to **recoup** enough cash flow in three years to construct the southeast shopping center in addition to financing the construction of the northeast shopping center, as well as the land development in its vicinity.

While the owner did not want the construction cost of the northwest shopping center to run wild, it apparently was satisfied with the cost estimate based on the detailed plans of the southeast shopping center. Thus, the owner had a general idea of what the construction cost of the northwest shopping center would be, and did not wish to wait for a more refined cost estimate until the detailed plans for that center were ready. To the owner, the **timeliness** of completing the construction of the northwest shopping center was far more important than reducing the construction cost in fulfilling its investment objectives.

Example 3-2: Resource Constraints for Mega Projects

A major problem with mega projects is the severe strain placed on the environment, particularly on the resources in the immediate area of a construction project. "Mega" or "macro" projects involve construction of very large facilities such as the Alaska pipeline constructed in the 1970's or the Panama Canal constructed in the 1900's. The limitations in some or all of the basic elements required for the successful completion of a mega project include:

- Engineering design professionals to provide sufficient manpower to complete the design within a reasonable time limit.
- Construction supervisors with capacity and experience to direct large projects.
- The number of construction workers with proper skills to do the work.
- The market to supply materials in sufficient quantities and of required quality on time.
- The ability of the local infrastructure to support the large number of workers over an extended period of time, including housing, transportation and other services.

To compound the problem, mega projects are often constructed in remote environments away from major population centers and subject to severe climate conditions. Consequently, special features of each mega project must be evaluated carefully. [5]

New Words and Phrases

forego　放弃
legitimate　合法的，正当的
reimbursable　可补偿的，可收回的
timeliness　及时
sacrifice　牺牲，祭品，供奉
recoup　收回，恢复，偿还，扣除
planning and feasibility study　项目规划和可行性研究
technology intensive industry　技术密集型项目
construction cost　建设成本

Notes

[1] Among various types of construction, the influence of market pressure on the timing of initiating a facility is most obvious in industrial construction.

在各类建设项目当中,市场压力对启动一个项目在时间紧迫性上的影响,在工业项目上最为明显。

[2] Generally, if the owner can derive reasonable profits from the operation of a completed facility, the project is considered a success even if construction costs far exceed the estimate based on an inadequate scope definition.

总的来说,如果业主能从完成的项目运营当中获得合理的利润,即使建设成本因为缺乏详细的范围定义而大大超支,仍认为这个项目是成功的。

[3] The owner or facility sponsor holds the key to influence the construction costs of a project because any decision made at the beginning stage of a project life cycle has far greater influence than those made at later stages.

正是因为在项目生命周期的前期阶段所做的任何决策都远比后期阶段所做的决策有影响力,所以业主或项目发起人对项目建设成本的影响可谓举足轻重。

[4] For very large projects, it may bid up the price of engineering services as well as the costs of materials and equipment and the contract prices of all types.

对于特大型项目,与其材料和设备价格及各种合同价格一样,设计咨询价格有可能被抬高很多。

[5] To compound the problem, mega projects are often constructed in remote environments away from major population centers and subject to severe climate conditions. Consequently, special features of each mega project must be evaluated carefully.

为协调这个问题,特大型项目一般建设在远离人口密集区、比较偏远的地方,同时易受恶劣气候的影响。因此,每一个特大型项目的具体特征都应予以仔细评估。

Exercises

I. Translate the following phrases into English.

1. 概念规划和可行性研究
2. 采购和施工
3. 工程设计
4. 运营与维护
5. 建设成本
6. 项目进度

II. Translate the following sentences into Chinese.

1. With intensive competition for national and international markets, the trend of industrial construction moves toward shorter project life cycles, particularly in technology intensive industries.

2. However, some projects, notably some nuclear power plants, are clearly unsuccessful and abandoned before completion, and their demise must be attributed at least in part to inadequate planning and poor feasibility studies.

3. Many owners do not maintain an in-house engineering and construction management capability, and they should consider the establishment of an ongoing relationship with outside consultants in order to respond

quickly to requests.

4. While the owner did not want the construction cost of the northwest shopping center to run wild, it apparently was satisfied with the cost estimate based on the detailed plans of the southeast shopping center.

Project Life Cycle and Economic Feasibility

Facility investment decisions represent major commitments of corporate resources and have serious consequences on the profitability and financial stability of a corporation. In the public sector, such decisions also affect the viability of facility investment programs and the credibility of the agency in charge of the programs. It is important to evaluate facilities rationally with regard to both the economic feasibility of individual projects and the relative net benefits of alternative and mutually exclusive projects.

The cycle begins with the initial conception of the project and continues though planning, design, procurement, construction, start-up, operation and maintenance. It ends with the disposal of a facility when it is no longer productive or useful. Four major aspects of economic evaluation will be examined:

• The basic concepts of facility investment evaluation, including time preference for consumption, **opportunity cost, minimum attractive rate of return, cash flows over the planning horizon** and profit measures.

• Methods of economic evaluation, including **the net present value method, the equivalent uniform annual value method, the benefit-cost ratio method**, and **the internal rate of return method**.

• Factors affecting **cash flows**, including depreciation and tax effects, price level changes, and treatment of risk and uncertainty.

• Effects of different methods of financing on the selection of projects, including types of financing and risk, public policies on regulation and subsidies, the effects of project financial planning, and the interaction between operational and financial planning.

It is important to distinguish between the economic evaluation of alternative physical facilities and the evaluation of alternative financing plans for a project. The former refers to the evaluation of the cash flow representing the benefits and costs associated with the acquisition and operation of the facility, and this cash flow over the planning horizon is referred to as the economic cash flow or the operating cash flow. The latter refers to the evaluation of the cash flow representing the incomes and expenditures as a result of adopting a specific financing plan for funding the project, and this cash flow over the planning horizon is referred to as the financial cash flow. In general, economic evaluation and financial evaluation are carried out by different groups in an organization since economic evaluation is related to design, construction, operations and maintenance of the facility while financial evaluations require knowledge of financial assets such as equities, bonds, notes and mortgages. The separation of economic evaluation and financial evaluation does not necessarily mean one should ignore the interaction of different designs and financing requirements over time which may influence the relative desirability of specific design/financing combinations.

All such combinations can be duly considered. In practice, however, the division of labor among two groups of specialists generally leads to sequential decisions without adequate communication for analyzing the interaction of various design/financing combinations because of the timing of separate analyses.

As long as the significance of the interaction of design/financing combinations is understood, it is convenient first to consider the economic evaluation and financial evaluation separately, and then combine the results of both evaluations to reach a final conclusion.

<h2 style="text-align:center">New Words and Phrases</h2>

opportunity cost   机会成本
minimum attractive rate of return   基准贴现率
cash flows over the planning horizon   规划周期现金流
the net present value method   净现值法
the equivalent uniform annual value method   等值年法
the benefit-cost ratio method   成本收益法
the internal rate of return method   内部成本收益法
cash flow   资金流动

Basic Concepts of Economic Evaluation

A **systematic** approach for economic evaluation of facilities consists of the following major steps:
- Generate a set of projects or purchases for investment consideration.
- Establish **the planning horizon** for economic analysis.
- Estimate the **cash flow profile** for each project.
- Specify the **minimum attractive rate of return** (**MARR**).
- Establish the criterion for accepting or rejecting a proposal, or for selecting the best among a group of **mutually exclusive proposals**, on the basis of the objective of the investment.
- Perform **sensitivity** or uncertainty analysis.
- Accept or reject a proposal on the basis of the established criterion.

It is important to emphasize that many assumptions and policies, some **implicit** and some **explicit**, are introduced in economic evaluation by the decision maker. The decision making process will be influenced by the subjective judgment of the management as much as by the result of systematic analysis.

The period of time to which the management of a firm or agency wishes to look ahead is referred to as the planning horizon. Since the future is uncertain, the period of time selected is limited by the ability to forecast with some degree of accuracy. For capital investment, the selection of the planning horizon is often influenced by the useful life of facilities, since the disposal of usable assets, once acquired, generally involves suffering financial losses.

In economic evaluations, project alternatives are represented by their cash flow profiles over the n years or periods in the planning horizon. Thus, the interest periods are normally assumed to be in years ($t = 0$, 1, 2, ..., n), $t = 0$ representing the present time. Let $B_{t,x}$ be the annual benefit at the end of year t for a investment project x where $x = 1, 2, ...$ refer to projects No. 1, No. 2, etc., respectively. Let $C_{t,x}$ be the annual cost at the end of year t for the same investment project x. The **net annual cash flow** is defined as the annual benefit in excess of the annual cost, and is denoted by $A_{t,x}$ at the end of year t for an investment project x. Then, for $t = 0, 1, \ldots, n$:

$$A_{t,x} = B_{t,x} - C_{t,x} \qquad (3.1)$$

Where $A_{t,x}$ is positive, negative or zero depends on the values of $B_{t,x}$ and $C_{t,x}$, both of which are defined as positive quantities.

Once the management has committed funds to a specific project, it must forego other investment opportunities which might have been undertaken by using the same funds. The opportunity cost reflects the return that can be earned from the best alternative investment opportunity foregone. The foregone opportunities may include not only capital projects but also financial investments or other socially desirable programs. Management should invest in a proposed project only if it will yield a return at least equal to the minimum attractive rate of return (MARR) from foregone opportunities as envisioned by the organization.

In general, the MARR specified by the top management in a private firm reflects the opportunity cost of capital of the firm, the market interest rates for lending and borrowing, and the risks associated with investment opportunities. For public projects, the MARR is specified by a government agency, such as the Office of Management and Budget or the Congress of the United States. The public MARR thus specified reflects social and economic welfare considerations, and is referred to as the **social rate of discount**.

Regardless of how the MARR is determined by an organization, the MARR specified for the economic evaluation of investment proposals is critically important in determining whether any investment proposal is worthwhile from the standpoint of the organization. Since the MARR of an organization often cannot be determined accurately, it is advisable to use several values of the MARR to assess the sensitivity of the potential of the project to variations of the MARR value.

The objective of facility investment in the private sector is generally understood to be profit maximization within a specific time frame. Similarly, the objective in the public sector is the maximization of net social benefit which is **analogous** to **profit maximization** in private organizations. Given this objective, a method of economic analysis will be judged by the reliability and ease with which a correct conclusion may be reached in project selection.

The **basic principle** underlying the decision for accepting and selecting investment projects is that if an organization can lend or borrow as much money as it wishes at the MARR, the goal of profit maximization is best served by accepting all independent projects whose net present values based on the specified MARR are **nonnegative**, or by selecting the project with the maximum nonnegative net present value among a set mutually exclusive proposals. The net present value criterion reflects this principle and is most straightforward and unambiguous when there is no **budget constraint**. Various methods of economic evaluation, when properly applied, will produce the same result if the net present value criterion is used as the basis for decision.

Net Present Value Method

Let BPV_x be the present value of benefits of a project x and CPV_x be the present value of costs of the project x. Then, for MARR = i over a planning horizon of n years,

$$BPV_x = \sum_{t=0}^{n} B_{t,x}(1+i)^{-t} = \sum_{t=0}^{n} B_{t,x}(P \mid F, i, t) \qquad (3.2)$$

Unit 3 Construction Project of Planning and Decision

$$CPV_x = \sum_{t=0}^{n} C_{t,x}(1+i)^{-t} = \sum_{t=0}^{n} C_{t,x}(P\mid F,i,t) \tag{3.3}$$

where the symbol $(P\mid F,i,t)$ is a discount factor equal to $(1+i)^{-t}$ and reads as follows: "To find the present value P, given the future value $F=1$, discounted at an annual discount rate i over a period of t years." when the benefit or cost in year t is multiplied by this factor, the present value is obtained. Then, the net present value of the project x is calculated as:

$$NPV_x = BPV_x - CPV_x \tag{3.4}$$

or

$$NPV_x = \sum_{t=0}^{n}(B_{t,x} - C_{t,x})(P\mid F,i,t) = \sum_{t=0}^{n} A_{t,x}(P\mid F,i,t) \tag{3.5}$$

If there is no budget constraint, then all independent projects having net present values greater than or equal to zero are acceptable. That is, project x is acceptable as long as

$$NPV_x \geq 0 \tag{3.6}$$

For mutually exclusive proposals ($x = 1, 2, \ldots, m$), a proposal j should be selected if it has the maximum nonnegative net present value among all m proposals, i, e.

$$NPV_j = \max_{x \in m}\{NPV_x\} \tag{3.7}$$

provided that $NPV_j \geq 0$.

Net Future Value Method

Since the cash flow profile of an investment can be represented by its equivalent value at any specified reference point in time, the net future value (NFV_x) of a series of cash flows $A_{t,x}$ (for $t = 0, 1, 2, \ldots, n$) for project x is as good a measure of economic potential as the net present value. Equivalent future values are obtained by multiplying a present value by the **compound interest factor** $(F\mid P,i,n)$ which is $(1+i)^n$. Specifically,

$$NFV_x = NPV_x(1+i)^n = NPV_x(F\mid P,i,n) \tag{3.8}$$

Consequently, if $NPV_x \geq 0$, it follows that $NFV_x \geq 0$, and **vice vera**.

Net Equivalent Uniform Annual Value Method

The net equivalent uniform annual value (NUV_x) refers to a uniform series over a planning horizon of n years whose net present value is that of a series of cash flow $A_{t,x}$ (for $t = 0, 1, 2, \ldots, n$) representing project x. That is,

$$NUV_x = NPV_x \frac{i(1+i)^n}{(1+i)^n - 1} = NPV_x(U\mid P,i,n) \tag{3.9}$$

where the symbol $(U\mid P,i,n)$ is referred to as the capital recovery factor and reads as follows: "To find the equivalent annual uniform amount U, given the present value $P=1$, discounted at an annual discount rate i over a period of t years." Hence, if $NPV_x \geq 0$, it follows that $NUV_x \geq 0$, and vice versa.

Benefit-Cost Ratio Method

The benefit-cost ratio method is not as straightforward and unambiguous as the net resent value method but, if applied correctly, will produce the same results as the net present value method. While this method is often used in the evaluation of public projects, the results may be misleading if proper care is not exercised in its application to mutually exclusive proposals.

The benefit-cost ratio is defined as the ratio of the discounted benefits to the discounted cost at the same point in time. In view of Eqs. (3.2) and (3.3), it follows that the criterion for accepting an independent project on the basis of the benefit-cost ratio is whether or not the benefit-cost ratio is greater than or equal to one:

$$\frac{BPV_x}{CPV_x} \geq 1 \tag{3.10}$$

However, a project with the maximum benefit-cost ratio among a group of mutually exclusive proposals generally does not necessarily lead to the maximum net benefit. Consequently, it is necessary to perform **incremental analysis** through **pairwise comparisons** of such proposals in selecting the best in the group. In effect, pairwise comparisons are used to determine if incremental increases in costs between projects yields larger incremental increases in benefits. This approach is not recommended for use in selecting the best among mutually exclusive proposals.

Internal Rate of Return Method

The term **internal rate of return method** has been used by different analysis to mean somewhat different procedures or economic evaluation. The method is often misunderstood and misused, and its popularity among analysis in the private sectors undeserved even when the method is defined and interpreted in the most favorable light. The method is usually applied by comparing the MARR to the internal rate of return value (s) for a project or a set of projects.

A major difficulty in applying the internal rate of return method to economic evaluation is the possible existence of multiple values of IRR when there are two or more changes of sign in the cash flow profile $A_{t,x}$ (for $t = 0, 1, 2, \ldots, n$). When that happens, the method is generally not applicable either in determining the acceptance of independent projects or for selection of the best among a group of mutually exclusive proposals unless a set of well defined decision rules are introduced for incremental analysis. In any case, no advantage is gained by using this method since the procedure is cumbersome even if the method is correctly applied. This method is not recommended for use either in accepting independent projects or in selecting the best among mutually exclusive proposals.

New Words and Phrases

evaluation 评价；评估；估价；求值
systematic 系统的；体系的；分类的；一贯的，惯常的
mutually 互相地；互助
sensitivity 敏感；敏感性；过敏
implicit 含蓄的；暗示的；盲从的
explicit 明确的；清楚的；直率的；详述的
analogous 类似的
nonnegative 正的，非负的

Unit 3 Construction Project of Planning and Decision

economic evaluation 经济评价
the planning horizon 规划期
cash flow profile 现金流量图
minimum attractive rate of return（MARR） 最低收益率
mutually exclusive proposals 互斥方案
net annual cash flow 年净现金流量
social rate of discount 社会贴现率
profit maximization 利润最大化
basic principle 基本原理
budget constraint 预算限制
compound interest factor 复利因子
vice versa 反之亦然
incremental analysis 增量分析
pairwise comparison 成对比较
internal rate of return method 内部收益率法

Part II Speaking

Talks Between the Owner and the Program Manager

Dialogue 1

A: We have studied your proposal, and we think your management approach is best suited to the requirements of this project.
B: Thank you. We are pleased to provide professional construction management service for this project.
A: About the **project duration** what's your opinion?
B: It certainly is difficult to complete so big a project in such a short period of time. Our plan is to use a **fixed-price construction contract** and encourage the contractor to finish the exterior of the building before winter.
A: So you are quite confident of the completion date.
B: Yes. We can continue the interior work during the cold season and make possible your occupancy on schedule next spring.

Dialogue 2

A: We plan to invest $1 million in the project.
B: Well, that's around the **cost estimate** the project.
A: I'd like to know more about the cost estimate.
B: Well, that's just a rough estimate. A best estimate will be provided later. Are all the **appropriations**

available now?

A: Not yet. We need some more details about the budget.

B: No problem. Further information about cost estimate, **cost criteria** and **budget considerations** will be included in our document.

New Words and Phrases

appropriation   经费，专款
project duration   工期
cost estimate   造价估算，成本估计
cost criteria   造价依据
budget considerations   概（预）算根据
fixed-price construction contract   定价施工合同

Unit 4
Bidding and Tendering of Construction Projects

Part I Reading and Translating

1. 建筑工程招标：是指建筑单位（业主）就拟建的工程发布通告，用法定方式吸引建筑项目的承包单位参加竞争，进而通过法定程序从中选择条件优越者来完成工程建筑任务的一种法律行为。

2. 建筑工程投标：是指经过特定审查而获得投标资格的建筑项目承包单位，按照招标文件的要求，在规定的时间内向招标单位填报投标书，争取中标的法律行为。

3. 工程招标制度：也称为工程招标承包制，它是指在市场经济的条件下，采用招投标方式以实现工程承包的一种工程管理制度。工程招投标制的建立与实行是对计划经济条件下单纯运用行政办法分配建设任务的一项重大改革措施，是保护市场竞争、反对市场垄断和发展市场经济的一个重要标志。

Text

Standard Bidding/Tendering Documents

The aim of studying standard bidding documents for procurement of works is to assist practitioners to thoroughly understand biding processes and its documents. It provides an **at a glance** description of bidding documents and biding activities, which occur from the decision to request bidders through to the award of a **contract or engagement**. The other types of bidding documents may vary from little to great extent; however, understanding of standard bidding documents is the necessity to the contractors competing in the international market.

The standard bidding documents for procurement of works have been prepared by the World Bank to be used for the procurement of admeasurement (**unit price or rate**) type of works through **international competitive bidding** in projects that are financed in whole or in part by the World Bank.[1] These bidding documents are not suitable for lump sum contracts without substantial changes to the method of payment and price adjustment, and to the bill of quantities, schedules of activities, and so forth.

The process of prequalification shall follow the procedure indicated in standard prequalification documents: procurement of works, issued by the World Bank. Prequalification is usually used for all major works or complex works. After obtaining approval of the World Bank (post-qualification might be appropriate), an alternative section III, evaluation and qualification criteria could possibly be applied as an exception.

PART 1—BIDDING PROCEDURES
Section I Instructions to Bidders (ITB)

This section provides relevant information to help bidders prepare their bids. Information is also provided on the submission, opening, and evaluation of bids and on the award of contracts. Section I contains provisions are to be used without modification, if the project is wholly or partially funded by the World Bank.

Contents of Clauses of Section I

A. General
1. Scope of Bid
2. Source of Funds
3. Fraud and Corruption
4. Eligible Bidders
5. Eligible Materials, Equipment, and Services

B. Contents of Bidding Document
6. Sections of Bidding Documents
7. Clarification of Bidding Documents, Site Visit, Pre-Bid Meeting
8. Amendment of Bidding Documents

C. Preparation of Bids
9. Cost of Bidding
10. Language of Bid
11. Documents Comprising the Bid
12. Letter of Bid and Schedules
13. Alternative Bids
14. Bid Prices and Discounts
15. Currencies of Bid and Payment
16. Documents Comprising the Technical Proposal
17. Documents Establishing the Qualifications of the Bidder
18. Period of Validity of Bids
19. **Bid Security**
20. Format and Signing of Bid

D. Submission and Opening of Bids
21. **Sealing and Marking of Bids**
22. Deadline for Submission of Bids

23. Late Bids
24. Withdrawal, Substitution, and Modification of Bids
25. Bid Opening

E. Evaluation and Comparison of Bids
26. Confidentiality
27. Clarification of Bids
28. Deviations, Reservations, and Omissions
29. Determination of Responsiveness
30. Nonmaterial Non-conformities
31. Correction of Arithmetical Errors
32. Conversion to Single Currency
33. **Margin of Preference**
34. Evaluation of Bids
35. Comparison of Bid
36. Qualification of the Bidder
37. Employer's Right to Accept Any Bid, and to Reject Any or All Bids

F. Award of Contract
38. Award Criteria
39. Notification of Award
40. Signing of Contract
41. Performance Security

Section Ⅱ Bid Data Sheet (BDS)

This section consists of provisions that are specific to every procurement, and that supplement the information or requirements included in instructions to bidders are also specific to each procurement. The employer must specify in the bid data sheet only the information that the instructions to bidders requests are specified in the bid data sheet. To facilitate the preparation of the bid data sheet, its clauses are numbered with the same numbers as the corresponding instructions to bidders clause.

Section Ⅲ Evaluation and Qualification Criteria

This section contains all the criteria that the employer will use to evaluate bids and qualify bidders. In accordance with instruction to bidders, no other methods, criteria and factors will be used. The bidder shall provide all the information requested in the forms included in Section Ⅳ (bidding forms).

The World Bank requires bidders to be qualified by meeting predefined, precise and minimum requirements. The method entails setting pass-fail criteria, which, if not met by the bidder, results in disqualification. Therefore, it will be necessary to ensure that a bidder's risk of having its bid rejected on grounds of qualification is remote, if due diligence is exercised by the bidder during bid preparation. For this purpose, clear-cut, fail-pass qualification criteria need to be specified in order to enable bidders to make an informed decision whether to pursue a specific contract and if so, either as a single entity or in joint venture. The criteria adopted must relate to characteristics that are essential to ensure satisfactory execution of the contract, and must be stated in unambiguous terms.

Contents of Criteria of Section Ⅲ
1. Evaluation
1.1 Adequacy of **Technical Proposal**
1.2 Multiple Contracts
1.3 Completion Time
1.4 Technical Alternatives
1.5 Domestic Preference
2. Qualification
2.1 Update of Information
2.2 Financial Resources
2.3 Personnel
2.4 Equipment

1.1 Adequacy of Technical Proposal

Evaluation of the bidder's technical proposal will include an assessment of the bidder's technical capacity to mobilize key equipment and personnel for the contract consistent with its proposal, regarding work methods, scheduling, and material sourcing insufficient detail and fully in accordance with the requirements stipulated in Section Ⅵ (employer's requirements).

1.2 Multiple Contracts

Works are grouped in multiple contracts and pursuant to the instructions to bidders, the employer will evaluate and compare bids on the basis of a contract, or a combination of contracts, or as a total of contracts in order to arrive at the least cost combination for the employer by taking into account discounts offered by bidders in case of award of multiple contracts.

2.1 Update of Information

The bidder shall continue to meet the criteria used at the time of prequalification. Updating and reassessment of the following in formation which was previously considered during prequalification will be required:

(a) Eligibility
(b) Pending Litigation
(c) Financial Situation

2.2 Financial Resources

Using the relevant forms in section Ⅳ (bidding forms) the bidder must demonstrate access to, or availability of, financial resources such as liquid assets, unencumbered real assets, lines of credit, and other financial means.

2.3 Personnel

The bidder shall provide details of the proposed personnel and their experience records in the relevant information forms included in section Ⅳ (bidding forms).

Because the managerial and technical competence of a contractor is largely related to the key personnel on site, the bidder should demonstrate having staff with extensive experience, and should be limited to those requiring critical operational or technical skills. The **prequalification criteria** will refer to a limited number of such key personnel, for instance, the project or contract manager and those superintendents working under the project manager who will be responsible for major components (e.g., superintendents specialized in dredging, piling, or earthworks, as required for each particular project).

2.4 Equipment

The bidder must demonstrate that it has the key equipment listed. In most cases bidders can readily purchase, lease, or hire equipment; thus, it is usually unnecessary to assess a contractor's qualification which depends on the contractor's owning readily available items of equipment. The pass-fail criteria adopted will be limited only to those bulky or specialized items that are critical for the type of project to be implemented, and that may be difficult for the contractor to obtain quickly, such as heavy lift cranes and piling barges, dredgers, asphalt mixing plants, etc. Even in such cases, contractors may not own the specialized items of equipment, and may rely on specialist subcontractors or equipment-hire firms, or the availability of such subcontractors.

Section IV   Bidding Forms

This section contains the forms which are to be completed by the bidder and submitted as part of his bid.

The employer will include in the bidding documents all bidding forms that the bidder shall fill out and include in his bid. As specified in section IV of the bidding documents, these forms are the bid submission sheet and relevant schedules, the bid security, the **bill of quantities**, the technical proposal form, and the bidder's qualification information form for which two options are attached. [2]

Section V   Eligible Countries

This section contains information regarding eligible countries, ineligible counties' contractor will be excluded. Consistent with international law, the proceeds of the World Bank's loans, equity investment or guarantees shall not be used for payment to persons or entities or for any import of goods, if such payment or import is prohibited by a decision of **the United Nations Security Council** taken under Chapter VII of the charter of the United Nations. [3] Persons or entities, or suppliers offering goods and services, covered by such prohibition shall therefore not be eligible for the award of World Bank-Financed contracts.

PART 2—Works Requirements

Section VI   Works Requirements

This section contains the specification, the drawings, and supplementary information that describe the works to be procured.

PART 3—CONDITIONS OF CONTRACT AND CONTRACT FORMS

Section VII   General Conditions (GC)

This section contains the general clauses to be applied in all contracts. The text of the clauses in this section shall not be modified.

Section VIII   Particular Conditions (PC)

As the standard text of the general conditions chosen must be retained intact, any amendments and additions to the general conditions will be introduced in the particular conditions.

The contents of this section supplement the general conditions and will be prepared by the employer. Whenever there is a conflict, the provisions herein shall prevail over those in the general conditions.

The use of standard conditions of contract for all civil works will ensure comprehensiveness of coverage, better balance of rights or obligations between employer and contractor, general acceptability of its provisions, and savings in time and cost for bid preparation and review, leading to more economical prices. [4]

The particular conditions take precedence over the general conditions. It is good practice to have a list of tax and custom regulations applicable in the country, to be provided as non-binding general information, attached to the bidding documents.

Section IX Annex to the Particular Conditions—Contract Forms

This section contains forms, which shall be completed by bidders, will form part of the contract. Section IX of the bidding documents also contains forms for the contract agreement, the performance security, and the **advance payment security**. After notification of award, the employer will prepare the contract agreement using the contract agreement form and send it to the successful bidder. The successful bidder shall sign the contract agreement and return it to the employer together with the performance security and the advance payment security, using the respective forms provided in section IX.[5]

The notification of award will be the basis for formation of the contract as described in instructions to bidders. This standard form will be filled in and sent to the successful bidder, after evaluation of bids has been completed.

New Words and Phrases

at a glance   一瞥，看一眼
contract or engagement   合同
unit price or rate   单位价格或费率
international competitive bidding   国际上竞争性招标
bid security   招标担保
sealing and marking of bids   投标文件封档
margin of preference   优惠幅度
bid data sheet   投标资料表
technical proposal   技术标
prequalification criteria   资格预审标准
bill of quantity   工程量清单
the United Nations Security Council   联合国安全理事会
advance payment security   预付款担保

Notes

[1] The standard bidding documents for procurement of works have been prepared by the World Bank to be used for the procurement of admeasurement (unit price or rate) type of works through international competitive bidding in projects that are financed in whole or in part by the World Bank.

项目采购的标准招标文件（SBDPW）由世界银行编制，世界银行完全或部分提供资金的项目需通过国际竞争性招标，这些标准文件用于单价（单位价格或费率）类型的采购。

[2] As specified in section IV of the bidding documents, these forms are the bid submission sheet and relevant schedules, the bid security, the bill of quantities, the technical proposal form, and the bidder's qualification information form for which two options are attached.

正如投标文件第四节所规定的，这些表格是标书提交总表及相关的表格、投标担保、工程量清单、技术方案表及投标人资格信息表，这些表格中包括两种选择。

[3] Consistent with international law, the proceeds of the World Bank's loans, equity investment or guarantees shall not be used for payment to persons or entities or for any import of goods, if such payment or

import is prohibited by a decision of the United Nations Security Council taken under Chapter Ⅶ of the charter of the United Nations.

与国际法一致，世界银行贷款的盈利、产权投资或者担保将不被用于对自然人或者实体或者针对任何商品进口的付款，如果这样的付款或者进口被联合国安全理事会根据联合国宪章第七章的规定做出的决议所禁止的话。

[4] The use of standard conditions of contract for all civil works will ensure comprehensiveness of coverage, better balance of rights or obligations between employer and contractor, general acceptability of its provisions, and savings in time and cost for bid preparation and review, leading to more economical prices.

土木工程合同标准条件的使用将确保合同覆盖范围的广度、雇主和承包商之间权利和义务的更均衡、其条款的广泛接受性、标书编制和审查的时间和成本的节约，从而实现更经济的价格。

[5] The successful bidder shall sign the contract agreement and return it to the employer together with the performance security and the advance payment security, using the respective forms provided in section Ⅸ.

中标人将使用第九节中提供的表格签署合同协议并连同履约担保、预付款担保一起返还给雇主。

Exercises

I. Translate the following phrases into English.

1. 低的固定资本需求
2. 初步费用
3. 现金流的短缺
4. 政府干预
5. 绩效责任
6. 供应链

II. Translate the following sentences into Chinese.

1. It will be necessary to plot income against expenditure using the programme of works and the bill of quantities-activity schedule-payments in arrears and retentions, both from the employer and to subcontractors must be considered. Upon completion of the review, the contractor will grade the bid based on the interest to the company and recommend whether or not to bid.

2. The bidding strategies of some contractors are influenced by a policy of minimum percentage markup for general overhead and profit.

3. A true story relating to translation resulted, not in the subcontract, but the subcontractor being executed.

4. Nowadays, international contractors are mitigating risk by declining work perceived as too risky, subcontracting large portions of their work to others, and apportioning risk in wage structures. In essence, contractors are passing risk on to others in the supply chain; therefore, they seem adept at managing risk.

Passage A

The Bidding/Tendering Process

Introduction

A bid is the final price or "offer" which is submitted to the client by the contractor, is a sum of money for which he prepared to carry out the work, and will include not only the estimate, but also the margin of overheads and profit. Bidding is the process by which an employer/client procures a building project.

The biding process typically engages a number of parties, each of whom invests considerable time and money in the competition for a **construction contract**. Most of the rules of the competition are set out in the bid package. But the process also involves implied obligations and duties of fairness which do not appear in documents and are not easily defined. For these reasons, the bidding process is one of the most **contentious** and highly-litigated aspects of the construction process.

Equally, it represents a high-risk area for the consultants who are retained to guide employers through this **complicated process**. The bidders compete not only with each other, but also with the employers to protect their profit. This is almost certainly as a result of the cost and uncertainty that is inherent in any competitive process. It is the very nature of a bidding process that all parties are in competition with each other and, each is fully entitled to act in their own interests.

Prequalification

Prequalification is a method of determining **bidder responsibility** before soliciting bids. Employers can use prequalification to restrict the bidding to a group of bidders who meet **predetermined responsibility standards**. Procedures are not rigid, and employers rate bidders according to their own special requirements. Responsibility standards may include the bidder's **integrity**, ability, experience, past performance, financial ability, safety record, bonding capacity, **claims record**, and available staff. Employers can use prequalification by projects or for a stated time.

The major international agencies such as the World Bank and the Asian Development Bank etc., typically will request all bidders to pass prequalification (some of the projects indicating post-qualification requirement). The successful execution of contracts for are buildings, **civil engineering**, supply and installation, **turnkey**, and design-and-build projects requires that contracts are awarded only to firms, or combinations of firms, that are suitably experienced in the type of work and **construction technology** involved, that are financially and managerially sound, and that can provide all the equipment required in a timely manner. Prequalification usually consists of the following stages:

- Advertisement and notification.
- Preparing and issuing **a prequalification document**.
- Preparation and submission of applications.

- Opening and evaluation of applications.
- Updating and confirmation of bidder's qualification.

The notification will be given in sufficient time to enable prospective bidders to obtain prequalification or bidding documents and prepare and submit their responses. Where large works or complex items of equipment are involved, this period will generally be not less than twelve weeks to enable prospective bidders to conduct investigations before submitting their bids. Various **construction industry associations** have excellent publications available for references on competitive bidding.

Bidding/Tendering Process

All qualified bidders will be rendered further instructions or information to bid. The **International Competitive Bidding (ICB) process** includes the following stages:

Preparing and Issuing a Bidding Document

For **open bidding**, employers publish an advertisement for bids newspapers and trade papers. This advertisement notifies all qualified bidders of the project in the international market.

When preparing and issuing of the bidding document, the employer will use the standard bidding documents issued by the World Bank, as it is **mandatory requirement** for contracts financed by the World Bank. The Section I Instructions to Bidders (ITB) and Section VII General Conditions of Contract (GCC) are subject to no modification or without suppressing or adding text to the document.

Bid Preparation and Submission

During this stage, the bidding documents may need modification. The employer will promptly respond to requests for **clarifications** from bidders and amend if needed, and **addenda** issued by the architect/engineer or employer transmits notice of modifications to all prospective bidders. The bidder is responsible for the preparation and submission of its bid. The conversion of the estimate into bid is undertaken by the bidder for all aspects of the project evaluation, other than **pure costs** are considered. Preparation during a bid process is not without risk, as the invitation to bid document is an invitation to treat (albeit creating a separate contract); the bid is hopefully an offer, capable of acceptance within a prescribed time, and the acceptance creates a binding contract.

Pre-bid Meeting/Conference

The employer will usually develop from submitted prequalification materials a selected list of qualified bidders, and conduct pre-bid meetings with prequalified bidders to familiarize bidders with the necessary documents and agreements relating to the project. Large or complicated projects usually require a pre-bid meeting, while small straightforward projects usually do not require a pre-bid meeting. The employer and architect/engineer conduct the pre-bid meeting to familiarize bidders with specifics of the project. Topics to address at the pre-bid meeting include the following:

- Introduction of the architect/engineer and employer's construction representatives.
- Project details and requirements.
- Employer's bidding documents and **construction procedures**.
- Unusual project requirements.
- Question and answer period.
- **Site tour.**

At the pre-bid meeting, the architect/engineer presents the project's details, conducts the question-and-answer session, and leads a tour of the project site. If necessary the architect/engineer will prepare records of the items discussed at the pre-bid meetings, issue an addendum to answer questions asked at the presentation or project site tour, including questions and answers, and distribute to all prospective bidders.

Bid Opening

Bid opening will be at a specified time, usually immediately after the receipt of bids. Attendance may be limited to the employer and architect/engineer, or the employer may also invite bidders. Bid opening is a critical event in the bidding process; the employer will appoint experienced staff to conduct the bid opening strictly following the procedures as specified in the instruction to bidders for all bids received not later than the date and time of the bid submission deadline. A bid for which a bid withdrawal or bid **substitution** notice was received on time shall not be opened, but returned unopened to the bidder. If encounter unexpected delay or unforeseeable circumstances, the employer may require cancellation of the bidding process and put off the procedures before bid opening.

The sequence in which bids are handled and opened is crucial. The employer will, however, verify at bid opening the validity of the documentation (power of attorney) or other acceptable equivalent document as specified in instruction to bidders, confirming the validity of a bid modification, bid withdrawal, or bid substitution as the case may be, because a withdrawn or substituted bid shall not be opened and not read out consequently and, therefore, they shall not be further considered by the employer. Similarly, a bid modification shall be opened and read out to modify a bid that was received on time.

Bid Evaluation/Review

The employer is responsible for bid evaluation and contract award. The employer will appoint experienced architect/engineer to conduct the evaluation of the bids. The architect/engineer will review all bids received for responsiveness, participate in investigating the lowest and best responsible bidders and deliver a written recommendation to the employer about the award of, or rejection of any bids for each construction contract. The architect/engineer and employer will have sole **discretion** to make the final decision on bid awards.

Usually, the architect/engineer and employer will conduct pre-award conferences with apparently successful bidders and will gather documentation for contract execution from such bidders. This is a matter of assessing the intention of the parties. Where the signing of a formal document is envisaged, the parties did not intend to be bound until the formal documentation has been prepared and signed. Making a **counter-offer** will have the effect of negating the original bid, if the bidder is asked to confirm that the bid remains open for acceptance on the revised basis.

Contract Award

After selecting the bidders, the employer prepares a notice of award (letter of intention) and sends it to the successful bidder. Attached to the notice are the construction agreement, the conditions of contracts, **construction bonds**, **insurance requirements**, and other documents. This notice **sets forth** the conditions regarding contract award and the time allowed to sign and to return the agreement and other required documents. However, the notice does not authorize the start of construction. Construction starts after both parties execute the construction agreement and the employer issues a notice to proceed.

After the employer receives the signed agreement and other documents and finds everything satisfactory, the employer will execute the contract by signing the agreement. The employer then will send a copy of the executed contract to the successful bidder, now the contractor. If the successful bidder does not return the signed agreement and required documents within the time allowed, or if the required documents are not satisfactory, then the employer usually has the right to reject the bid and start proceedings with the next lowest bidder.

New Words and Phrases

contentious 有争议的,诉讼的
integrity 完整;廉正;诚实,正直
turnkey 工程总承包
clarification 澄清
addenda 附录,附加物
substitution 代替,代替物;置换
discretion 考虑周到,自由裁决权
the bidding/tendering process 投标过程
construction contract 建筑工程承包合同
complicated process 复杂的程序
bidder responsibility 投标责任
predetermined responsibility standard 预定的责任标准
claims record 索赔记录
civil engineering 土木工程
construction technology 施工技术
prequalification document 资格预审文件
construction industry association 建筑行业协会
International Competitive Bidding (ICB) process 国际竞争投标过程
open bidding 公开招标
mandatory requirement 硬性要求,强制性的要求
pure cost 纯粹成本,净成本
construction procedures 施工程序
site tour 场地参观
bid opening 开标
bid evaluation/review 评标
counter-offer 还价
contract award 合同授予
construction bonds 施工契约
insurance requirement 保险要求
set forth 陈列;出发,宣布

Bidding Procedure of Construction Projects

The implementing agencies of borrowing countries can use a variety of procurement methods on World

Bank-financed projects. The method selected depends on a number of factors including the type of goods or services being procured, the value of the goods or services being procured, the potential interest of foreign bidders and even the cost of the procurement process itself. The overall objective of the **guidelines** how to select procurement methods is to allow borrowing countries to buy high quality goods and services as economically as possible. In the World Bank's experience, this objective is best achieved through **transparent**, formal **competitive bidding**. For the procurement of equipment and civil works, International Competitive Bidding (ICB) is the procurement method the World Bank encourages its borrowers to use in the majority of cases. Under ICB, cost is the primary factor in determining a **winning bid**. Other methods for procuring goods and civil works include **limited international bidding**, **national competitive bidding**, **international shopping**, and **direct contracting**. This section outlines the bidding process of International Competitive Bidding.

The objective of International Competitive Bidding (ICB) is to provide all eligible prospective bidders with timely and adequate notification of a borrower's requirements and an equal opportunity to bid for the required goods and works.

Notification

Timely notification of bidding opportunities is essential in competitive bidding. For projects which include procurement on the basis of ICB, the borrower is required to prepare and submit to the bank a draft general procurement notice. The bank will arrange for its publication in Development Business (UNDB). The notice shall contain information concerning the borrower (or prospective borrower), amount and purpose of the loan, scope of procurement under ICB, and the name and address of the borrower's agency responsible for procurement and the address of the website where specific procurement notices will be posted. If known, the scheduled date for availability of prequalification or bidding documents should be indicated. The borrower shall maintain a list of responses to the notice. The related prequalification or bidding documents, as the case may be, shall not be released to the public earlier than eight weeks after the date of publication of the notice. The general procurement notice shall be updated annually for all outstanding procurement.

Prequalification of Bidders

Prequalification is usually necessary for large or complex works, or in any other circumstances in which the high costs of preparing detailed bids could discourage competition, such as custom-designed equipment, industrial plant, specialized services, and contracts to be let under turnkey, design and build, or management contracting. This also ensures that invitations to bid are extended only to those who have adequate capabilities and resources. Prequalification may also be useful to determine eligibility for preference for domestic contractors where this is allowed. Prequalification shall be based entirely upon the capability and resources of prospective bidders to perform the particular contract satisfactorily, taking into account their (a) experience and past performance on similar contracts, (b) capabilities with respect to personnel, equipment, and construction or manufacturing facilities, and (c) financial position.

Borrowers shall inform all applicants of the results of prequalification. As soon as prequalification is completed, the bidding documents shall be made available to the qualified prospective bidders. For prequalification for groups of contracts to be awarded over a period of time, a limit for the number or total value of awards to any one bidder may be made on the basis of the bidder's resources. The list of prequalified firms in such instances shall be updated periodically. Verification of the information provided in the submission for prequalification shall be confirmed at the time of award of contract, and award may be denied to a bidder that is judged to no longer have the capability or resources to successfully perform the contract.

Preparation of the Bidding Documents

The bidding documents shall furnish all information necessary for a prospective bidder to prepare a bid for the goods and works to be provided. While the detail and complexity of these documents may vary with the size and nature of the proposed bid package and contract, they generally include: invitation to bid; instructions to bidders; form of bid; form of contract; conditions of contract, both general and special; specifications and drawings; relevant technical data (including of geological and environmental nature); list of goods or bill of quantities; delivery time or schedule of completion; and necessary appendices, such as formats for various securities. The basis for bid evaluation and selection of the lowest evaluated bid shall be clearly outlined in the instructions to bidders and/or the specifications. If a fee is charged for the bidding documents, it shall be reasonable and reflect only the cost of their printing and delivery to prospective bidders, and shall not be so high as to discourage qualified bidders.

The bidding documents shall be so worded as to permit and encourage international competition and shall set forth clearly and precisely the work to be carried out, the location of the work, the goods to be supplied, the place of delivery or installation, the schedule for delivery or completion, minimum performance requirements, and the warranty and maintenance requirements, as well as any other pertinent terms and conditions. In addition, the bidding documents, where appropriate, shall define the tests, standards, and methods that will be employed to judge the conformity of equipment as delivered, or works as performed, with the specifications. Drawings shall be consistent with the text of the specifications, and an order of precedence between two shall be specified.

The bidding documents shall specify any factors, in addition to price, which will be taken into account in evaluating bids, and how such factors will be quantified or otherwise evaluated. If bids based on alternative designs, materials, completion schedules, payment terms, etc., are permitted, conditions for their acceptability and the method of their evaluation shall be expressly stated. Any additional information, clarification, correction of errors, or modifications of bidding documents shall be sent to each recipient of the original bidding documents in sufficient time before the deadline for receipt of bids to enable bidders to take appropriate actions. If necessary, the deadline shall be extended. The bank shall receive a copy (in hard copy format or sent electronically) and be consulted for issuing a "no objection" when the contract is subject to prior review.

Specific Procurement Notices (invitation to Bid)

The international community shall also be notified in a timely manner of the opportunities to bid for specific contracts. To that end, invitations to prequalify or to bid, as the case may be, shall be advertised as specific procurement notices in at least one newspaper of national circulation in the borrower's country (and in the official gazette, if any). Such invitations shall also be transmitted to those who have expressed interest in bidding in response to the general procurement Notice. Publication of the invitations in the development business is also encouraged. Borrowers are also strongly encouraged to transmit such invitations to embassies and trade representatives of countries of likely suppliers and contractors. Additionally, for large, specialized or important contracts, borrowers shall advertise the invitations in development business and/or well-known technical magazines, newspapers and trade publications of wide international circulation. Notification shall be given in sufficient time to enable prospective bidders to obtain prequalification or bidding documents and prepare and submit their responses.

Borrowers shall provide reasonable access to project sites for visits by prospective bidders. For works or complex supply contracts, particularly for those requiring refurbishing existing works or equipment, a pre-bid conference may be arranged whereby potential bidders may meet with borrower representatives to seek clarifications. Minutes of the conference shall be provided to all prospective bidders with a copy to the bank (in hard copy or sent electronically). The deadline and place for receipt of bids shall be specified in the invitation to bid.

Time for Preparation of Bids

The time allowed for the preparation and submission of bids shall be determined with due consideration of the particular circumstances of the project and the magnitude and complexity of the contract. Generally, not less than six weeks from the date of the invitation to bid or the date of availability of bidding documents, whichever is later, shall be allowed for ICB. Where large works or complex items of equipment are involved, this period shall generally be not less than twelve weeks to enable prospective bidders to conduct investigations before submitting their bids. In such cases, the borrower is encouraged to convene pre-bid conferences and arrange site visits. Bidders shall be permitted to submit bids by mail or by hand.

Opening of Bids

The time for the bid opening shall be the same as for the deadline for receipt of bids or promptly thereafter, and shall be announced, together with the place for bid opening, in the invitation to bid. The borrower shall open all bids at the stipulated time and place. Bids shall be opened in public; that is, bidders or their representatives shall be allowed to be present. The name of the bidder and total amount of each bid, and of any alternative bids if they have been requested or permitted, shall be read aloud and recorded when opened and a copy of this record shall be promptly sent to the bank. bids received after the time stipulated, as well as those not opened and read out at bid opening, shall not be considered.

Evaluation of Bids

Firstly, the borrower shall examine the bids to ascertain whether the bids (a) meet the eligibility requirements specified in the guidelines, (b) have been properly signed, (c) are accompanied by the required securities, (d) are substantially responsive to the bidding documents, and (e) are otherwise generally in order. If a bid is not substantially responsive, that is, it contains material deviations from or reservations to the terms, conditions and specifications in the bidding documents, it shall not be considered further. The bidder shall not be permitted to correct or withdraw material deviations or reservations once bids have been opened.

The next step is to apply the evaluation criteria specified in the bidding documents and adjust each bid as appropriate using the evaluation criteria. Only the criteria specified in the bid document can be applied. No new criteria must be introduced at evaluation, and the specified criteria must be applied wherever appropriate. Specified criteria cannot be waived during evaluation.

The Borrower shall prepare a detailed report on the evaluation and comparison of bids setting forth the specific reasons on which the recommendation is based for the award of the contract.

Post Qualification of Bidders

If bidders have not been prequalified, the Borrower shall determine whether the bidder whose bid has been determined to offer the lowest evaluated cost has the capability and resources to effectively carry out the contract as offered in the bid. The criteria to be met shall be set out in the bidding documents, and if the bidder does not meet them, the bid shall be rejected. In such an event, the Borrower shall make a similar determination for the next lowest evaluated bidder.

Award of Contract or Rejection of All Bids

The borrower shall award the contract, within the period of the validity of bids, to the bidder who meets the appropriate standards of capability and resources and whose bid has been determined (a) to be substantially responsive to the bidding documents and (b) to offer the lowest evaluated cost. A bidder shall not be required, as a condition of award, to undertake responsibilities for work not stipulated in the bidding documents or otherwise to modify the bid as originally submitted.

Bidding documents usually provide that borrowers may reject all bids. Rejection of all bids is justified when there is lack of effective competition, or bids are not substantially responsive. If all bids are rejected, the borrower shall review the causes justifying the rejection and consider making revisions to the conditions of contract, design and specifications, scope of the contract, or a combination of these, before inviting new bids. All bids shall not be rejected if new bids invited on the same bidding and contract documents are solely for the purpose of obtaining lower prices. The bank's prior concurrence shall be obtained before rejecting all bids, soliciting new bids or entering into negotiations with the lowest evaluated bidder.

New Words and Phrases

guideline 指南；指引；指导方针
transparent 透明的；显然的；坦率的；易懂的
competitive bidding 竞标
winning bid 中标
limited international bidding 有限国际招标

national competitive bidding　　国内竞争性招标
international shopping　　国际询价采购
direct contracting　　直接采购
prequalification of bidder　　投标人资格预审
post qualification of bidder　　对投标人的资格后审
award of contract or rejection of all bid　　授予合同或拒绝所有投标

Part II　Speaking

Collecting Tender Document

A: Excuse me, may I collect a tender document here?

B: Was your company qualified in the prequalification?

A: Yes, we were informed by your office two days ago.

B: Which company are you from?

A: China Construction Group.

B: Please show me your company authorization letter for collecting the tender document and your name card.

A: Here you are.

B: Okay, that's fine. The tender document includes three booklets and thirty-six sheets of tender drawing. This is Booklet 1; it includes Instructions to the Tenders, **Form of Tender**, **Articles of Agreement**, **General Conditions of Contract** and **Special Conditions of Contract**.

A: What is the **Performance Bond** requirement?

B: 10% of the Contract Sum. The main points of concern in the Conditions of Contract, such as **Construction Duration**, **Liquidated Damages**, **Percentage of Retention** and **Maintenance Period** are abstracted in Appendix A to Form of Tender. Form of Performance Bond is shown in Appendix B to Form of Tender.

A: I see. What about Booklets 2 and 3?

B: Booklet 2 contains all the Specifications.

A: Is the Finishing Schedule also included in Booklet 2?

B: Yes, you can find it in the chapter for architectural works. Method of Measurement and **Bill of Quantities** are included in Booklet 3. This is a list of tender drawings. You can check the tender drawings against the list.

A: Thirty-six sheets of tender drawings, exactly.

B: Please sign here for my record.

New Words and Phrases

instruction to tender　　投标须知
form of tender　　投标书
articles of agreement　　协议书
general conditions of contract　　通用合同条件
special conditions of contract　　专用合同条件

performance bond　履约保函
construction duration　工期
liquidated damage　误期罚款
percentage of retention　滞留金百分比
maintenance period　保修期
bill of quantities　工程量清单

Unit 5
Contract Management of Construction Projects

Part I Reading and Translating

Professional Knowledge Guidance

1. 建设工程合同：是指承包人进行工程建设，发包人支付价款的合同。建设工程合同包括工程勘察、设计、施工合同。建设工程合同是一种诺成合同，合同订立生效后双方应当严格履行。建设工程合同也是一种双务、有偿合同，当事人双方在合同中都有各自的权利和义务，在享有权利的同时必须履行义务。

2. 建设工程合同的双方当事人：分别称为承包人和发包人。承包人，是指在建设工程合同中负责工程的勘察、设计、施工任务的一方当事人，承包人最主要的义务是进行工程建设，即进行工程的勘察、设计、施工等工作。发包人是指在建设工程合同中委托承包人进行工程的勘察、设计、施工任务的建设单位（或业主、项目法人），发包人最主要的义务是向承包人支付相应的价款。

3. 合同管理：企业的经济往来，主要是通过合同形式进行的。一个企业的经营成败和合同及合同管理有密切关系。企业合同管理是指企业对以自身为当事人的合同依法进行订立、履行、变更、解除、转让、终止及审查、监督、控制等一系列行为的总称。其中订立、履行、变更、解除、转让、终止是合同管理的内容；审查、监督、控制是合同管理的手段。合同管理必须是全过程的、系统性的、动态性的。

Project Contract Management

Introduction

Contract management plays a significant role in construction project management system, since construction project management involves groups of people representing different **disciplines**, from project managers, contract managers, and division managers to subcontractors, architects, engineers, suppliers, and clients—all trying to collaborate on a multitude of issues and changes while **juggling** multiple documents and contracts. [1] From the signing of the contract, the **implementation** of the contract, and finally the **termination** of the contract, main contractor must guarantee the project running smoothly and they receive the final expected result.

Construction contract management involves the activities necessary to effect and determine the fulfillment of the contract requirements by the parties to the construction contract. Construction contract management begins when the agreement between the employer and contractor is executed and ends when final payment is accepted by the contractor.

Contract managers must monitor cost, scope, quality, and time frame and must ensure that all contract conditions are met. This important work affects both the financial and the actual success of the project or company. Contract management must ensure that:

- The employer's interests are protected and its obligations are met.
- The contractual obligations of the service provider are met.
- Contract milestones are duly **discharged**.
- Key **deliverables** are received.
- Contract related processes are completed.
- Any variations, claims, issues, disputes, and any additional funding requirements are managed.

The Targets of Contract Management

The important targets of a contract are to manage the contract within the following constraints: time, cost, and quality.

Cost is the responsibility of quantity surveyor whether you are contractor's quantity surveyor the consultant's **quantity surveyor**. There is a close relationship between planning and management. [2] The quantity surveyor uses the **bill of quantity** as the management tool in managing the project.

In managing the time of a construction project, a construction program prepared by the contractor and accepted by the engineer is used to manage the time, since all the activities required to complete the project is identified, and relationships between different activities and durations are identified and can be easily monitored. If **deviations** occur, the **remedial** action could be taken to **mitigate** the delay. There is a close relationship between cost and time. Delay in the completion of the project inevitably means increases in cost. The costs on a project depend on the quantity of the work, duration of the work and site establishment costs. Moreover, it is apparent that nonconformance of quality will cause many secondary problems such as schedule delay, cost overruns, sub-contractor insolvency etc.

The Contract Documents

Incomplete or inaccurate contract documents require additional time and effort on the part of project participants, and progress may be delayed while interpretations or revisions are being prepared. Contract modifications are typically required to resolve issues resulting from incomplete or inaccurate contract documents. The time and effort required to prepare and respond to the contract modifications may distract contractor from concentrating on the project. Negotiating price and time revisions often result in disagreement or conflict.

Contract Documents

The contract documents are listed and enumerated in the agreement and referred to in the conditions of the contract for the work to be performed. They are the legal documents which describe the work requirement. The contract documents describe the proposed construction works that result performing services, furnishing labor, and supplying and incorporating materials and equipment into the construction works.

Contract and Agreements

Contract documents consist of both written and graphic element and typically include the following:

These include contracting forms (agreement) and conditions of contract (general and supplementary conditions, or employer furnished general or particular special conditions) as well as various named attachments and forms.[3] Revisions, clarifications and modifications are changes applicable to the contract documents such as addenda issued during the procurement process or change orders issued during the course of the work.

Specifications

These include specific written requirements for the work. Specifications define the quality requirements for products, materials and workmanship upon which the contract is based and establish requirements for administration and performance of the project.

Contract Drawings

Contract drawings are those named in the agreement and can be supplemented by various forms of interpretations and modifications including small-size sketches. These include large graphic illustrations of the physical form of the work to be performed. They show the quantitative extent and relationships of elements to one another. They help to establish the extent of the work and are complementary with the specifications. Contract drawings are general bound separately because of their larger size.

Record Drawings

The contract documents may require record drawings. Often the architect may issue new versions of drawings to indicate changes and field conditions. Concealed conditions and utility locations are the most common information required. The contract documents indicate the type of information required to be included on the record drawings. These record drawings are as a permanent record of the actual conditions of the completed work.

There are several types of drawings, reports, and specifications that may be utilized during construction but may not be included with the contract documents. These may include surveys, hazardous material reports, assessments, and geotechnical data. The contract documents are interrelated and they provide different types of information required to carry out the work.

The contract documents consist of in order of **precedence** the following:

- **Letter of acceptance.**
- Contract agreement.
- **MOU** if any.
- Particular conditions of contract.
- Contract data.

- General conditions of contract.
- Copies of guarantees and bonds.
- Insurance.
- Drawings.
- Specifications.
- Bills of quantities.
- Any other **pertaining** documents.

The Main Objects of Contract Management

Finance Management

The main tasks of financial management include resource planning, cost estimation, cost planning and cost control. Before signing a contract, everything possible has to be taken into account, to assure that every party has its own responsibilities lined up more specifically than its **financial obligations**. According to the cost planning measures would be taken to any deviations that are bound to occur, maximize the financial benefit for the project.

Subcontract Management

It will probably take a huge amount of the main contractor's time and energy to manage subcontractors, including **designated subcontractor**, **nominated subcontractor** and **domestic subcontractors**. The main contractor takes equivalent responsibilities or obligations consistent with those undertaken by any subcontractor. The main contractor may be held liable for defective work carried out by a subcontractor and responsible for the acts, **defaults** and neglects of any subcontractor as fully as if they were deemed as the defaults or neglects of the main contractor. The main contractor is also responsible for health and safety on the building site.

Progress Management

A construction contract will generally set a period for completion of the works. That period may be specified in the tender documents or otherwise agreed with the contractor before a contract is awarded. The contract may impose **liquidated** damages, in the form of a charge per day or per week on the contractor, for failing to meet the **specified completion time**. In order to finish the project on time, the importance of progress management is to makes sure certain tasks are finished on schedule.

Tasks in progress management include schedule making, **project follow-ups**, schedule updates, and reports. These tasks usually take place in the control department, and are assorted into the engineering department, the procurement department, the construction department, and the quality department. If a delay occurs that is not within the contractor's control, the main contractor is entitled to request for the time for completion to be extended.

Quality Management

Maintaining good quality is one of the main objectives of construction management in addition to meeting designated schedule and cost. In addition, quality is one of the important factors considered when determining the success of a project. Quality in construction projects can be classified in various ways. There are various objects and methods of quality control according to phases of the project life cycle. Quality management includes the processes required to ensure that the project will satisfy the needs for which it was undertaken.

It includes all activities of the overall management function that determine the quality policy, objectives, and responsibilities and implements them by means such as quality planning, quality control, quality assurance, and quality improvement, within the quality system. Documentation quality management contributes to smoothness or otherwise of the construction process, and may influence cost and time to a degree.

Health, Safety and Environment Management

The target of health, safety and environment management is to guarantee people's health and safety, protect nature, reduce pollution, and stimulate **sustainable development**. When a project management organization is established, the parties' obligations are largely set out in the contract documents, however, there are also **regulatory requirements** created by government law that will not be specified in the contract documents. The regulatory requirements of the health, safety and environment protection are different in different countries. The contractor is liable for compliance with all **statutory requirements**, if the contractor just follow the domestic requirements without paying attention to the local requirements; this may cause the project to fail when examined. The contractor is responsible for the giving of all notices necessary to comply with regulatory requirements and the payment of all necessary fees, charges and other **imposts** other than those notices and imposts to be given or paid by the client under the contract.

Managing Variations and Claims

If the client's representative or engineer instructs (directs) a variation, the contractor is obliged to carry out the instruction. A variation becomes part of the contract and all the contract conditions apply to the changed work, including provisions for extensions of time and site conditions (if applicable). There is a risk that actions of the client may delay the completion of a construction contract, thus it is therefore important to manage variations effectively in order to reduce the risk of exceeding the budget and completing the project late. Variations are one of the main reasons for cost and time **overruns** in construction contracts (please refer to last unit for more information).

The contractor will be entitled to claims for additional payment and for an extension to the period for completion following a variation instruction. The additional payment may include additional costs for delay, acceleration and/or disruption associated with the variation.[4] Construction contracts involve various matters for which the contractor may **make a claim against** the client. Most frequently, these claims are for payment and/or additional time. Claims for additional payment can arise for a multitude of reasons including disputes over variations, changes in circumstances, prolongation claims and disruption claims.

Summary

In brief, contract management should contain the following characteristics:

- Control construction project's contracts, budgets, forecast costs, and deliverables.
- Collaborate between project managers, contract managers, administrators, subcontractors, architects, engineers, suppliers, and clients.
- Ensure project changes are resolved, payment is made, and claims are avoided.
- Be prepared for the unexpected and have the information necessary to negotiate cost and schedule details to final resolution.
- Track daily reports, meeting minutes, and materials delivered against **purchase orders**.
- Instantly reflect cost or schedule impact of any change, and identify which contractors are impacted.

● Analyze **comparative trends** and cause/effect among projects to maximize efficiency while minimizing project costs, risks and safety issues.

● Manage, implement, administer, conduct, and guide effective contract administration function for the organization from proposal through contract close.

New Words and Phrases

discipline　学科；纪律，惩罚；训练，训导
juggling　欺骗的，变戏法的；欺骗，杂耍
implementation　履行，实现；安装启用
termination　结束，终止
discharge　免除，放出；排除，流出
deliverable　可交付使用的，可以传达的
deviation　偏差，偏离，偏向
remedial　补救的，治疗的；矫正的
mitigate　减轻，缓和下来；使缓和，使减轻
precedence　优先，居先
MOU　谅解备忘录
pertaining　有关的，附属的；关于
default　违约；拖欠，不到场；缺席，缺乏
liquidate　清理，清算（破产的企业）；清偿，了债（债务等）；肃清，消灭
impost　关税，税款
overrun　超出限度；泛滥成灾
quantity surveyor　预算师或造价师
bill of quantity　工料清单，工程量清单
letter of acceptance　接收函
finance management　财务管理
financial obligations　财务责任
subcontract management　分包管理
designated subcontractor　指定的分包商
nominated subcontractor　被提名的分包商
domestic subcontractor　国内的分包商
progress management　进度管理
specified completion time　指定的完成时间
project follow-ups　工程随访
sustainable development　可持续发展
regulatory requirement　监管要求
statutory requirements　法规要求，法令要求
make a claim against　向……索赔
purchase orders　订单
comparative trend　比较趋势

Notes

[1] Contract management plays a significant role in construction project management system, since construction project management involves groups of people representing different disciplines, from project managers, contract managers, and division managers to subcontractors, architects, engineers, suppliers, and clients—all trying to collaborate on a multitude of issues and changes while juggling multiple documents and contracts.

在建设项目管理系统中,合同管理扮演着极其重要的角色,由于建设项目管理涉及代表不同专业学科的团队,从项目经理、合同经理及部门经理到分包商、建筑师、工程师、供应商和业主——全体人员都在设法尽力应对多种文件和合同的同时,在大量争端和变更上面进行协作。

[2] Cost is the responsibility of quantity survey or whether you are contractor's quantity surveyor or the consultant's quantity surveyor. There is a close relationship between planning and management.

工程造价是工程造价师的职责,无论你是承包商的造价师,还是咨询企业的造价师,工程进度与工程管理存在着密切的联系。

[3] These include contracting forms (agreement) and conditions of contract (general and supplementary conditions, or employer furnished general or particular special conditions) as well as various named attachments and forms.

合同文件还包括签约形式(协议)及合同条件(总体和辅助条件,或者业主提供的总体或特殊条件),以及若干指定的附件和表格。

[4] The contractor will be entitled to claims for additional payment and for an extension to the period for completion following a variation instruction. The additional payment may include additional costs for delay, acceleration and/or disruption associated with the variation.

承包商有权对遵守变更指令后发生的额外付款和变更延期进行索赔。额外付款可能包括针对与变更有关的延误索赔、加速索赔和终止索赔的额外成本。

Exercises

I. Translate the following phrases into English.

1. 合同履行与签订
2. 工程量清单计价规则
3. 竣工结算时间
4. 对客户进行索赔
5. 工程跟踪调查与随访

II. Translate the following sentences into Chinese.

1. In managing the time of a construction project, a construction program prepared by the contractor and accepted by the engineer is used to manage the time, since all the activities required to complete the project is identified, and relationships between different activities and durations are identified and can be easily monitored.

2. The main contractor may be held liable for defective work carried out by a subcontractor and responsible for the acts, defaults and neglects of any subcontractor as fully as if they were deemed as the defaults or neglects of the main contractor.

3. The contractor is responsible for the giving of all notices necessary to comply with regulatory

requirements and the payment of all necessary fees, charges and other imposts, other than those notices and imposts to be given or paid by the client under the contract.

Types of Contracts

In recent years the role of many general contractors has **evolved** from that of master builders, who actually built an entire project by directly hiring the labor and purchasing and installing the materials, to that of manager and coordinator of all the different types of construction work that must go into a project. The construction work itself is now performed substantially by speciality contractors and subcontractors. Today's **general contractor** no longer attempts to be an expert in all the different trades, and he **parcels out** much of the work to separate subcontractors, each specializing in his own particular trade. By subcontracting, the general contractor also shifts the legal responsibility for performance of each portion of the work to the speciality subcontractor and establishes a firm price for each portion of the subcontracted work.

There are several areas of basic concern to a general contractor which should be covered in his contract with an owner. The general contractor must have an adequate amount of money due and payable at the proper time to enable him to finance the work of each of his subcontractors as well as the work which he will perform directly. The general contract must specify the amount, method, and time of payments to be made by the owner to the general contractor and the percentage of **retention** (if any) to be withheld from progress payments by the owner. The general contract must also specify accurately the scope of the work to be performed and the time within which the work must be completed. In addition, provisions are necessary to establish fair and precise procedures for handling changes in the work to be performed. Other provisions may include a definition of the rights of both parties on a default or termination of the contracts.

In answer to the question "How much is the contractor to be paid?" the general contract must specify the total amount of payment in the contract which will **be entitled** for performance of the construction. Although there are variations in payment clauses, there are three basic ways of calculating the compensation that the contractor will receive under the contract: a lump sum or fixed price, unit pricing, and cost plus a fee.

Fixed price Contracts

The most common form of general contract is a lump-sum agreement in which the owner and general contractor agree with a fixed amount to be paid to the contractor for the performance of the entire contract work. The contractor takes the risk of being able to perform all the work for the amount specified in the contract. The general contractor's profit, if any, is realized by the difference between the **lump-sum** contract and the cost of the construction, including **overhead** and indirect costs. Therefore, the contractor must add an adequate amount to cover the risk of increased costs.

In estimating work under a fixed-price contract, the bidding contractor considers the worst conditions that might affect costs and relates those to the price the considers necessary to obtain the work through the low bid process. The owner normally pays lump-sum prices which are **guarded to varying degrees** doesn't exceed maximum anticipated costs, whether or not the maximum costs are actually incurred. The contractor can't usually receive any **escalation** of the contract prices for inflated costs if there is no escalation clause in the contract. However, this doesn't **preclude** the contractor from sustaining a claim for equitable adjustment in the event that his costs are increased by changes in the contract requirements, or by other acts of the owner and his agents.

To the extent competitive conditions allow, this risk factor must be contained in the general contractor's price to the owner. An owner typically desires a fixed-price general contract if he needs to fix a specific financial commitment for financing the project. A commonly used lump-sum contract is that AIA Standard Form of Agreement between owner and contractor.

Lump-sum payment provisions may be used in conjunction with a variety of flexible payment combinations. For example, the contract may provide that the fixed price be reduced if the contractor doesn't meet certain performance requirements, such as no completing the work within the contract time; the contract may provide that the fixed price be increased if the contractor exceeds a performance standard.

Unit-price Contracts

Under unit pricing of construction general contracts, the general contractor is paid a fixed amount for each unit of work performed. To avoid disputes over how much work has in fact been performed, each "unit" of work must be precisely defined.

In using the unit-price method the owner assumes the risk of the amount of work that is to be done. This includes the risk that the estimates of **prospective** work made by the owner or the architect are accurate and therefore that the total cost of the construction is accurately predicted. The contractor bears the risk that the cost of each unit of work will not rise above the unit prices specified in the contract.

When the general contractor bids on the units of work, he bases his price on the cost of performing the quantity of work anticipated. If, during the course of performance, the number of units of a particular type of work is substantially decreased, the cost per unit to the contractor will normally be much greater than **contemplated**. Conversely, if the amount of a particular unit of work is substantially increased, the contractor's cost per unit performed may decrease so that the original unit price becomes unfairly high.

A construction contract may combine a basic lump-sum-payment method with a supplemental unit-price arrangement for certain types of work, such as rock excavation.

In order to obtain larger payments early during a construction project to help finance the remainder of the work, contractors sometimes bid disproportionately high unit price on the work to be performed early and correspondingly low unit prices on subsequent work. The use of this practice may return to **haunt** the contractor in certain circumstances. If the owner decides to reduce the number of units of the early work, the contractor will lose the entire unit-price compensation on the eliminated work, including the amount he had shifted to the early work from the later work. The owner may also use change order to rearrange the work, which could upset the financing plans of the contractor.

Cost-plus-a-fee Contracts

Under a cost-plus-a-fee-compensation arrangement, the owner pays the general contractor for costs necessarily incurred in the construction and either a fixed fee or a fee based on a percentage of the cost of construction. Using the cost-plus-a-fee contract, an owner assumes the risk of greater construction costs than originally estimated. The owner may desire to set an outside limit on this risk by requiring the general contractor to guarantee the maximum cost of the contract and thereby fix a limit on the amount of the owner's investment in the project. The cost-plus-a-fee contract is also useful to the owner who doesn't know at the time of contracting whether or not a construction project will be completed in full or who wishes to begin on the construction before the plans and specifications are finally completed. This method normally allows the contractor to accept a smaller profit margin than under a lump-sum contract because the contractor doesn't have to assume the risk of cost increase. The addition of a maximum guaranteed cost provides a sharing of this risk by the parties, and the contractor must be able to determine from the plans and specifications if he can perform the work within the guaranteed maximum cost.

Another clause which may be inserted along with the guaranteed maximum cost is the savings clause. Using this combination the contractor is paid on completion of the contract a certain percentage of the amount by which the actual cost of performance falls below the guaranteed maximum cost. This incentive is a bonus besides the contractor's fee. The contractor should be aware that there does not have to be a savings clause in a contract with a guaranteed maximum cost under the law.

The main questions which should be resolved are proper language in the cost-plus-a-fee construction contract for identification of those costs that are **reimbursable**, those that are not reimbursable, and those that are included in the base figure from which the percentage fee is calculated. The reimbursable cost figure and base figure from which the percentage fee is calculated are not necessarily identical.

The contract should specify in great detail which costs are to be reimbursed, which costs are not reimbursable and which costs and services are covered in the fee. The reason such care is necessary becomes apparent upon the examination of cases where the contract covered the matter in general terms only, such as "the contractor shall be paid the cost of the building plus 10 percent." The courts vary widely in what they consider the undefined term "costs" to mean. A frequent source of **discrepancy** is whether overhead is a cost or to be chargeable as costs, whereas others reason that it is an indirect expense which is difficult to compute and therefore should be recovered through the fee. Most courts don't consider general overhead to be a cost.

New Words and Phrases

evolve 发展,展开;进化,演化
retention 保留额,自留额
overhead 一般管理费用,经常费用,间接费用
guard 保护（使不受伤害）
escalation 逐步上升,逐步升级,逐步增强
preclude 排除
prospective 预期的,未来的
contemplate 期待,期望;反复打算,凝思,沉思
haunt 缠住
reimburse 偿还
discrepancy 相差,差异,矛盾

general contractor 总承包商
parcel out 把……分成小部分
be entitled 有权（做某事，得到某物），有……的资格
lump-sum 金额一次总付的，一次付清
to varying degrees 在不同程度上
cost-plus-a-fee contract 成本加费用合同

Contract Provisions for Risk Allocation

Provisions for the allocation of risk among parties to a contract can appear in numerous areas in addition to the total construction price. Typically, these provisions assign responsibility for covering the costs of possible or unforeseen occurrences. A partial list of responsibilities with concomitant risk that can be assigned to different parties would include:

- Force majeure (i.e. this provision absolves an owner or a contractor for payment for costs due to "Acts of God" and other external events such as war or labor strikes).
- Indemnification (i.e. this provision absolves the **indemnified** party from any payment for losses and damages incurred by a third party such as adjacent property owners).
- Liens (i.e. assurances that third party claims are settled such as "mechanics liens" for worker wages).
- Labor laws (i.e. payments for any violation of labor laws and regulations on the job site).
- Differing site conditions (i.e. responsibility for extra costs due to unexpected site conditions).
- Delays and extensions of time.
- **Liquidated damages** (i.e. payments for any facility defects with payment amounts agreed to in advance).
- **Consequential damages** (i.e. payments for actual damage costs assessed upon impact of facility defects).
- Occupational safety and health of workers.
- Permits, licenses, laws, and regulations.
- Equal employment opportunity regulations.
- Termination for default by contractor.
- Suspension of work.
- Warranties and guarantees.

The language used for specifying the risk assignments in these areas must conform to legal requirements and past interpretations which may vary in different **jurisdictions** or over time. Without using standard legal language, contract provisions may be unenforceable. Unfortunately, standard legal language for this purpose may be difficult to understand. As a result, project managers often have difficulty in interpreting their particular responsibilities. Competent legal counsel is required to advise the different parties to an agreement about their respective responsibilities.

Standard forms for contracts can be obtained from numerous sources, such as the **American Institute of Architects (AIA)** or the **Associated General Contractors (AGC)**. These standard forms may include risk and responsibility allocations which are unacceptable to one or more of the contracting parties. In particular, standard forms may be biased to reduce the risk and responsibility of the originating organization or group. Parties to a contract should read and review all contract documents carefully.

The three examples appearing below illustrate contract language resulting in different risk assignments between a contractor (CONTRACTOR) and an owner (COMPANY). Each contract provision allocates different levels of indemnification risk to the contractor.

Example 5-1: A Contract Provision Example with **High Contractor Risk**

"Except where the sole negligence of COMPANY is involved or alleged, CONTRACTOR shall indemnify and hold harmless COMPANY, its officers, agents and employees, from and against any and all loss, damage, and liability and from any and all claims for damages on account of or by reason of bodily injury, including death, not limited to the employees of CONTRACTOR, COMPANY, and of any subcontractor or CONTRACTOR, and from and against any and all damages to property, including property of COMPANY and third parties, direct and/or consequential, caused by or arising out of, in while or in part, or claimed to have been caused by or to have arisen out of, in whole or in part, an act of omission of CONTRACTOR or its agents, employees, vendors, or subcontractors, of their employees or agents in connection with the performance of the contract documents, whether or not insured against; and CONTRACTOR shall, at its own cost and expense, defend any claim, suit, action or proceeding, whether groundless or not, which may be commenced against COMPANY by reason thereof or in connection therewith, and CONTRACTOR shall pay any and all judgments which may be recovered in such action, claim, proceeding or suit, and defray any and all expenses, including costs and attorney's fees which may be incurred by reason of such actions, claims, proceedings, or suits."

Comment: This is a very burdensome provision for the contractor. It makes the contractor responsible for practically every conceivable occurrence and type of damage, except when a claim for loss or damages is due to the sole negligence of the owner. As a practical matter, sole negligence on a construction project is very difficult to ascertain because the work is so inter-twined. Since there is no dollar limitation to the contractor's exposure, sufficient liability coverage to cover worst scenario risks will be difficult to obtain. The best the contractor can do is to obtain as complete and broad excess liability insurance coverage as can be purchased. This insurance is costly, so the contractor should insure the contract price is sufficiently high to cover the expense.

Example 5-2: An Example Contract Provision with Medium Risk Allocation to Contractor

"CONTRACTOR shall protect, defend, hold harmless, and indemnify COMPANY from and against any loss, damage, claim, action, liability, or demand whatsoever (including, with limitation, costs, expenses, and attorney's fees, whether for appeals or otherwise, in connection therewith), arising out of any personal injury (including, without limitation, injury to any employee of COMPANY, CONTRACTOR or any subcontractor), arising out of any personal injury (including, without limitation, injury to any employee of COMPANY, CONTRACTOR, or any subcontractor), including death resulting therefrom or out of any damage to or loss or destruction of property, real and or personal (including property of COMPANY, CONTRACTOR, and any subcontractor, and including tools and equipment whether owned, rented, or used by CONTRACTOR, any subcontractor, or any workman) in any manner based upon, occasioned by, or attributable or related to the performance, whether by the CONTRACTOR or any subcontractor, of the work or any part thereof, and CONTRACTOR shall at its own expense defend any and all actions based thereon, except where personal injury or property damage is caused by the negligence of COMPANY or COMPANY's employees. Any loss, damage, cost expense or attorney's fees incurred by COMPANY in connection with the foregoing may, in addition to other remedies, be deducted from CONTRACTOR's compensation, then due or thereafter to become due. COMPANY shall effect for the benefit of CONTRACTOR a waiver of subrogation on the existing facilities, including consequential damages such as, but not by way of limitation, loss of profit and loss of product or plant downtime, but excluding any deductibles which shall exist as at the date of this CONTRACT; provided, however, that said waiver of subrogation shall be expanded to include all said deductible amounts on the acceptance of the work by COMPANY."

Comment: This clause provides the contractor considerable relief. He still has unlimited exposure for injury to all persons and third party property but only to the extent caused by the contractor's negligence. The "sole" negligence issue does not arise. Furthermore, the contractor's liability for damages to the owner's property—a major concern for contractors working in petrochemical complexes, at times worth billions—is limited to the owner's insurance deductible, and the owner's insurance carriers have no right of recourse against the contractor. The contractor's limited exposure regarding the owner's facilities ends on completion of the work.

Example 5-3: An Example Contract Provision with Low Risk Allocation to Contractor

"CONTRACTOR hereby agrees to indemnify and hold COMPANY and/or any parent, subsidiary, or affiliate, or COMPANY and/or officers, agents, or employees of any of them, harmless from and against any loss or liability arising directly or indirectly out of any claim or cause of action for loss or damage to property including, but not limited to, CONTRACTOR's property and COMPANY's property and for injuries to or death of persons including but not limited to CONTRACTOR's employees, caused by or resulting from the performance of the work by CONTRACTOR, its employees, agents, and subcontractors and shall, at the option of COMPANY, defend COMPANY at CONTRACTOR't sole expense in any litigation involving the same regardless of whether such work is performed by CONTRACTOR, its employees, or by its subcontractors, their employees, or all or either of them. In all instances, CONTRACTOR't indemnity to COMPANY shall be limited to the proceeds of CONTRACTOR't umbrella liability insurance coverage."

Comment: With respect to indemnifying the owner, the contractor in this provision has minimal out-of-pocket risk. Exposure is limited to whatever can be collected from the contractor's insurance company.

New Words and Phrases

indemnify　赔偿；保护；使免于受罚
jurisdiction　可法办，审判权，管辖权；权限，权力
liquidated damages　先约赔偿金
consequential damages　后果赔偿金
American Institute of Architects (AIA)　美国建筑师协会
Associated General Contractors (AGC)　承包商联合会
high contractor risk　高承包商风险

Part II Speaking

The Owner Hands Over the Site Late

(Mr. Bian, Project Manager from the Contractor, and Mr. Cheng, **Chief Engineer**, are talking to the Owner's Representative, Mr. Sukhnandan, who looks very young and energetic, and the **Consultant**, Mr. Shaw, who seems to be quite experienced.)

Bian: Last week, we sent you a letter, asking you to **hand over** the whole site to us, including the **access road**. But we haven't received a reply yet. The contract is quite **specific about** this in its special conditions: Possession of the site shall be given to the Contractor on the date named in the Appendix 1, which is April 20, 1992. Today is April 26. It's already one week late.

Sukh: I'm sorry about this, Mr. Bian. Unfortunately we have met with some difficulty in **requisitioning** the land on the left bank of the river for the site areas. You know, some of the land is privately owned and the owners won't agree to sell the land. Nor do they want to **grant** us **permission** to use it because they are afraid that the project will disturb their peaceful life.

Shaw: Some people here **are obsessed with** their traditional life, They don't want to have a change of their life! You will never understand them.

Cheng: It's so puzzling! They should know that they will get benefit from this project. At least they could get the **lighting power** easily, at a much lower price.

Sukh: We've already promised to provide them with electric power for lighting free of charge. In return, they let us use their land for nothing.

Bian: When do you think you can solve the problem and make the whole site and the access road available to us? This is what **was concerned about**.

Shaw: At present, the access road has been built up to the **dam site** and we are beginning to build the road to the **power-house** from the junction. It happens to be the rainy season and the rains have slowed down our progress, but we are making a great effort to finish it soon.

Sukh: So we can hand over to you the completed access road and the area on the right bank so that you can begin the preparation work there, you can have them from tomorrow. I'll give you a letter of confirmation right after this meeting. Once we solve our problem with the land owners, which I believe we can soon, we will hand over the remaining part of the site area.

Bian: Mr. Sukhnandan, let me make it plain to you. The delay in handing over the site area has adversely affected our construction plan. We have to request you to extend the completion time of this project accordingly. Meanwhile, we reserve the right to be reimbursed for any costs incurred because of the delay. Fifteen engineers and technicians are already here waiting eagerly to start their jobs. A lot of preparation work needs to be done by us, especially the traffic road within the site.

Sukh: I understand your position, Mr. Bian. As for the compensation, we'll try to settle this matter according to the contract.

Bian: To make this project a success, we need cooperation from each other.

Sukh: I couldn't agree more.

New Words and Phrases

consultant 咨询顾问
requisition 征用
chief engineer 总工程师
hand over 移交，交出
access road 进场道路
be specific about 对……有明确规定
grant permission 给予许可
be obsessed with 对……着迷，抱着……不放
lighting power 照明用电
be concerned about 对……关心
dam site 坝址
power-house 电站厂房

Unit 6 Management of Engineering Cost

Part I Reading and Translating

Professional Knowledge Guidance

1. **工程成本**：企业用于施工和管理的一切费用的总和，综合反映工程中的劳动消耗和物资消耗状况，是检查施工企业经营管理成果的一个综合性指标。工程成本分为直接成本、间接成本两部分。

2. **成本管理**：是企业生产经营过程中各项成本核算、成本分析、成本决策和成本控制等一系列科学管理行为的总称。成本管理由成本规划、成本计算、成本控制和业绩评价四项组成。

3. **成本估算**
   前期策划阶段的估算：参照过去同类工程信息匡算；按照国家或部门颁布的概算指标计算；专家咨询法；生产能力估算法。
   项目设计和计划阶段的概（预）算：使用定额资料，如概（预）算定额；直接按部分工程、专项的供应或服务进行询价；采用已完工的数据；合同价。

4. **成本控制**：是企业根据一定时期预先建立的成本管理目标，由成本控制主体在其职权范围内，在生产耗费发生以前和成本控制过程中，对各种影响成本的因素和条件采取的一系列预防和调节措施，以保证成本管理目标实现的管理行为。

Project Cost Estimate and Cost Control

Project Cost Management

Cost management is very much more than simply maintaining records of expenditure and issuing cost reports. Cost management means understanding how and why costs occur and promptly taking the necessary response in light of all the relevant information. Keeping a project within budget depends on the application of an efficient and effective system of cost control. From the information generated in the progress of the project, cost management should be not only to identity past trends, but also to forecast the likely consequence of future decisions including final out-turn cost, that is, the final account. <u>Cost management helps the project team to better establish the appropriate project contract strategy, and cost management should be placed in which contract and possibly the form of contract be adopted.</u> [1] Cost management can also help denity possible programme restraints both contract preparation and execution. Without an effective company-wide cost-control system this would result in substantial risk to any contractor's slender margins.

Project Cost Estimate

Cost estimating is one of the most important steps in project management. A cost estimate establishes the base line of the project cost at different stages of development of the project. A cost estimate at a given stage of project development represents a prediction provided by the cost engineer or estimator on the basis of available data. According to the American Association of Cost Engineers, cost engineering is defined as that area of engineering practice where engineering judgment and experience are utilized in the application of scientific principles and techniques to the problem of cost estimation, cost control and profitability.

Virtually all cost estimation is performed according to one or some combination of the following basic approaches:

Production Function

The relationship between the output of a process and the necessary resources is referred to as the production function. In construction, a production function relates the amount or volume of output to the various inputs of labor, material and equipment. The relationship between the size of a building project (expressed in square meter) and the input labor (expressed in labor hours per square meter) is an example of a production function for construction.

Empirical Cost Inference

Empirical estimation of cost functions requires statistical techniques which relate the cost of constructing or operating a facility to a few important characteristics or attributes of the system. The role of statistical inference is to estimate the best parameter values or constants in an assumed cost function. Usually, this is accomplished by means of regression analysis techniques.

Unit Costs for Bill of Quantities

A unit cost is assigned to each of the facility components or tasks as represented by the bill of quantities. The total cost is the summation of the quantities of the products multiplied by the corresponding unit costs. The unit cost method is straightforward in principle but quite laborious in application. The initial step is to break down or disaggregate a process into a number of tasks. Create Work Breakdown Structure (WBS) is the process of subdividing project deliverables and project work into smaller, more manageable components. Collectively, these tasks must be completed for the construction of a facility. Once these tasks are defined and quantities representing these tasks are assessed, a unit cost is assigned to each task and then the total cost is determined by summing the costs incurred in each task. The level of detail in decomposing into task will vary considerably from one estimate to another.

Unit 6 Management of Engineering Cost

Allocation of Joint Costs

Allocations of cost from existing accounts may be used to develop a cost function of an operation. The basic idea in this method is that each expenditure item can be assigned to particular characteristics of the operation. [2] In many instances, however, a causal relationship between the allocation factor and the cost item cannot be identified or may not exist. For example, in construction projects, the accounts for basic costs may be classified and allocated proportionally to various tasks which are subdivisions of a project. It usually according to labor, material, construction equipment, **construction supervision**, and general office overhead.

These basic costs may then be allocated proportionally to various tasks which are subdivisions of a project.

Detailed Estimating Method

Activity-based detailed or unit cost estimates are typically the most **definitive** estimating techniques, and use information down to the lowest level of detail available. They are also the most commonly understood and utilized estimating techniques. The accuracy of activity-based detailed or unit cost techniques depends on the accuracy of available information, resources spent to develop the cost estimate and the validity of the bases of the estimate. A **work statement** and set of drawings or specifications may be used to identify activities that make up the project. Each activity is further decomposed into detailed items (WBS) so that labor hours, material costs, equipment costs, and subcontract costs are **itemized** and quantified.

Cost estimates must consider the overall costs of the works, including labor, materials, equipment, services, facilities, **inflation allowance** or **contingency costs**. Moreover, cost estimates must also consider the causes of variation of the final estimate and various costing alternatives for purposes of better project management. It is necessary to analyse the project in as many individual work sections as can be identified, if possible, to prepare indicative quantities and consider the resources necessary to carry out the work, including location of project and access thereto, especially with regard to heavy and large loads, availability of labour and the possible need of accommodation for workmen, off-site construction, **temporary works**. Cost estimates may increase or decrease as the project progresses and additional detail become known. The accuracy of a cost estimate of a project will improve as the project progresses through its life cycle.

Cost Control

Cost control is the **manipulation** and analysis of all costs pertaining to the project. Cost control is also a method or system used to record, compare, track and effect the cost of the project for profitability. For control and monitoring purposes, the original detailed cost estimate is typically converted to a project budget, and the project budget is used subsequently as a guide for management. The final or detailed cost estimate provides a baseline for the **assessment of financial performance** during the project. To the extent, that costs are within the detailed cost estimate, then the project is thought to be under financial control. [3] Overruns in particular cost categories signal the possibility of problems and give an indication of exactly what problems are being encountered **expense oriented construction planning** and control focuses upon the categories included in the final cost estimation.

In general, construction cost control consists basically of monitoring actual performance against cost estimates and identifying variances. The cost control methods based on the detection of variances appears to assume that the causes of deviation will be apparent and the appropriate corrective action obvious. Cost control includes:

Project Performance Reviews

Project performance review is to compare cost performance over time, schedule activities or **work packages**, **planned value**, and **milestones**. The construction plan and the associated **cash flow** estimates can provide the baseline reference for subsequent project monitoring and control. For schedules, progress on individual activities and the achievement of milestone completions can be compared with the project schedule to monitor the progress of activities. Compares actual project performance to planned or **expected value**, and examines project performance over time to determine if performance is improving. Expenses inured during the course of a project are recorded in specific work elements cost accounts, and then comparing it with the original cost estimates in each category to ascertain if the budget is under control. Two related outcomes are expected from the periodic monitoring of costs:

- Identification of any work items whose actual costs are exceeding their budgeted costs, with subsequent actions to try to bring those costs into **conformance** with the budget.
- Estimating the total cost of the project at completion, based on the cost record so far and expectations of the cost to complete unfinished items.

Variance Analysis

The purpose of variance analysis is to describe how cost variances are managed, such as monitoring cost performance to detect and understand variances from plan, ensuring changes are acted on time, preventing unauthorized changes from being included, managing the actual changes when and as they occur, then ensure the acceptable range of variance decreases as the project progresses.

Project Management Estimating Software

Project management estimating software is computerized **cost accounting** and integrated cost control system which is used to track planned cost versus actual cost and to forecast the effects of cost changes. Project management software spreadsheets and simulation/statistical tools are widely used to assist with cost estimating; it can simplify the use of the techniques and facilitate more rapid consideration of costing alternatives, provide a means of comparing actual with budgeted expenses in a timely manner, develop a database of productivity and **cost-performance data** for use in estimating the costs of operations that are deviating from the project budget, and generate data for valuing variations and changes to the contact and potential claims for **additional payments**. [4]

Summary

In conclusion, an elective cost-control management should contain the following characteristics:

- A detailed budget for the project set with a contingency sum to be used at the **discretion** of the project manager.
- Costs should be forecast before decisions are made to allow for the consideration of all possible courses of action.
- The cost-recording system should be cost-effective to operate, the actual costs should be compared with forecasted costs at appropriate periods to ensure **conformity with** the budget and to allow for corrective action if necessary and if possible.
- Actual costs should be subject to variance analysis to determine reasons for any deviation from the budget.

- The cost implications of time and quality should **be incorporated into** rate into the decision-making process.

New Words and Phrases

definitive　确切的，准确的
itemize　分条列述，详细列表
manipulation　操纵，操控
milestone　里程碑
conformance　符合；顺应，一致性
discretion　自由裁决权；考虑周到；谨慎，判断力
project cost estimate　项目成本估算
production function　生产函数
empirical cost inference　实证成本推理，经验成本推理
construction supervision　建设监理
work statement　工作报表
inflation allowance　通胀准备金；物价补贴
contingency cost　意外成本；应急费；不可预见费
temporary work　临时工程
assessment of financial performance　财务业绩评价，财务状况评价
expense oriented construction planning　以费用为导向的建设规划，面向成本的建设规划
project performance reviews　项目绩效考核（审查）
work package　工作包
planned value　计划值
cash flow　现金流量
expected value　期望值
variance analysis　方差分析
cost accounting　成本会计
cost-performance data　性价比数据
additional payment　额外支出；追加付款
conformity with　符合；顺应，与……一致
be incorporated into　纳入；使成为……的一部分

Notes

[1] Cost management helps the project team to better establish the appropriate project contract strategy, and cost management should be placed in which contract and possibly the form of contract be adopted.

成本管理有助于项目小组更好地制订合适的项目合同策略，成本管理应贯穿于合同谈判到合同终结的全过程。

[2] Allocations of cost from existing accounts may be used to develop a cost function of an operation. The basic idea in this method is that each expenditure item can be assigned to particular characteristics of the operation.

有时需要从现有的会计账目上去进行成本分解，从而确定某项具体操作的成本函数。这种方

法的基本思想是，每一项花费都能对应地分配到操作过程中的某一特定步骤。

[3] To the extent, that costs are within the detailed cost estimate, then the project is thought to be under financial control.

在某种程度上，如果项目造价包括在详细成本预算之内，则项目被认为已处于财务控制之中。

[4] Project management software spreadsheets and simulation/statistical tools are widely used to assist with cost estimating; it can simplify the use of the techniques and facilitate more rapid consideration of costing alternatives, provide a means of comparing actual with budgeted expenses in a timely manner, develop a database of productivity and cost-performance data for use in estimating the costs of operations that are deviating from the project budget, and generate data for valuing variations and changes to the contact and potential claims for additional payments.

项目管理软件电子数据表和模拟/统计工具已广泛用于辅助成本预算，且它可以简化技术的使用，促进以成本替代方案更快形成，提供一种以及时的方式将预算费用与实际费用进行对比的方法，开发一个以生产量和性价比数据来评估执行成本偏离项目预算的数据库，生成可以对合同变更和变化及额外支出的潜在索赔进行计量的数据。

Exercises

I. Translate the following phrases into English.

1. 实证成本推理
2. 建设施工监理
3. 财务业绩评价
4. 项目绩效考核
5. 费用为导向的建设规划

II. Translate the following sentences into Chinese.

1. Keeping a project within budget depends on the application of an efficient and effective system of cost control. From the information generated in the progress of the project, cost management should be not only to identify past trends but also forecast the likely consequence of future decisions including final out-turn cost, that is, the final account.

2. Major projects often have substantial elements that are unique and for which there is no relevant historic data. The role of statistical inference is to estimate the best parameter values or constants in an assumed cost function.

3. Activity-based, detailed or unit cost estimates are typically the most definitive of the estimating techniques and use information down to the lowest level of detail available.

4. It is necessary to analyze the project in as many individual work sections as can be identified, if possible, to prepare indicative quantities and consider the resources necessary to carry out the work, include location of project and access thereto, especially with regard to heavy and large loads, availability of labor and the possible need of accommodation for workmen, off-site construction, temporary works.

5. Compares actual project performance to planned or expected value, examines project performance over time to determine if performance is improving, expenses incurred during the course of a project are recorded in specific work elements cost accounts to be compared with the original cost estimates in each category to ascertain if the budget is under control.

Unit 6 Management of Engineering Cost

Cost Estimate

Every project has to prepare feasibility studies, like **cost-benefit analysis.** The methods of assessing benefits are very specific for each type of infrastructure and to describe them would go beyond the scope of this document. On the other hand every construction project estimates the costs applying more or less the same method.

Basically there are three types of cost estimates, all with different level of accuracy:
- Rough estimate.
- Indicative estimate.
- Detailed estimate.

Every type of estimate should include optimistic, pessimistic and the most likely estimates. The ranges between these figures depend on the accuracy of the estimate and the accuracy of the information on which the estimate is based. Obviously the less accurate the estimate or information, the bigger the range between the optimistic, most likely and pessimistic figures. For example the level of soil investigation influences the accuracy of the estimate. Rough estimates for ground works are often based on desk studies and assumptions alone, while the detailed estimate may be based on soil investigations as good as 1 : 10,000 ratio.

The most likely scenario is seldom enough for a client to make its judgement. The client needs to check if it can afford the pessimistic scenario. As construction budgets are large, unforeseen extreme high cost may result in bankruptcy of the project and perhaps the client. Large clients with many infrastructure projects, like the national road authority, develop alternative plans to utilize financial godsends. They may develop several small contracts that can be implemented within a few months before the end of the budget year, utilizing the unspent cash prior the deadline to return it to the treasury.

The choice between the levels of estimate depends on the needs of the client and the available information. Most clients need the most accurate cost estimate possible, prior financially-committing themselves. However it may not always be possible to develop a detailed cost estimate for the construction at an early stage of the project.

Rough Estimates

Rough estimates are usually used during the initial stage of the project and is based on unit rates for whole constructions.

The constructions are classified on basis of a few simple indicators, like:
- Number of household connecting to a sewer pipe.
- Height of elevation, number of lanes and number of elevated crossings of elevated motorway.
- Location, number of floors, volume of building and garden of the building.

This type of unit rates often includes the costs to design, prepare and supervise the construction.

Indicative Cost

Indicative cost estimates at least require a preliminary design, but preferably a detailed design. The design is broken down in specific **semi-finished products**, like walls, floors, roofs, foundations, windows, doors, etc. The amount of each semi-finished product, e. g. volume of foundation, is multiplied with a unit rate that includes the direct, indirect costs, profit and supervision costs. Alternatively the unit rates may only include the direct costs. The total direct cost to build the construction is subsequently multiplied with ratios for indirect costs, profit, and design and supervision inputs.

Detailed Cost Estimate

Consultants or contractors that bid for a certain contract usually develop the detailed cost estimate, but clients who aware of the financial risks may also prepare detailed cost estimates. First of all the client need to add the cost of its supervision inputs to the cost estimate of the potential contractors. Secondly the bidders may increase their demand for profit or willing to take a loss depending on their market situation. Loss making contractors may go bankrupt or may not be able advance the construction costs. The profit/loss is usually a percentage of total direct and indirect costs. Thirdly bidders will base their cost price on their financial risk assessment. But because most civil engineering contracts are based on remeasurement payment arrangements, and have a certain degree of unknown in it, the client is interested in its financial risks. Information the client cannot obtain from the bidders' quotations.

The preparation of the detailed cost estimate separates the direct and the indirect costs and profit. The direct costs are the costs that can be assigned to construction of a certain semi-finished product, like a wall.

Indirect Costs

The indirect costs are the project costs that cannot be assigned to a specific construction element. In a way the production unit of the specific construction elements (walls, floors, roofs etc.) all share these resource covered under the indirect costs. Typical examples of indirect costs are:

- Site management.
- Offices, sheds, storage.
- Access roads.
- Transport of workers.
- **Water and sanitation service.**
- **Health and safety provisions.**
- Insurance.
- Bonds.
- Tools, scaffolds.
- Company costs.

Site Management

The site management cost is based on the duration and number of site managers.

Offices, Sheds and Stores

The contractor may either hire the necessary offices, sheds and stores, usually for the whole project duration or may have purchased **mobile buildings**. In the latter case the cost depend on the utilization degree, depreciation and the duration of the use of the buildings.

In formula:

Costs for buildings = duration × annual depreciation × 100/utilization degree

Where: Duration [years]

Utilisation degree [percentage of time building is in use]

Annual depreciation [local currency]

Unit 6 Management of Engineering Cost

Access Roads
Many construction sites are inaccessible for motorised transport and it is necessary to construct an access road. The access road may be a simple dirt road, but when heavy equipment is expected, concrete and metal slabs are more appropriate.

Transport of Workers
It is very common that the project has to pick up workers from neighbouring villages. The transport of the workers costs fuel, wage of the drivers and depreciation of the vehicles.

The cost of the fuel is usually calculated by multiplying of the number of trips during project duration, average length of a trip [km], fuel consumption rate [1/km] and the fuel cost per litre [$/1] with each other.

The wage of the driver is calculated with the following equation: No. of Trips × average trip duration [hour] × wage per hour.

And the depreciation of the vehicles is calculated with the formula: No. of Trips × average trip duration [year] × annual depreciation × 100/utilization degree.

Health and Safety Provisions
The cost of the health and safety provisions depends on the number of workers on site and the technology. Experienced contractors will have unit rates to calculate the costs of health and safety provisions.

Tools
Tools and plant will wear and tear. Its cost is estimated on basis of its depreciation rates and utilization degree.

Bonds and Insurances
Bonds and insurances are usually purchased per project and contractor will obtain quotations from their insurance companies.

Company Costs
There are various company costs like staff salaries; office rent, or depreciation and O&M costs; vehicles; loan interests.

The company costs are usually divided over the number of expected projects that are running at the same time.

Staff Salaries
The staff salaries are the salaries paid to the office staff, like the director, secretary, bookkeepers and others. It also includes the additional benefits and allowances paid to the permanent staff of the company.

Direct Costs
The direct costs are the costs of all the inputs that can be directly and solely linked to a certain activity or construction of a certain semi-finished product. It includes risk allowances. Typical inputs are human resources, equipment, and materials.

Direct Cost Calculation
To calculate the direct costs, the construction is divided in semi-finished products like walls, floors, roofs, doors, foundations etc. Ideally the construction is broken down as detailed as possible.

The production of each semi-finished product is analysed. The quantities for the materials, human and equipment resources are estimated but also the risks of the production process of that particular semi-finished product are described. The quantities of materials are often expressed in volumes, weight or length units.

The quantities of human resources are expressed in the number of work days, weeks or months. Because most workers receive different salaries, depending on their skills and responsibilities, it is necessary to differentiate the human resource inputs of the various salary scales, e.g. unskilled, semi-skilled and skilled activities. The quantity of equipment is described in consumption of time. The risk allowances are often expressed in a percentage, for example 10% for groundwork and 2% for a mason wall.

The direct costs per semi-finished product are calculated with the following formula:

$$\text{Direct costs} = (1 + RA/100\%) \times \sum Q_i \times UR_i$$

Where:

RA: Risk allowance [%]

Q_i: Quantity of (i)

i: Material, human resource or equipment

UR: Unit rate [local currency]

The quantities are multiplied with their respective unit rates. The unit rates of the human resources are based on the gross salaries, benefits and bonuses. The unit rates of the equipment are based on the lease rates or the depreciation and utilization rates (when the equipment is owned). And the unit rates of the materials include delivery costs.

New Words and Phrases

cost-benefit analysis   成本效益分析
semi-finished product   半成品
indirect cost   间接成本
water and sanitation service   供水及卫生设施
health and safety provision   健康与安全措施
mobile building   活动房屋
direct cost   直接成本

The Construction Project Budget

For cost control on a project, the construction plan and the associated cash flow estimates can provide the **baseline** reference for subsequent project monitoring and control. For schedules, progress on individual activities can be compared with the project schedule to monitor the process of activities. Contract and job specifications provide the criteria by which to assess and assure the required quality of construction. The final or detailed cost estimate provides a baseline for the assessment of financial performance during the project. To the extent that costs are within the detailed cost estimate, then the project is thought to be under financial control. **Overruns** in particular cost categories signal the possibility of problems and give an indication of exactly what problems are being encountered. Expense oriented construction planning and control focused upon the categories included in the final cost estimation.

For control and monitoring purposes, the original detailed cost estimate is typically converted to a project budget, and the project budget is used subsequently as a guide for management. Specific items in the detailed cost estimate become job cost elements. Expenses incurred during the course of a project are recorded in specific job cost accounts to be compared with the original cost estimates in each category. Thus, individual job cost accounts generally represent the basic unit for cost control. Alternatively, job cost accounts may be disaggregated or divided into work elements which are related both to particular scheduled activities and to particular cost accounts.

In addition to cost amounts, information on material quantities and labor inputs within each job account is also typically retained in the project budget. With this information, actual materials usage and labor employed can be compared to the expected requirements. As a result, cost overruns or savings on particular items can be identified as due to changes in unit prices, labor productivity or in the amount of material consumed.

The number of cost accounts associated with a particular project can vary considerably. For constructors, on the order of 400 separate cost accounts might be used on a small project. These accounts record all the **transactions** associated with a project. Thus, separate accounts might exist for different types of materials, equipment use, payroll, project office, etc. Both physical and non-physical resources are represented, including overhead items such as computer use or interest charges. Table 6-1 summarizes a typical set of cost accounts that might be used in building construction. Note that this set of accounts is organized **hierarchically**, with seven major divisions (accounts 201 to 207) and numerous subdivisions under each division. This hierarchical structure facilitates aggregation of costs into predefined categories; for example, costs associated with the superstructure (account 204) would be the sum of the underlying subdivisions (i.e. 204.1, 204.2, etc.). The subdivision accounts in Table 6-1 could be further divided into personnel, material and other resource costs for the purpose of financial accounting.

Table 6-1 Illustrative Set of Project Cost Accounts

201	Clearing and Preparing Site
202	Substructure
202.1	Excavation and Shoring
202.2	Piling
202.3	Concrete Masonry
202.31	Mixing and Placing
202.32	Formwork
202.33	Reinforcing
203	Outside Utilities (water, gas, sewer, etc.)
204	Superstructure
204.1	Masonry Construction
204.2	Structural Steel
204.3	Wood framing, Partitions, etc.
204.4	Exterior Finishes (brickwork, terra cotta, cut stone, etc.)
204.5	Roofing, Drains, Gutters, Flashing, etc.
204.6	Interior Finish and Trim
204.61	Finish Flooring, Stairs, Doors, Trim
204.62	Glass Windows, Glazing
204.63	Marble, Tile, Terrazzo
204.64	Lathing and Plastering

(续)

204.65	Soundproofing and Insulation	
204.66	Finish Hardware	
204.67	Painting and Decoration	
204.68	Waterproofing	
204.69	Sprinklers and Fire Protection	
204.7	Service work	
204.71	Electrical work	
204.72	Heating and Ventilating	
204.73	Plumbing and Sewage	
204.74	Air Conditioning	
204.75	Fire Alarm, Telephone, Security, Miscellaneous	
205	Paving, Curbs, Walks	
206	Installed Equipment (elevators, revolving doors, mail chutes, etc.)	
207	Fencing	

In developing or implementing a system of cost accounts, an appropriate numbering or coding system is essential to facilitate communication of information and proper aggregation of cost information. Particular cost accounts are used to indicate the expenditures associated with specific projects and to indicate the expenditures on particular items throughout the organization.

One particular problem informing a project budget in terms of cost accounts is the treatment of **contingency** amounts. These allowances are included in project cost estimates to accommodate unforeseen events and the resulting costs. However, in advance of project completion, the source of contingency expenses is not known. Realistically, a budget accounting item for contingency allowance should be established whenever a contingency amount was included in the final cost estimate.

A second problem in forming a project budget is the treatment of inflation. Typically, final cost estimates are formed **in terms of** real dollars and an item reflecting inflation costs is added on as s percentage. This inflation allowance would then be allocated to individual cost items in relation to the actual expected inflation over the period for which costs will be incurred.

An Example of Project Budget for a Constructor

A summary budget for a constructor is illustrated in Table 6-2. This budget is developed from a project to construct a **wharf**. The costs are divided into direct and indirect expenses. Within direct cost, expenses are divided into material, subcontract, and temporary work and machinery cost. This budget indicates aggregate amounts for the various categories. Cost details associated with particular cost accounts would supplement and support the aggregate budget shown in Table 6-2. A profit and a contingency amount might be added to the basic budget of $ 1, 7 15, 147 shown in Table 6-2 for completeness.

Table 6-2 An Example of a Project Budget for a Wharf Project ($)

	Material Cost	Subcontract Work	Temporary Work	Machinery Cost	Total cost
Steel Piling	292 172	129 178	16 389	0	437 739
Tie-Rod	88 233	29 254	0	0	117 487
Anchor-Wall	13 0281	60 873	0	0	191 154
Backfill	242 230	27 919	0	0	300 149
Coping	42 880	22 307	13 171	0	78 358
Dredging	0	111 650	0	0	111 650
Fender	48 996	10 344	0	1 750	61 090
Other	5 000	32 250	0	0	37 250
Sub-total	849 800	423 775	29 560	1 750	1 304 885

Unit 6 Management of Engineering Cost

(续)

	Material Cost	Subcontract Work	Temporary Work	Machinery Cost	Total cost
Summary					
Total of Direct Cost					1 304 885
Indirect Cost					
Common Temporary Work					19 320
Common Machinery					80 934
Transportation					15 550
Office Operating Costs					294 458
Total of Indirect Cost					410 262
Total of Project Cost					1 715 147

New Words and Phrases

baseline　基线；底线
overrun　超出限度
transaction　交易，业务；办理，执行
hierarchically　分层次地，分等级地
wharf　码头；停泊处
contingency　偶然性；意外事故；可能性
construction project budget　建设项目预算
in terms of　依据，根据；在……方面，关于……

Part II Speaking

Project Estimating

A: Charles and Bobby, have you received quotations from the subcontractors and suppliers?

B: Yes, all the quotations have been received and analyzed. We have chosen the most reasonable ones for inclusion into each item of the works.

A: Good. But please be aware that you can take the prices provided by the subcontractors only as our **cost prices**, not our **selling prices**.

C: We have entered the data into the computers. The prices from the subcontractors and suppliers have been filled into the "Cost Price" column in our **Estimation Format**.

B: How can we obtain the "Selling Price" from the "Cost Price"?

A: A few coefficients will be derived from the percentages of insurance, **surety bonds**, contingencies, company overheads and profit. Then, Cost Price multiplied by the coefficient equals Selling Price. Regarding insurance and surety bonds, I am making inquiries from the insurance companies and banks, 2% or 3% is usually taken for our company overheads. The top management of our company will make the final decision on contingencies and profit.

C: The structural subcontractor included **tower cranes** and **scaffolding** in his quotation. May introduce his prices directly into Estimation Format?

A: No, you shouldn't insert his prices directly into the "Cost Price" column before deducting tower crane, scaffolding cost and **batching plant**, because these costs have been already included in Preliminaries.

C: There is an item called "**Provisional Sums**" in BOQ. What does it mean?

A: "Provisional Sums" is a certain amount of money in provision and may be expended in whole or in part as directed by the engineer or wholly deducted from the contract sum if not required. We should simply include such sums in the **Tender Summary**.

New Words and Phrases

cost price　成本价
selling price　销售价
estimation format　估算表
surety bond　担保函
tower crane　塔式起重机
scaffolding　脚手架
batching plant　搅拌站
provisional sums　暂估金额
tender summary　标价汇总

Unit 7 Project Planning and Scheduling

Part I Reading and Translating

Professional Knowledge Guidance

1. 建设工程进度控制：是指对工程项目各建设阶段的工作内容、工作程序、工作持续时间和衔接关系编制计划，将该计划付诸实施，在实施过程中经常检查实际进度是否按计划要求进行，对出现的偏差分析原因，采取措施或调整、修改原计划，直至工程竣工，交付使用。这样不断地计划、执行、检查、分析、调整计划的动态循环过程，就是进度控制。

2. 施工计划种类：包括日计划，周计划，月计划。建筑施工企业应该充分合理利用本身的人力、物力、财力等资源，在总目标的规划组织管理下，确保是施工进度计划按部就班，以实现预期的任务，并且提高经济效益。

3. 影响进度的因素：归纳为人为因素，技术因素，设备与构配件因素，水文地质与气象因素，其他环境、社会因素以及难以预料的因素等。其中人为因素是最大的干扰因素。

Construction Planing

Construction planning is a fundamental and challenging activity in the management and execution of construction projects. It involves **the choice of technology, the definition of work tasks**, and the estimation of the required resources and durations for individual tasks, and the identification of any interactions among the different work tasks. A good construction plan is the basis for developing the budget and the schedule for work. Developing the construction plan is a critical task in the management of construction, even if the plan is not written or otherwise formally recorded. [1] In addition to these technical aspects of construction planning, it may also be necessary to make organizational decisions about the relationships between project participants and even which organizations to include in a project. For example, the extent to which subcontractors will be used on a project is often determined during construction planning.

Forming a construction plan is a highly challenging task. As Sherlock Holmes noted:

Most people, if you describe a train of events to them, will tell you what the result would be. They can put those events together in their minds, and argue from them that something will come to pass. There are few people, however, who, if you told them a result would be able to evolve from their own inner consciousness what the steps were which led up to that result. This power is what I mean when I talk of **reasoning backward**.

Like a detective, a planner begins with a result (i.e. a facility design) and must synthesize the steps required to yield this result. Essential aspects of construction planning include the generation of required activities, analysis of the implications of these activities, and choice among the various alternative means of performing activities.[2] In contrast to a detective discovering a single train of events, however, construction planners also face the **normative problem** of choosing the best among numerous alternative plans. Moreover, a detective is faced with an observable result, whereas a planner must imagine the final facility as described in the plans and specifications.

In developing a construction plan, it is common to adopt a primary emphasis on either cost control or on **schedule control** as illustrated in Figure 7-1. Some projects are primarily divided into expense categories with associated costs. In these cases, construction planning is cost or expense oriented. Within the categories of expenditure, a distinction is made between costs incurred directly in the performance of an activity and indirectly for the accomplishment of the project. For example, borrowing expenses for project financing and overhead items are commonly treated as indirect costs. For other projects, scheduling of work activities over time is critical and is emphasized in the planning process. In this case, the planner insures that the proper precedence among activities are maintained and that efficient scheduling of the **available** resources **prevails**. Traditional scheduling procedures emphasize the maintenance of task precedence (resulting in **critical path scheduling procedures**) or efficient use of resources over time (resulting in **job shop scheduling procedures**).[3] Finally, most complex projects require consideration of both cost and scheduling over time, so that planning, monitoring and record keeping must consider both dimensions. In these cases, the integration of schedule and budget information is a major concern.

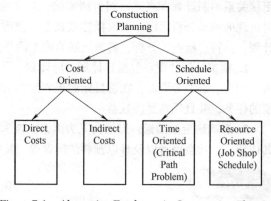

Figure 7-1 Alternative Emphases in Construction Planning

We shall consider the functional requirements for construction planning such as technology choice, **work breakdown**, and budgeting. Construction planning is not an activity which is restricted to the period after the award of a contract for construction. It should be an essential activity during the facility design. Also, if problems arise during construction, re-planning is required.

New Words and Phrases

available   可获得的;可购得的;可找到的;有空的

prevail 盛行，流行；战胜，获胜
construction planning 施工计划
the choice of technology 施工技术的选择
the definition of work task 工作任务的定义
reasoning backward 逆向推理
normative problem 规范性问题
schedule control 进度控制
critical path scheduling procedure 关键路径进度控制程序
job shop scheduling procedure 工作现场进度控制程序
work breakdown 工作分解

Notes

[1] A good construction plan is the basis for developing the budget and the schedule for work. Developing the construction plan is a critical task in the management of construction, even if the plan is not written or otherwise formally recorded.

一个好的施工计划是预算和进度工作的基础。建设项目管理的重要任务是制定好施工计划，即使这个施工计划不是书面的或其他正式记录的形式。

[2] Essential aspects of construction planning include the generation of required activities, analysis of the implications of these activities, and choice among the various alternative means of performing activities.

施工计划的基本内容包括定义所需要的各项活动，分析这些活动之间的内在联系，以及从完成这些活动的多种可替代方法中做出选择。

[3] Traditional scheduling procedures emphasize the maintenance of task precedence (resulting in critical path scheduling procedures) or efficient use of resources over time (resulting in job shop scheduling procedures).

传统的进度控制程序强调保持任务先后顺序（结果是形成了关键路径进度控制程序）或随时间推移有效利用资源（结果是形成了工作现场进度控制程序）。

Exercises

I. Translate the following phrases into English.

1. 资源和工作持续时间估算
2. 制定施工计划
3. 施工技术层面问题
4. 施工计划基本内容
5. 直接成本和间接成本

II. Translate the following sentences into Chinese.

1. It involves the choice of technology, the definition of work tasks, and the estimation of the required resources and durations for individual tasks and the identification of any interactions among the different work tasks.

2. Developing the construction plan is a critical task in the management of construction, even if the plan is not written or otherwise formally recorded.

3. In addition to these technical aspects of construction planning, it may also be necessary to make

organizational decisions about the relationships between project participants and even which organizations to include in a project.

4. For example, borrowing expenses for project financing and over head items are commonly treated as indirect costs. For, other projects, scheduling of work activities over time is critical and is emphasized in the planning process.

Defining Work Tasks

At the same time that the choice of technology and general method are considered, a parallel step in the planning process is to define the various work tasks that must be accomplished. These work tasks represent the necessary framework to permit scheduling of construction activities, along with estimating the resources required by the individual work tasks, and any necessary precedence or required sequence among the tasks. The terms work "tasks" or "activities" are often used **interchangeably** in construction plans to refer to specific, defined items of work. In job shop or manufacturing terminology, a project would be called a "job" and an activity called an "operation", but the sense of the terms is equivalent. The scheduling problem is to determine an appropriate set of activity start time, resource allocations and completion times that will result in completion of the project in a timely and efficient fashion. Construction planning is the necessary fore-runner to scheduling. In this planning, defining work tasks, technology and construction method is typically done either simultaneously or in a series of iterations.

The definition of appropriate work tasks can be a laborious and **tedious** process, yet it represents the necessary information for application of formal scheduling procedures. Since construction projects can involve thousands of individual work tasks, this definition phase can also be expensive and time consuming. Fortunately, many tasks may be repeated in different parts of the facility or past facility construction plans can be used as general models for new projects. For example, the tasks involved in the construction of a building floor may be repeated with only minor differences for each of the floors in the building. Also, standard definitions and **nomenclatures** for most tasks exist. As a result, the individual planner defining work tasks does not have to approach each **facet** of the project entirely from scratch.

While repetition of activities in different locations or reproduction of activities from past projects reduces the work involved, there are very few computer aids for the process of defining activities. For the scheduling process itself, numerous computer programs are available. But for the important task of defining activities, reliance on the skill, judgment and experience of the construction planner is likely to continue.

More formally, an activity is any subdivision of project tasks. The set of activities defined for a project should be comprehensive or completely exhaustive so that all necessary work tasks are included in one or more activities. Typically, each design element in the planned facility will have one or more associated project activities. Execution of an activity requires time and resources, including manpower and equipment, as described in the next section. The time required to perform an activity is called the duration of the activity. The beginning and the end of activities are signposts or milestones, indicating the progress of the project. Occasionally, it is useful to define activities which have no duration to mark important events. For example, **receipt** of equipment on the construction site may be defined as an activity since other activities would depend upon the equipment availability and the project manager might appreciate formal notice of the arrival. Similarly, receipt of regulatory approvals would also be specially marked in the project plan.

The extent of work involved in any one activity can vary tremendously in construction project plans. Indeed, it is common to begin with fairly coarse definitions of activities and then to further sub-divide tasks as the plan becomes better defined. As a result, the definition of activities evolves during the preparation of the plan. A result of this process is a natural **hierarchy** of activities with large, abstract functional activities repeatedly sub-divided into more and more specific sub-tasks. For example, the problem of placing concrete on site would have sub-activities associated with **placing forms, installing reinforcing steel, pouring concrete, finishing the concrete, removing forms** and others. Even more specifically, sub-tasks such as removal and cleaning of forms after concrete placement can be defined. Even further, the sub-task "clean concrete forms" could be subdivided into the various operations:

1. Transport forms from on-site storage and unload onto the cleaning station.
2. Position forms on the cleaning station.
3. Wash forms with water.
4. Clean concrete debris from the form's surface.
5. Coat the form surface with an oil release agent for the next use.
6. Unload the form from the cleaning station and transport to the storage location.

This detailed task breakdown of the activity "clean concrete forms" would not generally be done in standard construction planning, but it is essential in the process of programming or designing a robot to undertake this activity since the various specific tasks must be well defined for a robot implementation.

It is generally advantageous to introduce an explicit hierarchy of work activities for the purpose of simplifying the presentation and development of a schedule. For example, the initial plan might define a single activity associated with "site clearance." Later, this single activity might be sub-divided into "re-locating utilities", "removing vegetation", "grading", etc. However, these activities could continue to be identified as sub-activities under the general activity of "site clearance." This hierarchical structure also facilitates the preparation of summary charts and reports in which detailed operations are combined into aggregate or "super" -activities.

More formally, a hierarchical approach to work task definition decomposes the work activity into component parts in the form of a tree. Higher levels in the tree represent decision nodes or summary activities, while branches in the tree lead to smaller components and work activities. A variety of constraints among the various nodes may be defined or imposed, including precedence relationships among different tasks as defined below. Technology choices may be decomposed to decisions made at particular nodes in the tree. For example, choices on plumbing technology might be made without reference to choices for other functional activities.

Of course, numerous different activity hierarchies can be defined for each construction plan. For example, upper level activities might be related to facility components such as foundation elements, and then lower level activity divisions into the required construction operations might be made. Alternatively, upper level divisions might represent general types of activities such as electrical work, while lower work divisions represent the application of these operations to specific facility components. As a third alternative, initial divisions might represent different **spatial locations** in the planned facility. The choice of a hierarchy depends upon the desired scheme for summarizing work information and on the convenience of the planner. In computerized databases, multiple hierarchies can be stored so that different aggregations or views of the work breakdown structure can be obtained.

The number and detail of the activities in a construction plan is a matter of judgment or convention. Construction plans can easily range between less than a hundred to many thousand defined tasks, depending on the planner's decisions and the scope of the project. If sub-divided activities are too refined, the size of the network becomes **unwieldy** and the cost of planning excessive. Sub-division yields no benefit if reasonably accurate estimates of activity durations and the required resources cannot be made at the detailed work breakdown level. On the other hand, if the specified activities are too coarse, it is impossible to develop realistic schedules and details of resource requirements during the project. More detailed task definitions permit better control and more realistic scheduling. It is useful to define separate work tasks for those activities which involve different resources, or those activities which do not require continuous performance.

For example, the activity "prepare and check shop drawings" should be divided into a task for preparation and a task for checking since different individuals are involved in the two tasks and there may be a time lag between preparation and checking.

In practice, the proper level of detail will depend upon the size, importance and difficulty of the project as well as the specific scheduling and accounting procedures which are adopted. However, it is generally the case that most schedules are prepared with too little detail than too much. It is important to keep in mind that task definition will serve as the basis for scheduling, for communicating the construction plan and for construction monitoring. Completion of tasks will also often serve as a basis for progress payments from the owner. Thus, more detailed task definitions can be quite useful. But more detailed task breakdowns are only valuable to the extent that the resources required, durations and activity relationships are realistically estimated for each activity. Providing detailed work task breakdowns is not helpful without a **commensurate** effort to provide realistic resource requirement estimates. As more powerful, computer-based scheduling and monitoring procedures are introduced, the ease of defining and manipulating tasks will increase, and the number of work tasks can reasonably be expected to expand.

Example 7-1: Task Definition for a Road Building Project

As an example of construction planning, suppose that we wish to develop a plan for a road construction project including two culverts. Initially, we divide project activities into three categories as shown in Figure 7-2: structures, roadway, and general. This division is based on the major types of design elements to be constructed. Within the roadway work, a further sub-division is into earthwork and pavement. Within these sub-divisions, we identify clearing, excavation, filling and finishing (including seeding and sodding) associated with earthwork, and we define watering, compaction and paving sub-activities associated with pavement. Finally, we note that the roadway segment is fairly long, and so individual activities can be defined for different physical segments along the roadway path. In Figure 7-2, we divide each paving and earthwork activity into activities specific to each of two roadway segments. For the culvert construction, we define the sub-divisions of structural excavation, concreting, and reinforcing. Even more specifically, structural excavation is divided into excavation itself and the required backfill and compaction. Similarly, concreting is divided into placing concrete forms, pouring concrete, stripping forms, and curing the concrete. As a final step in the structural planning, detailed activities are defined for reinforcing each of the two culverts. General work activities are defined for move in, general supervision, and clean up. As a result of this planning, over thirty different detailed activities have been defined.

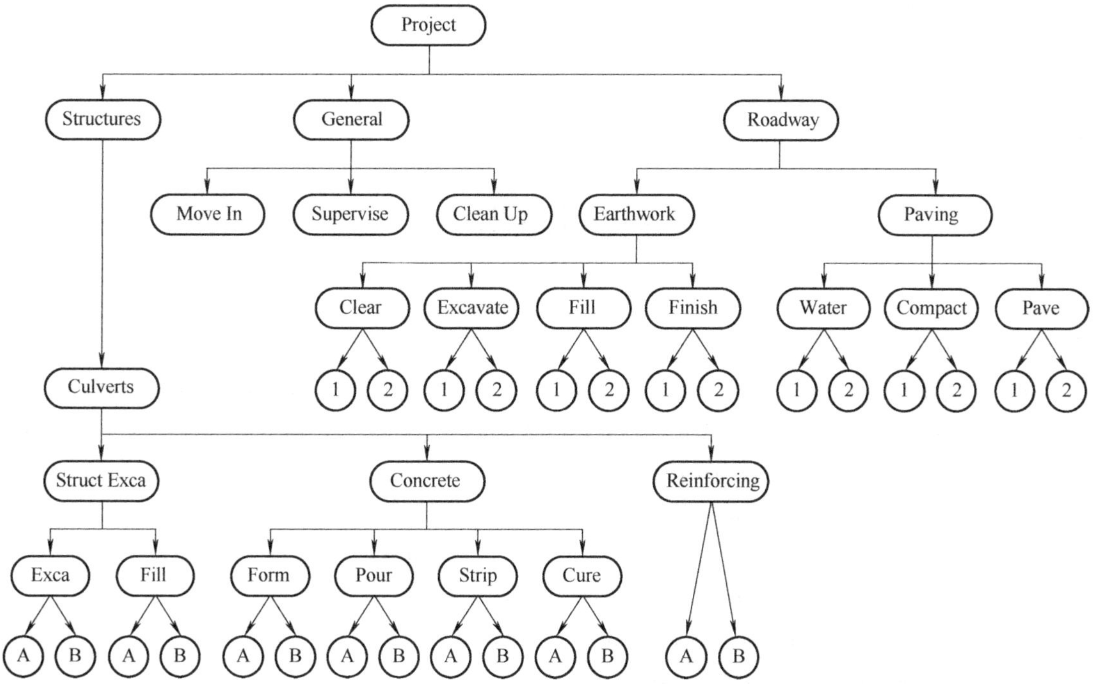

Figure 7-2 Illustrative Hierarchical Activity Divisions for a Roadway Project

At the option of the planner, additional activities might also be defined for this project. For example, materials ordering or lane striping might be included as separate activities. It might also be the case that a planner would define a different hierarchy of work breakdowns than that shown in Figure 7-2. For example, placing reinforcing might have been a sub-activity under concreting for culverts. One reason for separating reinforcement placement might be to emphasize the different material and resources required for this activity. Also, the division into separate roadway segments and culverts might have been introduced early in the hierarchy. With all these potential differences, the important aspect is to insure that all necessary activities are included somewhere in the final plan.

New Words and Phrases

interchangeably   可交换地，可交替地
tedious   冗长乏味的，沉闷的，单调乏味的
nomenclature   术语，专门名词；术语表，术语集
facet   面，方面；在……上的琢面
receipt   收到；收据；收入
hierarchy   层级，等级制度
unwieldy   笨重的；笨拙的；不灵便的
commensurate   相称的；同量的；同样大小的
placing form   支设模板
installing reinforcing steel   绑扎钢筋
pouring concrete   浇筑混凝土

finishing the concrete　养护混凝土
removing forms　拆模
spatial location　空间位置

Work Plan

Work Plan

After the project is structured in phases, the project manager has to develop a work plan for the project. For the first coming phase this work plan has be very detailed. Later phases require fewer details. A work plan shows all tasks that have to be carried out to produce all necessary outputs/services. It describes who are involved in these activities and when the activity takes place. A good work plan also presents the relationships between the different tasks (successors and predecessors).

Typical ways of presenting work plans are network plans and chant charts.

Network plans can be presented in two ways:

- **Activity on the arrow (critical path method).**
- **Activity in the node (PERT chart).**

Figures 7-3 respectively present the legend for the activity on the arrow chart, an example of a Gant chart.

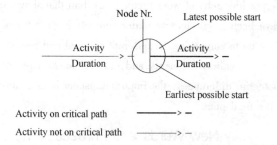

Figure 7-3　Legend for the Activity on the Arrow Chart

First Draft

Preparing work plans is an **iterative** process. It is almost impossible to provide immediately accurate answers on every questions, like for example, when key resources are needed, are available, how much time an activity will need etc. The planner will usually start with rough estimates to prepare a first version and modify this when more accurate information becomes available. Planners will have to make notes on their assumptions, which influence the plan. Important considerations during the planning exercises are:

- Relationships with other projects or departments: If the project depends on the work of others, do the others understand the project's dependency and agree to the **hand-off dates**?
- Resources availability and usage (including people, materials, and equipment): Who manages the

resources?

- Activity duration's: What is the base of Activity duration estimates?
- Project costs: What is the base of the project/activity costs? Who approves the budget?
- Available time: Is the deadline for the task fixed or flexible?
- Deliverables.

Schedule a Project

Projects are scheduled from the start date when the project finish date is not yet determined. This is usually the situation for most infrastructure projects. However some infrastructure projects, for example school buildings, have to be completed before a certain deadline and are therefore scheduled from the finish date. Scheduling from the finish date means that the project will be scheduled backwards from a particular date, with each activity finishing as late as possible while still making the end date.

Activity Duration and Dependencies

The project manager determines which activities are necessary, and makes an estimate about the duration of these activities, the amount of resources needed and relationship between these activities. The number of labourers and type of equipment often determine the duration of an activity. However the duration of some activities depends also on other factors, like for example of curing of concrete or ordering of materials. These activities have so-called lead-times.

Activity Dependencies

The nature of the relationship between two linked activities defines a dependency between their finish and start dates. For example, the "Preparation of Contract document" activity must finish before the start of the "Signing contract" activity. There are four kinds of activity dependencies:

Act. Dependency	Description
Finish-to-start (FS)	Activity (B) cannot start until Activity (A) finishes
Start-to-start (SS)	Activity (B) cannot start until activity (A) starts
Finish-to-finish (FF)	Activity (B) cannot finish until activity (A) finishes
Start-to-finish (SF)	Activity (B) cannot finish until activity (A) starts

Activities can also be related to specific dates. For example production of asphalt concrete should not take place during the rainy season or the blasting of an old **viaduct** should be done on Sunday October 13, etc.

Sequence of Activities

Sometimes a succeeding activity cannot immediately start after the completion of the preceding activity, like for example casting of concrete and removing of formwork. The minimum time between the finish date of the preceding and the earliest possible start date of succeeding activity is called **lag time**.

Plan for and Procure Resources

Estimate Resources Needed

After all activities and tasks have been determined, the project manager may start allocating resources to activities and specific tasks.

Historical Data

(S) He may obtain the data from a manual, but an update from other historical resources is always highly recommended to adjust the duration information to the specific circumstances. Professional organizations collect historical information from old project files, databases, and from people who have worked on similar projects on regular intervals. Smaller, more pioneering organizations may try to review any available post-mortem information from previous projects. Project managers should in particular search for information on the types and numbers of resources used.

Refine Duration Estimates

It goes without saying that the duration estimates should be upgraded, when more accurate information comes forward or when the allocation of resources is changed.

Resource Graphs

Resource graphs shows what resources are needed and when. It is aso shows when certain resources are over allocated. Typical resource graphs are **labour schedules**, **plant and transport schedules** and materials schedules. A typical **resource graph** is presented below.

Labour Schedules

The construction of infrastructure requires besides flexible unskilled labourers also many specialised labourers. Those labourers with the same qualifications are positioned in the same so-called labour pool. To avoid reduction in productivity due to reduced motivation and start and finish periods it is advisable to aim for an even workload for each of the labour-pools. This is even more of interest for those organizations, which have employed the labour-force on a permanent basis. This is achieved by a continuing exchange between the labour schedule and the chant chart or network plan. The labour schedules are drawn up using the chant charts already prepared. For each activity the number of workers from each labour pool is recorded.

Plant and Transport Schedules

Expensive plant and transport vehicles are generally planned to be 100% utilized. Cheaper plant and transport vehicles are generally planned to fit in with the prepared plan.

Besides for aiming at constant utilization of the different resource pools, the project manager (in particular during the **implementation phase**) wants to avoid that a succeeding activity will overtake a preceding activity. The project manager prefers therefore that all activities will run at the same speed.

Material Schedule

Material schedules act as a guide for ordering materials, but also serves as a checklist of materials needed. It is usually minor items that get forgotten and cause temporarily delays.

Meeting Deadlines

Changing the duration is one method to help meeting deadlines, resolve resource over-allocations, and budget cuts. Another option to meet the deadlines is the creation of sub-projects. If a big project contains a number of outputs or an output, which can be segmented, it may be advisable to use this technique. Segmenting of road works will result in many production gangs undertaking the same activity at the same time.

Specify Resource Availability

Availability of resources refers to the availability of resources to work on the project, that is, whether the resource is working half time or full time on the project, whether there are two or three of the same resource, and whether the resource's availability changes at any point. Infrastructure projects may compete with the agricultural sector to attract workers during the harvest seasons.

The more familiar, project managers are with resource capabilities, the more efficiently and effectively these resources can be assigned to the different tasks. Project managers should also be familiar with equipment preventive maintenance schedules, especially when equipment is not rented. A special plan should be developed to present the rate of consumption for materials, their costs and specifically when they need to be purchased. If the project does not purchase from regular suppliers, time should be allocated for the selection of these suppliers.

New Words and Phrases

iterative　迭代的；重复的；反复的
viaduct　高架桥；高架铁路，高架公路
activity on the arrow (critical path method)　箭头代号（关键路径法）
activity in the node (PERT chart)　节点（计划评审技术图）
hand-off date　交付日期
lag time　滞后时间；迟延时间
labour schedule　劳动力安排
plant and transport schedule　工厂和运输时间表
resource graph　资源图
material schedule　材料日程表
implementation phase　实施阶段
meeting deadline　截止日

Part II Speaking

Project Programming

B: Good morning, Mr. Armstrong.
A: Good morning, Mr. Bao Lin. As specified in the contract, you are required to submit your project program not later than tomorrow. I guess you are going to submit it now.
B: Yes, but before our formal submission, may I ask for your advice and comments on our **draft program**?
A: Why not? I like to have discussions with our contractors about their programs.
B: Here is the copy for you.
A: It looks fine. All the activities in the chart are shown in color bars. It shows the links between an activity and its **preceding activities** as well as succeeding ones.
B: Though we have already made **network analysis** of the program, our eventual schedule of the works is still presented in **linked bar chart** form for easy understanding.
A: How did you decide the level of detail of the activities in the program?
B: In order to measure the works according to the Contract Document, we just took the items shown in B. O. Q. as the activities.
A: Where can I find the activities regarding **shop-drawing** design and equipment procurement?

B: I am sorry. We did not include such activities in the program.
A: I think such important activities should have been included in your schedule. Designing, submission and approval of shop drawings and equipment procurement always take a long time. If these activities are not properly scheduled, surely the implementation of your program will be in a mess.
B: You are perfectly right. I will revise this program accordingly this afternoon and submit the revised one to you tomorrow morning.
A: Please remember that a more detailed three-month **rolling program** is required to be submitted within seven days.
B: The preparation of the three-month rolling program is on the way. I will submit it to you on time. Thank you.

New Words and Phrases

draft program 计划草稿
preceding activity 紧前工作（succeeding activity 紧后工作）
network analysis 网络分析
linked bar chart 关联横道图
shop-drawing 加工图，施工详图
rolling program 滚动计划

Unit 8
Construction Site Management

Part I Reading and Translating

Professional Knowledge Guidance

1. 建筑业劳动生产率：是指建筑业劳动者在报告期内生产出建筑业产品的效率。它以建筑产品产量或价值和其相适应的劳动消耗量的比值来表示，是考核建筑业企业生产效率的提高和劳动节约情况的重要指标。

2. 建筑材料管理：是建筑材料的计划、供应、使用等管理工作的总称。建筑材料构成建筑产品实体，是建筑生产的劳动对象。合理地组织建筑材料的计划、供应与使用，保证建筑材料从生产企业按品种、数量、质量、期限进入建筑工地，减少流转环节，防止积压浪费，对缩短建设工期，加快建设速度，降低工程成本有重要意义。

3. 建筑机械：是工程建设和城乡建设所用机械设备的总称，它包括挖掘机械、铲土运输机械、压实机械、工程起重机械、桩工机械、路面机械、混凝土机械、混凝土制品机械、钢筋级预应力机械、装修机械、高空作业机械等。

Factors Affecting Job-Site Productivity

Job-site productivity is influenced by many factors which can be characterized either as labor characteristics, project work conditions or as **non-productive activities**.[1] The labor characteristics include:
- Age, skill and experience of workforce.
- **Leadership and motivation** of workforce.

The project work conditions include among other factors:
- Job size and complexity.
- Job site accessibility.
- Labor availability.

- Equipment utilization.
- **Contractual agreements.**
- Local climate.
- Local cultural characteristics, particularly in foreign operations.

The non-productive activities associated with a project may or may not be paid by the owner, but they nevertheless take up potential labor resources which can otherwise be directed to the project. The non-productive activities include among other factors:

- Indirect labor required to maintain the progress of the project.
- Rework for correcting unsatisfactory work.
- Temporary work stoppage due to inclement weather or material shortage.
- Time off for union activities.
- Absent time, including late start and early quits.
- Non-working holidays.
- Strikes.

Each category of factors affects the productive labor available to a project as well as the on-site labor efficiency.

Labor Characteristics

Performance analysis is a common tool for assessing worker quality and contribution. Factors that might be evaluated include:

- Quality of work—**caliber** of work produced or accomplished.
- Quantity of work—volume of acceptable work.
- Job knowledge—demonstrated knowledge of requirements, methods, techniques and skills involved in doing the job and in applying these to increase productivity.
- Related work knowledge—knowledge of effects of work upon other areas and knowledge of related areas which have influence on assigned work.
- Judgment—soundness of conclusions, decisions and actions.
- Initiative—ability to take effective action without being hold.
- Resource utilization—ability to **delineate** project needs and locate, plan and effectively use all resources available.

These different factors could each be assessed on three point scale: recognized strength, meets expectation, and area needing improvement

Examples of work performance in these areas might also be provided.

Project Work Conditions

Job-site labor productivity can be estimated either for each craft (**carpenter**, **bricklayer**, etc.) or each type of construction (residential housing, processing plant, etc.) under a specific set of work conditions. A **base labor productivity** may be defined for a set of work conditions specified by the owner or contractor who wishes to observe and measure the labor performance **over a period of time** under such conditions. [2] A **labor productivity index** may then be defined as the ratio of the job-site labor productivity under a different set of work conditions to the base labor productivity, and is measured of the relative labor efficiency of a project under this new set of work conditions.

The effects of various factors related to work conditions on a new project can be estimated in advance, some more accurately than others. For example, for very large construction projects, the labor productivity index tends to decrease as the project size and/or complexity increase because of logistic problems and the "learning" that work force must undergo before adjusting to the new environment. [3] Job-site accessibility often may reduce the labor productivity index if the workers must perform their jobs in round about ways, such as avoiding traffic in **repaving** the highway surface or maintaining the operation of a plant during renovation. Labor availability is another factor. Shortage of local labor will force the contractor to bring in non-local market labor or schedule overtime work or both. In either case, the labor efficiency will be reduced in addition to incurring additional expenses. The degree of equipment utilization and mechanization of a construction project clearly will have direct bearing on job-site labor productivity. The **contractual arrangements play an important role in** the utilization of union or non-union labor, the use of subcontractors and the degree of field supervision, all of which will impact job-site labor productivity. Since on-site construction essentially involves outdoor activities, the local climate will influence the efficiency of workers directly. In foreign operations, the cultural characteristics of the host country should be observed in assessing the labor efficiency.

Non-Productive Activities

The non-productive activities associated with a project should also be examined in order to examine the **productivity labor yield**, which is defined as the ratio of direct labor hour devoted to the completion of a project to the potential labor hours. The direct labor hour are estimated **on the basis of** the best possible conditions at a job site by excluding all factors which may reduce the productive labor yield. For example, in the repaving of highway surface, the flagmen required to divert traffic represent indirect labor which does not contribute to the labor efficiency of the paving crew if the highway is closed to the traffic. Similarly, for large projects in remote areas, indirect labor may be used to provide housing and infrastructure for the workers hired to supply the direct labor for a project. The labor hours spent on rework to correct unsatisfactory original work represent extra time taken away from potential labor hours. The labor hours related to such activities must be deduced from the potential hours in order to obtain the actual productive labor yield.

Example 8-1: Effects of job size on productivity

A contractor has established that under a set of "standard" work conditions for building construction, a job requiring 500,000 labor hours is considered standard in determining the base labor productivity. All other factors being the same, the labor productivity index will increase to 1.1 or 110% for a job requiring only 400,000 labor-hours. Assuming that a linear relation exists for the range between jobs requiring 300,000 to 700,000 labor hours as shown in Figure 8-1, determine the labor productivity index for a new job requiring 650,000 labor hours under otherwise the same set of work conditions. [4]

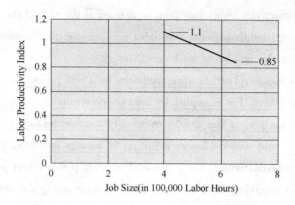

Figure 8-1 Illustrative Relationship between Productivity Index and Job Size

New Words and Phrases

caliber　　[军] 口径；才干；水准；器量
delineate　　描绘，描写，画……的轮廓
carpenter　　木工，木匠；制作；当木匠
bricklayer　　砖瓦匠，泥水匠
repave　　重新铺砌；再铺
non-productive activity　　非生产因素
leadership and motivation　　领导与激励
contractual agreement　　合同协议
performance analysis　　技术性能分析
job-site labor productivity　　现场（工地）劳动生产率
base labor productivity　　基准劳动生产率
over a period of time　　在一定期间内
labor productivity index　　劳动生产率指数
contractual arrangement　　合同安排
play an important role in...　　在……方面发挥重要作用
productive labor yield　　有效劳动产出
on the basis of...　　在……基础上

Notes

[1] Job-site productivity is influenced by many factors which can be characterized either as labor characteristics, project work conditions or as non-productive activities.
　　影响现场生产率的因素很多，大致分为劳动力特性、工程工作条件（环境）或非生产性活动。

[2] A base labor productivity may be defined for a set of work conditions specified by the owner or contractor who wishes to observe and measure the labor performance over a period of time under such conditions.
　　基准劳动生产率可以定义为在给定的工作条件（环境）下，业主或承包商期望观测和衡量（此条件下）的一段时期内的劳动绩效。

[3] The effects of various factors related to work conditions on a new project can be estimated in

advance, some more accurately than others. For example, for very large construction projects, the labor productivity index tends to decrease as the project size and/or complexity increase because of logistic problems and the "learning" that work force must undergo before adjusting to the new environment.

劳动生产率指数（可以）比其他指标更准确地预估与新项目工作条件相关的各种影响因素。例如，对于特大型的建设项目，因为后勤问题和劳动力在适应新环境前必须经过的学习过程，随着项目规模和/或复杂性的增长，劳动生产力指数趋于下降。

［4］ Assuming that a linear relation exists for the range between jobs requiring 300,000 to 700,000 labor hours as shown in Figure 8-1, determine the labor productivity index for a new job requiring 650,000 labor hours under otherwise the same set of work conditions.

假如在某项工作所需的300000～70000工时范围内工时与劳动生产率指数存在线性关系，如图8-1所示，在完全相同的工作条件下，确定某项新工作需要650000工时的劳动生产率指数。

Exercises

I. Translate the following phrases into English.

1. 现场劳动生产率
2. 技术性能分析
3. 有效劳动产出
4. 劳动生产率指数
5. 资源利用

II. Translate the following sentences into Chinese.

1. Under ordinary circumstances, the constructor will handle the procurement to shop or materials with the best price/performance characteristics specified by the designer.

2. In general, if the work can be done in the shop where working conditions can better be controlled, it is advisable to do so, provided that the fabricated members or units can be shipped to the construction site in a satisfactory manner at a reasonable cost.

3. As a further step to simplify field assembly, an entire wall panel including plumbing and wiring or even an entire room may be prefabricated and shipped to the site.

4 This multiple handling diverts scarce skilled craftsmen and contractor supervision into activities which do not directly contribute to construction.

5. In each of the locations, the contractor had supervision and construction labor to identify materials, unload from transport, determine where the material was going repackage if required to split shipments, and then re-load materials on outgoing transport.

Choice of Equipment and Standard Production Rates

Typically, construction equipment is used to perform essentially repetitive operations, and can be broadly classified according to two basic functions: (1) **operators such as cranes, graders, etc.** which stay within the confines of the construction site, and (2) **haulers such as dump trucks, ready mixed**

concrete truck, etc. which transport materials to and from the site. In both cases, the cycle of a piece of equipment is a sequence of tasks which is repeated to produce a unit of output. For example, the sequence of tasks for a crane might be to fit and install a **wall panel** (or a package of eight wall panels) on the side of a building; similarly, the sequence of tasks of a **ready mixed concrete truck** might be to load, haul and unload two cubic yards (or one truck load) of fresh concrete.

In order to increase job-site productivity, it is beneficial to select equipment with proper characteristics and a size most suitable for the work conditions at a construction site. In excavation for building construction, for examples, factors that could affect the selection of excavators include:

1. Size of the job. Larger volumes of excavation will require larger excavators, or smaller excavators in greater number.

2. Activity time constraints. Shortage of time for excavation may force contractors to increase the size or numbers of equipment for activities related to excavation.

3. Availability of equipment. Productivity of excavation activities will diminish if the equipment used to perform them is available but not the most adequate.

4. Cost of transportation of equipment. This cost depends on the size of the job, the distance of transportation, and the means of transportation.

5. Type of excavation. Principal types of excavation in building projects are cut and/or fill, excavation massive, and excavation for the elements of foundation. The most adequate equipment to perform one of these activities is not the most adequate to perform the others.

6. Soil characteristics. The type and condition of the soil is important when choosing the most adequate equipment since each piece of equipment has different outputs for different soils. Moreover, one excavation pit could have different soils at different stratums.

7. Geometric characteristics of elements to be excavated. Functional characteristics of different types of equipment make such considerations necessary.

8. Space constraints. The performance of equipment is influenced by the spatial limitations for the movement of excavators.

9. Characteristics of haul units. The size of an excavator will depend on the haul units if there is a constraint on the size and/or number of these units.

10. Location of dumping areas. The distance between the construction site and dumping areas could be relevant not only for selecting the type and number of haulers, but also the type of excavators.

11. Weather and temperature. Rain, snow and severe temperature conditions affect the job-site productivity of labor and equipment.

By comparing various types of machines for excavation, for example, **power shovels** are generally found to be the most suitable for excavating from a level surface and for attacking an existing digging surface or one created by the power shovel; furthermore, they have the capability of placing the excavated material directly onto the haulers. Another alternative is to use **bulldozers** for excavation.

The choice of the type and size of haulers is based on the consideration that the number of haulers selected must be capable of disposing of the excavated materials expeditiously. Factors which affect this selection include:

1. **Output of excavators**. The size and characteristics of the excavators selected will determine the output volume excavated per day.

2. **Distance to dump site.** Sometimes part of the excavated materials may be piled up in a corner at the job-site for use as backfill.

3. **Probable average speed.** The average speed of the haulers to and from the dumping site will determine the cycle time for each hauling trip.

4. **Volume of excavated materials.** The volume of excavated materials including the part to be piled up should be hauled away as soon as possible.

5. Spatial and weight constraints. The size and weight of the haulers must be feasible at the job site and over the route from the construction site to the dumping area.

Dump trucks are usually used as haulers for excavated materials as they can move freely with relatively high speeds on city streets as well as on highways.

New Words and Phrases

bulldozer 推土机
operators such as cranes, graders, etc. 操作设备（如起重机、平整机等）
haulers such as dump trucks, ready mixed concrete truck, etc. 运输设备（如自卸卡车、混凝土搅拌运输车等）
wall panel 护墙板
reddy mixed concrete truck 预拌混凝土卡车
power shovel 挖土机，机铲
output of excavator 开挖机械产量
distance to dump site 卸载地的距离
probable average speed 可能的平均速度
volume of excavated material 开挖材料的量

Material Procurement and Delivery

The main sources of information for **feedback** and control of material procurement are requisition, bids and **quotations**, **purchase orders** and subcontracts, shipping and receiving documents, and **invoices**. For projects involving the large scale use of critical resources, the owner may initiate the procurement procedure even before the selection of a constructor in order to avoid shortages and delays. Under ordinary circumstances, the constructor handles the procurement to shop for materials with the best price/performance characteristics specified by the designer. Some **overlapping** and **rehandling** in the procurement process is unavoidable, but it should be minimized to insure timely **delivery** of the materials in good condition.

The materials for delivery to and from a construction site may be broadly classified as **bulk materials**, Standard off-the-shelf materials, and **Fabricated members or units**.

The process of delivery, including transportation, field storage and installation will be different for these classes of materials. The equipment needed to handle and haul these classes of materials will also be different.

Bulk materials refer to materials in their natural or semi-processed state, such as earthwork to be excavated, wet concrete mix, etc. Which are usually encountered in large quantities in construction. Some bulk materials such as earthwork or gravels may be measured in bank (solid in site) volume. Obviously, the quantities of materials for delivery may be substantially different when expressed in different measures of volume, depending on the characteristics of such materials.

Standard piping and valves are typical examples of standard off-the-shelf materials which are used extensively in the chemical processing industry. Since standard off-the-shelf materials can easily be **stockpiled**, the delivery process is relatively simple.

Fabricated members such as steel beams and columns for buildings are pre-processed in a shop to simplify the field erection procedures. Welded or bolted connections are attached partially to the members which are cut to precise dimensions for adequate fit. Similarly, steel tanks and pressure vessels are often partly or fully fabricated before shipping to the field. In general, if the work can be done in the shop where working conditions can better be controlled, it is advisable to do so, provided that the fabricated members or units can be shipped to the construction site in a satisfactory manner at a reasonable cost.

As a further step to simplify field assembly, an entire wall panel including plumbing and wiring or even an entire room can be prefabricated and shipped to the site. While the field labor is greatly reduced in such cases, "materials" for delivery are in fact manufactured products with value added by another type of labor. With modern means of transporting construction materials and fabricated units, the percentage of costs on direct labor and materials for a project may change if more fabricated units are introduced in the construction process.

In the construction industry, materials used by a specific craft are generally handled by **craftsmen**, not by general labor. Thus, electricians handle electrical materials, pipe-fitters handle pipe materials, etc. This multiple handling diverts scarce skilled craftsmen and contractor supervision into activities which do not directly contribute to construction. Since contractors are not normally in the freight business, they do not perform the tasks of freight delivery efficiently. All these factors tend to **exacerbate** the problems of freight delivery for very large projects.

Example 8-2: Freight Delivery for the Alaska Pipeline Project

The freight delivery system for the Alaska pipeline project was set up to handle 600,000 tons of materials and supplies. This tonnage did not include the pipes which comprised another 500,000 tons and were shipped through a different routing system. The complexity of this delivery system is illustrated in Figure 8-2. The rectangular boxes denote geographical locations. The points of origin represent plants and factories throughout the U.S. and elsewhere. Some of the materials went to a primary staging point in Seattle and some went directly to Alaska. There were five ports of entry: Valdez, Anchorage, Whittier, Seward and Prudhoe Bay. There was a secondary staging area in Fairbanks and the pipeline itself was divided into six sections. Beyond the Yukon River, there was nothing available but a dirt road for hauling. The amounts of freight in thousands of tons shipped to and from various locations are indicated by the numbers near the network branches (with arrows allowing the directions of material flows) and the modes of transportation are noted above the branches. In each of the locations, the contractor had supervision and construction labor to identify materials, unload from transport, determine where the material was going, repackage if required to split shipments, and then re-load materials on outgoing transport.

Example 8-3: Process Plant Equipment Procurement

The procurement and delivery of bulk materials items such as purchasing electrical and structural

Unit 8 Construction Site Management

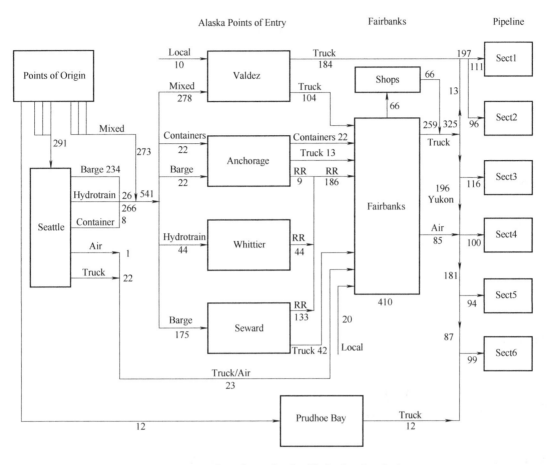

Figure 8-2 Freight Delivery for the Alaska Pipeline Project

elements involves a series of activities if such items are not standard and/or in stock. The times required for various activities in the procurement of such items might be estimated to be as follows:

Activities	Duration/days	Cumulative Duration
Requisition ready by designer	0	0
Owner approval	5	5
Inquiry issued to vendors	3	8
Vendor quotations received	15	23
Complete bid evaluation by designer	7	30
Owner approval	5	35
Place purchase order	5	40
Receive preliminary shop drawings	10	50
Receive final design drawings	10	60
Fabrication and delivery	60~200	120~260

As a result, this type of equipment procurement will typically require four to nine months. Slippage or contraction in this standard schedule is also possible, based on such factors as the extent to which a fabricator is busy.

New Words and Phrases

feedback　反馈
quotation　询价；引证，报价
invoice　发货，开发票
overlapping　搭接
procurement　采购
rehandle　重新处理，返工
delivery　交付
stockpile　储存
craftsmen　工匠
exacerbate　使……恶化
purchase order　购买指令
bulk material　大宗材料
fabricated member or unit　预制构件

Part II　Speaking

Field Management

Dialogue 1

A: I can see you are adopting the method of **soil consolidation works**.

B: Yes. This method worked very well with similar geological conditions in some works we did before.

A: But can you prove that this method is reliable for this project?

B: Yes. We have had some test operations, from which we estimate that after a certain time of vacuum prestressing, the area will sink and the **bearing capacity** will meet the requirement for the location of the main building.

A: Isn't the cost of the **vacuum pressure** more expensive than that of the **soil loading pressure**? Can we use the loading pressure instead of the vacuum pressure for this project?

B: I don't think we can. As you know, the soil loading pressure is much slower than the vacuum pressure for **soil compacting**, so it is not suitable for this project with such a tight schedule.

A: How long will it take by your present method?

B: We can shorten the construction period of the soil consolidation by 6 months.

Dialogue 2

A: I notice that you use 20,000 square meters for **precasting yard**. It seems that there will be not enough area for the **production facilities**.

B: No problem. We use that piece of land for the precasting yard only for a short period of time. After **piling works** goes on for 3 months, we will reduce the area for the precasting yard.

A: What will the area be used for after that?

B: We'll turn it into a warehouse, a repair workshop and a **steel embedment shop**.

A: How about the rebar yard?
B: The rebar yard also will be used only at the beginning stage of the construction. Other facilities can be set up later on that area.

New Words and Phrases

soil consolidation work　地基土固结处理
bearing capacity　承载力
vacuum pressure　真空预压
soil loading pressure　堆载预压
soil compacting　地基土固结
precasting yard　预制场
production facility　生产设施
piling work　桩基工程
steel embedment shop　预埋件车间

Unit 9
Quality Control and Safety During Construction

Part I Reading and Translating

Professional Knowledge Guidance

1. 工程项目质量：是指能够满足用户或社会需要并由工程合同、有关技术标准、设计文件、施工规范等详细设定其适用、安全、经济、美观等特性要求的工程实体质量与工程建设各阶段、各环节的工作质量的总和。

2. 工程项目施工质量控制：不但是施工监理重要的工作内容，也是工程项目质量控制的重点。监理工程师对工程施工的质量控制，就是按照合同赋予的权利，围绕影响工程质量的各种因素，对工程项目的施工进行有效的监督和管理。

3. 质量责任：包括参建各方主体和从业人员的质量责任，如建设单位的首要责任，勘察、设计、施工单位的主体责任。质量终身责任制是指五方主体项目负责人质量终身责任承诺、竣工后永久性标牌、质量终身责任信息档案等制度。

Text

Construction Quality Control and Management

Quality and Safety Concerns in Construction

Quality control and safety represent increasingly important concerns for project managers. **Defects** or failures in constructed facilities can result in very large costs. Even with minor defects, re-construction may be required and facility operations **impaired**. Increased costs and delays are the result. In the worst case, failures may cause **personal injuries** or fatalities. Accidents during the construction process can similarly result in personal injuries and large costs. Indirect costs of insurance, inspection and regulation are increasing rapidly due to these increased direct costs. Good project managers try to ensure that the job is done right the first time and that no major accidents occur on the project.

As with cost control, the most important decisions regarding the quality of a completed facility are made during the design and planning stages rather than during construction. [1] It is during these preliminary stages that component configurations, material **specifications** and functional performance are decided. Quality control during construction consists largely of insuring **conformance** to these original designs and planning decisions.

While conformance to existing design decisions is the primary focus of quality control, there are exceptions to this rule. First, **unforeseen** circumstances, incorrect design decisions or changes desired by an owner in the facility function may require **reevaluation of design decisions** during the course of construction. While these changes may be motivated by the concern for quality, they represent occasions for redesign with all the **attendant** objectives and constraints. As a second case some designs rely upon informed and appropriate decision making during the construction process itself. For example, some **tunneling methods** make decisions about the amount of shoring required at different locations based upon observation of soil conditions during the tunneling process. Since such decisions are based on better information concerning **actual site conditions**, the facility design may be more cost effective as a result. Any special case of redesign during construction requires the various considerations.

With the attention to conformance as the measure of quality during the construction process, the specification of quality requirements in the design and contract documentation becomes extremely important. Quality requirements should be clear and verifiable, so that all parties in the project can understand the requirements for conformance. Much of the discussion in this chapter relates to the development and the implications of different quality requirements for construction as well as the issues associated with insuring conformance.

Safety during the construction project is also influenced in large part by decisions made during the planning and design process. Some designs or construction plans are inherently difficult and dangerous to implement, whereas other, comparable plans may considerably reduce the possibility of accidents. For example, clear separation of traffic from construction zones during **roadway rehabilitation** can greatly reduce the possibility of accidental collisions. Beyond these design decisions, safety largely depends upon education, **vigilance** and cooperation during the construction process. [2] Workers should be constantly alert to the possibilities of accidents and avoid taking unnecessary risks.

Organizing for Quality and Safety

A variety of different organizations are possible for quality and safety control during construction. One common model is to have a group responsible for **quality assurance** and another group primarily responsible for safety within an organization. In large organizations, departments dedicated to quality assurance and to safety might assign specific individuals to assume responsibility for these functions on particular projects. For smaller projects, the project manager or an assistant might assume these and other responsibilities. In either case, insuring safe and quality construction is a concern of the project manager in overall charge of the project in addition to the concerns of personnel, cost, time and other management issues.

Inspectors and quality assurance personnel will be involved in a project to represent a variety of different organizations. Each of the parties directly concerned with the project may have their own quality and safety inspectors, including the owner, the engineer/architect, and the various constructor firms. These inspectors may be contractors from specialized quality assurance organizations. In addition to **on-site inspections**, samples of materials will commonly be tested by specialized laboratories to insure compliance. Inspectors to insure compliance with regulatory requirements will also be involved. Common examples are inspectors for the local government's building department, for environmental agencies, and for **occupational health and safety agencies**.

The **US Occupational Safety and Health Administration (OSHA)** routinely conduct site visits of work places in conjunction with approved state inspection agencies. OSHA inspectors are required by law to issue citations for all standard violations observed. Safety standards prescribe a variety of mechanical safeguards and procedures; for example, ladder safety is covered by over 140 regulations. In cases of extreme non-compliance with standards, OSHA inspectors can stop work on a project. However, only a small fraction of construction sites are visited by OSHA inspectors and most construction site accidents are not caused by **violations of existing standards**. As a result, safety is largely the responsibility of the managers on site rather than that of public inspectors.

While the multitude of participants involved in the construction process require the services of inspectors, it cannot be emphasized too strongly that inspectors are only a formal check on quality control. Quality control should be a primary objective for all the members of a project team. Managers should take responsibility for maintaining and improving quality control. Employee participation in quality control should be sought and rewarded, including the introduction of new ideas. Most important of all, quality improvement can serve as a **catalyst** for improved productivity. By suggesting new work methods, by avoiding rework, and by avoiding long term problems, good quality control can pay for itself. Owners should promote good quality control and seek out contractors who maintain such standards.

In addition to the various organizational bodies involved in quality control, issues of quality control arise in virtually all the functional areas of construction activities. For example, insuring accurate and useful information is an important part of maintaining quality performance. Other aspects of quality control include document control (including changes during the construction process), procurement, field inspection and testing, and final checkout of the facility. [3]

Work and Material Specifications

Specifications of work quality are an important feature of facility designs. Specifications of required quality and components represent part of the necessary documentation to describe a facility. Typically, this documentation includes any special provisions of the facility design as well as references to generally accepted specifications to be used during construction. [4]

General specifications of work quality are available in numerous fields and are issued in publications of organizations such as the American Society for Testing and Materials (ASTM), the American National Standards Institute (ANSI), or the Construction Specifications Institute (CSI). Distinct specifications are formalized for particular types of construction activities, such as welding standards issued by the American Welding Society, or for particular facility types, such as the Standard Specifications for Highway Bridges issued by the American Association of State Highway and Transportation Officials. These general specifications must be modified to reflect local conditions, policies, available materials, local regulations and other special circumstances.

Construction specifications normally consist of a series of instructions or prohibitions for specific operations. For example, the following passage illustrates a typical specification, in this case for excavation for structures:

Conform to elevations and dimensions shown on plan within a **tolerance** of plus or minus 0.10 foot, and extending a sufficient distance from footings and foundations to permit placing and removal of concrete formwork, installation of services, other construction, and for inspection. [5] In excavating for footings and foundations, take care not to disturb bottom of excavation. Excavate by hand to final grade just before concrete reinforcement is placed. Trim bottoms to required lines and grades to leave solid base to receive concrete.

This set of specifications requires judgment in application since some items are not precisely specified. For example, excavation must extend a "sufficient" distance to permit inspection and other activities. Obviously, the term "sufficient" in this case may be subject to varying interpretations. In contrast, a specification that tolerances are within plus or minus a tenth of a foot is subject to direct measurement. However, specific requirements of the facility or characteristics of the site may make the standard tolerance of a tenth of a foot inappropriate. Writing specifications typically requires a trade-off between assuming reasonable behavior on the part of all the parties concerned in interpreting words such as "sufficient" versus the effort and possible inaccuracy in pre-specifying all operations.

In recent years, performance specifications have been developed for many construction operations. Rather than specifying the required construction process, these specifications refer to the required performance or quality of the finished facility. The exact method by which this performance is obtained is left to the construction contractor. For example, traditional specifications for **asphalt** pavement specified the composition of the asphalt material, the asphalt temperature during paving, and compacting procedures. In contrast, a performance specification for asphalt would detail the desired performance of the pavement with respect to impermeability, strength, etc. How the desired performance level was attained would be up to the paving contractor. In some cases, the payment for asphalt paving might increase with better quality of asphalt beyond some minimum level of performance.

Example 9-1: Concrete Pavement Strength

Concrete pavements of superior strength result in cost savings by delaying the time at which repairs or reconstruction is required. In contrast, concrete of lower quality will necessitate more frequent overlays or other repair procedures. Contract provisions with adjustments to the amount of a contractor's compensation based on pavement quality have become increasingly common in recognition of the cost savings associated with higher quality construction. Even if a pavement does not meet the "ultimate" design standard, it is still worth using the lower quality pavement and resurfacing later rather than completely rejecting the pavement. Based on these life cycle cost considerations, a typical pay schedule might be Table 9-1.

Table 9-1 A Typical Pay Schedule

Load Ratio	Pay Factor	Load Ratio	Pay Factor
<0.50	Reject	1.10~1.29	1.05
0.50~0.69	0.90	1.30~1.49	1.10
0.70~0.89	0.95	>1.50	1.12
0.90~1.09	1.00		

In this table, the Load Ratio is the ratio of the actual pavement strength to the desired design strength and the Pay Factor is a fraction by which the total pavement contract amount is multiplied to obtain the appropriate compensation to the contractor. For example, if a contractor achieves concrete strength twenty percent greater than the design specification, then the load ratio is 1.20 and the appropriate pay factor is 1.05, so the contractor receives a five percent bonus. Load factors are computed after tests on the concrete actually used in a pavement. Note that a 90% pay factor exists in this case with even pavement quality only 50% of that originally desired. This high pay factor even with weak concrete strength might exist since much of the costs of pavements are incurred in preparing the pavement foundation. Concrete strengths of less then 50% are cause for complete rejection in this case, however.

New Words and Phrases

defect　缺点，缺陷；不足之处
impair　损害；削弱；减少
specification　规格；规范
conformance　符合
unforeseen　不可预见的，意料之外的
attendant　伴随的
vigilance　警觉，警惕
occupational　职业的
catalyst　推进剂
tolerance　公差，容差
asphalt　沥青
personal injury　人身伤害
reevaluation of design decision　设计决策的重新评估
tunneling method　隧道开掘方法
actual site condition　现场的实际状况
roadway rehabilitation　公路路面返修
quality assurance　质量保证
on-site inspection　现场监督检查
US Occupational Safety and Health Administration (OSHA)　美国职业安全与健康管理局
violations of existing standard　违反现行标准

Notes

[1] As with cost control, the most important decisions regarding the quality of a completed facility are

made during the design and planning stages rather than during construction.

与成本控制一样，对建成设施的质量来说，最重要的决策是在设计和规划阶段，而不是在施工阶段。

[2] For example, clear separation of traffic from construction zones during roadway rehabilitation can greatly reduce the possibility of accidental collisions. Beyond these design decisions, safety largely depends upon education, vigilance and cooperation during the construction process.

例如，在车行道翻修过程中，将施工区域进行明显的交通隔离可以大大降低意外碰撞的可能性。除了这些设计决策，在施工过程中安全在很大程度上取决于受教育程度、警惕性、合作性。

[3] Other aspects of quality control include document control (including changes during the construction process), procurement, field inspection and testing, and final checkout of the facility.

质量控制的其他方面还包括文档控制（包括施工过程中的变更控制）、采购管理、现场的监督与监测和设施的最终检查验收等内容。

[4] Specifications of work quality are an important feature of facility designs. Specifications of required quality and components represent part of the necessary documentation to describe a facility. Typically, this documentation includes any special provisions of the facility design as well as references to generally accepted specifications to be used during construction.

工作质量标准是建筑设施设计的重要内容。描述建筑设施所需文档的代表性部分是建筑设施需要区别的质量标准及其组成。这个文档通常不仅包括建筑设施设计的所有特别条款，还涉及在施工过程中采用的通用规范。

[5] Conform to elevations and dimensions shown on plan within a tolerance of plus or minus 0.10 foot, and extending a sufficient distance from footings and foundations to permit placing and removal of concrete formwork, installation of services, other construction, and for inspection.

按照平面图上的标高和尺寸施工，允许±0.10英寸的偏差，从基础边沿外放足够的距离以满足混凝土浇筑、构件安装、其他施工活动及施工检查等的需要。

Exercises

I. Translate the following phrases into English.

1. 质量控制和安全问题
2. 保险，检验和监管的间接成本
3. 检查人员和质量保证人员
4. 一系列指示或禁止特定的操作
5. 质量控制的各种组织机构

II. Translate the following sentences into Chinese.

1. In the worst case, failures may cause personal injuries or fatalities. Accidents during the construction process can similarly result in personal injuries and large costs.

2. Quality control during construction consists largely of insuring conformance to these original designs and planning decisions.

3. In large organizations, departments dedicated to quality assurance and to safety might assign specific individuals to assume responsibility for these functions on particular projects.

4. Each of the parties directly concerned with the project may have their own quality and safety inspectors, including the owner, the engineer/architect, and the various constructor firms.

Quality Control by Statistical Methods

An ideal quality control program might test all materials and work on a particular facility. For example, nondestructive techniques such as X-ray inspection of welds can be used throughout a facility. An on-site inspector can witness the appropriateness and adequacy of construction methods at all times. Even better, individual craftsmen can perform continuing inspection of materials and their own work. Exhaustive or 100% testing of all materials and work by inspectors can be exceedingly expensive, however. In many instances, testing requires the destruction of a material sample, so exhaustive testing is not even possible. As a result, small samples are used to establish the basis of accepting or rejecting a particular work item or shipment of materials. Statistical methods are used to interpret the results of test on a small sample to reach a conclusion concerning the acceptability of an entire lot or batch of materials or work products.

The use of statistics is essential in interpreting the results of testing on a small sample. Without adequate interpretation, small sample testing results can be quite misleading. As an example, suppose that there are ten **defective** pieces of material in a lot of one hundred. In taking a sample of five pieces, the inspector might not find any defective pieces or might have all sample pieces defective. Drawing a direct inference that none or all pieces in the population are defective on the basis of these samples would be incorrect. Due to this random nature of the sample selection process, testing results can vary substantially. It is only with statistical methods that issues such as the chance of different levels of defective items in the full lot can be fully analyzed from a small sample test.

There are two types of statistical sampling which are commonly used for the purpose of quality control in batches of work or materials:

1. The acceptance or rejection of a lot is based on the number of defective (bad) or nondefective (good) items in the sample. This is referred to as **sampling by attributes**.

2. Instead of using defective and nondefective classifications for an item, a quantitative quality measure or the value of a measured variable is used as a quality indicator. This testing procedure is referred to as **sampling by variables**.

Whatever sampling plan is used in testing, it is always assumed that the samples are representative of the entire population under consideration. Samples are expected to be chosen randomly so that each member of the population is equally likely to be chosen. Convenient sampling plans such as sampling every twentieth piece, choosing a sample every two hours, or picking the top piece on a delivery truck may be adequate to insure a random sample if pieces are randomly mixed in a stack or in use. However, some convenient sampling plans can be inappropriate. For example, checking only easily accessible joints in a building component is inappropriate since joints that are hard to reach may be more likely to have erection or fabrication problems.

Another assumption implicit in statistical quality control procedures is that the quality of materials or work is expected to vary from one piece to another. This is certainly true in the field of construction. While a designer may assume that all concrete is exactly the same in a building, the variations in material properties, manufacturing, handling, pouring, and temperature during setting insure that concrete is actually heterogeneous in quality. Reducing such variations to a minimum is one aspect of quality construction. Insuring that the materials actually placed achieve some minimum quality level with respect to average properties or fraction of defectives is the task of quality control.

New Words and Phrases

defective 有缺陷的
an ideal quality control program 理想化质量控制程序
sampling by attribute 特征抽样
sampling by variable 变量抽样

Quality Control And Quality Assurance

Quality control assures the reliability of performance of the designed system in accordance with assumed and expected reserve strengths in the design. To exercise "quality control" and achieve "quality assurance" **encompasses** monitoring the roles and producer, the laboratory tester, the constructor, and the user.

The reliability of performance of personnel involved in the various stages of creating a concrete structural system from conception through design, construction, and use depends on knowledge, training, and communication at all levels. A smooth flow of correct information among all participants and a shared systematic understanding of the developing problems lead to increased motivation toward improved solutions, hence improved quality control and a resulting high level of quality assurance. In summary, a **quality assurance system** needs to be provided based on the exercise of quality control at the various phases and interacting parameters of a total system.

Construction of a designed system is governed basically by five primary tasks: planning, design, materials selection, construction, and use (including maintenance). The process stars with the user, since the principal aim of a project is to satisfy the user's needs, and it **culminates** with the user as the primary beneficiary of the final product.

The User

Quality assurance is necessary to satisfy the user's needs and rights. It ensures that the activities influencing the final quality of a concrete structure are:

1. Based on clearly defined fundamental requirements that satisfy the operational, environmental, and boundary conditions set for the project at the outset.

2. Properly presented in accurate, well-dimensioned engineering working drawings based on optimal design procedures.

3. Correctly and efficiently carried out by competent personnel **in accordance with** predetermined plans and working drawing well supervised during the design stage.

4. Systematically executed in accordance with detailed specifications that conform to the applicable codes and local regulations.

Planning

In order to plan the successful execution of a proposed constructed system, all main and sub activities have to be clearly defined. This is accomplished through dividing the total project into a network plan of separately defined activities, relating each activity with time, analyzing the input control and the resulting output control, and expressing these conditions in the form of a checklist. In such a manner, the successful decision-making process concerning performance requirements becomes easier to accomplish. Such a process usually entails decisions on what function needs to be accomplished in a construction project, where and when that function will be executed, how the system will be constructed, and who the user will be. Correct determination of these factors leads to a decision as to the level of quality control needed and the degree of quality assurance that is expected to result.

Design

Quality control in design aims at verifying that the designed system has the safety, serviceability, and durability required for the use to which the system is intended as required by the applicable codes, and that such a design is correctly presented in the working drawing and the accompanying specifications. The degree of quality control depends on the type of system to be constructed; the more important the system, the more control that is required. As a minimum, a design must always be checked by an engineer other than the originating design engineer.

Since engineering working drawing are the primary link between the design process and the construction process, they should be a major object of design quality assurance. Consequently, the student has to be well acquainted with reading and interpreting working drawing and must be able to produce clear sketches that accurately express the design details if the constructed system is to reflect the actual design.

Materials Selection

It has to be emphasized at the outset that the quality of materials such as reinforced concrete is not determined only by **compressive or tensile strength** tests. Many other factors affect the quality of the finished product such as **water/cement ratio**, **cement content**, creep and shrinkage characteristics, freeze and thaw properties, and other durability aspects and conditions.

Construction

Construction is the execution stage of a project, which can be used to satisfy all design and specification requirements within prescribed time limits at minimum cost. To achieve the desired quality assurance, the construction phase has to be preceded by an **elaborate** and correct preparation stage, which can be part of the design phase. The preparation or planning phase is very critical since it gives an overall clear view of the various activities involved and the possible problems that could arise at the various phases of execution.

The human factor is of major significance at the construction phase. In most instances, the major site activities involve lab force use and scheduling of its utilization. An improved information flow system, clear **delineation** of the chain of command, and reward for superior performance increase motivation and lead to overall improvement in the entire quality assurance system and an optimization of the **efficiency/cost ratio** of a project.

New Words and Phrases

encompass　包含；包围；环绕；完成
culminate　使结束；使达到高潮；使达到顶点
elaborate　详尽的；精心制作的
delineation　勾画轮廓；描述，叙述；刻画，描写
quality assurance system　质量保证体系
in accordance with　与……一致
compressive or tensile strength　抗压或抗拉强度
water/cement ratio　水灰比
cement content　水泥含量
efficiency/cost ratio　效益成本比

Part II Speaking

Dialogue 1

A: We'd like to have a look at your **temporary site facilities**.
B: All right, I'll show you around. Let's first go to the **production area**.
A: Thank you.
B: Here we are. This is our **precast yard** for **the reinforcement concrete pile**. These two **gantry cranes** are set for handling of the piles.
A: What is the capacity of these cranes?
B: Each gantry crane in the production line can lift 10t. Here is the rebar yard. The **bending machine** and **cutting machine** can process the rebar with a diameter of 40 mm.
A: I think you should have a shed for the yard. In such a hot area, if works can work under a shed, it will certainly increase their efficiency.
B: That's a good suggestion. We'll make a shed as a roof for the rebar yard.

Dialogue 2

A: According to the **earthwork bid package** by the local architect, the bidders are required to **strip the top soil** up to 18 inches.
B: But in my observations, 6 inches is sufficient. My second visit to the job site yesterday gave me more reasons for my opinion.

A: If so, the bidder will have to **reappraise** their position.
B: Yes, they have to reduce their **quotations**.
A: In that way, the original estimate **contract price** for this item may decreased by 10%.
B: Let's obtain more details before we present it to the local architect and the owner.

New Words and Phrases

reappraise 重新估计
quotation 报价
site inspection 现场检查
temporary site facility 临时场地设施
production area 生产区
precast yard 钢筋混凝土预制场
reinforcement concrete pile 钢筋混凝土桩
gantry crane 门式起重机
bending machine 弯筋机
cutting machine 切断机
bid package 投标文件包
strip the top soil 除去表层土
contract price 合同价

Unit 10 Model Interoperability in Building Information

Part I Reading and Translating

Professional Knowledge Guidance

1. **工程项目的信息**：是在项目决策过程、实施过程（设计准备、设计、施工和物资采购过程等）和运行过程中产生的信息，以及其他与项目建设有关的信息，包括项目的组织类信息、管理类信息、经济类信息、技术类信息和法规类信息。

2. **BIM（Building Information Modeling）技术**：是在CAD之后发展起来的一种信息模型集成技术，它可以通过数字信息仿真模拟出建筑物真实存在时所具有的真实信息。BIM技术以三维数字技术为基础，通过一个共同的标准，目前主要是IFC（Industry Foundation Class），集成了建设工程项目各种相关信息的工程数据模型。BIM技术可以呈现出建筑全寿命周期的模型，当我们需要建筑内材料时，利用BIM技术提取起来比较方便。相对传统信息传递方法来说，BIM技术主要有可视化、协调性、模拟性及可出图性等特点。

Engineering Innovation—Building Information Modeling

Introduction

Building Information Modeling (BIM) —an innovative new approach to building design, construction, and management introduced by Autodesk in 2002—has changed the way industry professionals worldwide think about how technology can be applied to building design, construction, and management.[1] Building information modeling supports the continuous and immediate availability of project design scope, schedule,

and cost information that is high quality, reliable, integrated, and fully coordinated. Among the many competitive advantages it confers are:
- Increased speed of delivery (time saved).
- Better coordination (fewer errors).
- Decreased costs (money saved).
- Greater productivity.
- Higher-quality work.
- New revenue and business opportunities.

For each of the three major phases in the building lifecycle—design, construction, and management-building information modeling offers access to the following critical information:
- In the design phase—design, schedule, and budget information.
- In the construction phase—quality, schedule, safety and cost information.
- In the management phase—performance, utilization, and financial information.

The ability to keep this information up to date and accessible in an integrated digital environment gives architects, engineers, contractors, and employers a clear overall vision of their projects, as well as the ability to make better decisions faster—raising the quality and increasing the **profitability** of projects.

Although building information modeling is an approach and not a technology, it does require suitable technology to be implemented effectively. Examples of some of these technologies, in increasing order of effectiveness, include: CAD, Object CAD, and **Parametric Building Modeling**.

The concept of building information modeling is to build a building virtually, prior to building it physically, in order to work out problems, and simulate and analyze **potential impacts**. The heart of building information modeling is an authoritative building information model.

Building Information Modeling Benefits

Building Information Modeling (BIM) is used to refer to two different things: the process of building information modeling and the resulting model (the building information model). BIM is the development and use of a computer software model to simulate the construction and operation of a facility. The resulting model, a Building Information Modeling, is a data-rich, object-oriented intelligent and parametric digital representation of the facility, from which views and data appropriate to various users' needs can be extracted and analyzed to generate information, which can be used to make decisions and improve the process of delivering the facility.[2] Building information modeling is an approach to building design, construction, and management. Building information modeling is, essentially, the **intersection** of two critical ideas:

- Keeping critical design information in digital form makes it easier to update and share and more valuable to the firms creating and using it.

- Creating real-time, consistent relationships between digital design data-with innovative parametric building modeling technology—can save significant amounts of time and money and increase project productivity and quality.

BIM uses include visualization; scope clarification; partial trade's coordination; collision detection/avoidance; design validation; construction sequencing planning/phasing; plans/logistics; marketing presentations; options analysis, walk-throughs and fly-throughs; virtual mock-ups; and sight-line studies.

Unit 10 Model Interoperability in Building Information

BIM can help construction professionals create such a model for different interests, including architects, engineers, contractors, subcontractors, fabricators, suppliers and others offering myriad virtual details in the design, construction, and management phases of the building lifecycle, and sort out and work with the problems before hand. [3] For example, imagine walking into a building, walking through the lobby, removing the ceiling tiles and looking at the utilities in the ceiling space—before the building is even bit however, you will foresee what you need to tackle in advance.

BIM 4D Models

BIM 4D Models link components in 3D models with activities from the design, procurement, and construction schedules. The resulting 4D production model of a project allows project **stakeholders** to view the planned construction of a facility over time on the screen and to review a 3D model for any day, week, or month of the project.

4D models enable a diverse team of project participants to understand and comment on the project scope in a proactive and timely manner. They enable the exploration and improvement of the project executing strategy, improvements in **constructability** with corresponding gains in on-site productivity, and the rapid identification and resolution of time-space conflicts. 4D models have proven particularly helpful in projects that involve many stakeholders, in projects undergoing renovation during operation, and in projects with tight, urban site conditions. Tight site conditions, a must-met completion deadline, and many non-construction stakeholders have made the project idea for the application of 4D project management. The 4D model enabled the project team to produce a better set of specifications and design drawings for the construction of the project, resulting in fewer unplanned change orders, a smaller construction team, and a comfortable completion of the project ahead of schedule. [4]

BIM in Design

BIM is a very powerful architectural design and coordination tool for project-wide design and documentation. The project design team members typically rely on a number of purpose-built models including:
- 3D conceptual design model.
- Detailed geometric design model.
- Structural finite element analysis model.
- Structural steel fabrication model.
- Design coordination model.
- Construction planning and sequencing model.
- Equipment inventory model.
- Energy analysis model.
- Fire/life safety and **egress** model.
- Cost analysis model.

It is very rare that a single technology is being used on any one building project between different companies and/or across all phases of the project lifecycle. BIM has had a tremendous, positive impact on design, visualizing and communicating the **essence** of a complex facility to a broad audience. It helps designer solve a number of problems involving challenging geometry on plans, elevations and section drawings, and it can generate as "views" from a single design model, are always consistent. Structural engineers can have great success in sharing their concrete and steel 3D object models with architect to integrate into architectural model and data sharing.

BIM in Construction

In the construction phase of the building lifecycle, Building Information Modeling makes available concurrent in formation on building quality, safety, schedule, and cost. The contractor can accelerate the quantification of the building or estimating and value-engineering purposes and for the production of updated estimates and construction planning. The consequences of proposed or procured products can be studied and understood easily, and the contractor can quickly prepare plans showing site use or renovation phasing for the employer, thereby communicating and minimizing the impact of construction operations on the employer's operations and personnel. Building Information Modeling also means that less time and money are spent on process and administration issues in construction because document quality is higher and constriction planning better. The final result is that more of the employer's construction investment goes into the building than into administrative and overhead costs.

Cost Estimating

Both the main contractor and the subcontractor will benefit greatly from accurate take-off quantifies and a good construction-sequencing view to determine how crowded the site will be when they arrive. Such as an accurately detailed BIM 3D model will give wall and ceiling subcontractor not only the location and interrelation of each wall-and-ceiling item, but also the materials of what exactly comprises each component for an accurate take-off quantity, through visualizing the project contractors make sure all the constructing pieces are included.

Armed with this information, the experienced estimator will, and does work up an accurate quote without having to look around corners and imagining the architect as to what he or she really intended. Given this a clear view of the construction sequencing, the BIM 3D model will then afford the estimator a firm basis for a good bid.

Construction Quality and Safety

Public organizations and private companies in several countries have successfully led many BIM-based projects with considerable interest and effort. In fact, several public organizations have recommended delivering BIM data, which is checked with quality control according to BIM standards. The high quality control of BIM can be applied to both physical and logical conditions. From designing, a preliminary review of the quality of the functional, **aesthetic**, engineering and environmental aspects of the facilities can be carried out by using software tools prior to the final evaluation. Since the BIM quality check is based on BIM guidelines and standards, a quantitative review is possible, and in most cases, automatic verification can be done through the software itself. Such a system can help in the prevention of the initial selection of poor designs.

Construction safety professionals can use BIM to improve construction safety. Once a 3D model is created, it can be used for many purposes, including worker safety training and education, safety planning and employee involvement. Safety professionals need not be experts in model creation or its technical aspects; they simply need a basic understanding of BIM, which is essentially a 3D computer-aided design drawing. Craft men will be able to identify the sequence of activities, and material and tool requirements before work started. Pre-task planning offers the most opportunities to use BIM for construction safety. By virtually looking at the elements to be built, employees were able to better identify the hazards and control measures so the task could be completed faster and more safely. Such as duct works, which involve in identifying access as a significant concern and are able to bring in **aerial lifts**. The crew will identify falls as a hazard and devise control measures (e. g. fall protection devices). The piping will be installed in a tunnel and required much welding.

BIM in the Management

In the management phase of the building lifecycle, Building Information Modeling makes available concurrent information on the use or performance of the building, its occupants and contents, the life of the building over time, and the financial aspects of the building. Building Information Modeling provides a digital record of renovations and improves move planning and management. It accelerates the adaptation of standard building **prototypes** to site conditions for businesses, such as retail, that require the construction of similar buildings in many different locations. Physical information about the building, such as finishes, tenant or department assignments, furniture and equipment inventory, and financially important data about leasable areas and rental income or departmental cost allocations are all more easily managed and available. Consistent access to these types of information improves both revenue and cost management in the operation of the building.

In general, BIM is growingly changing the way employers, designers, engineers, contractors, subcontractors and fabricators approach building design, construction and operation[5].

Constructability Review

As projects get more and more complex, the issue of constructability becomes important. Constructability **infiltrates** all parts of a project, especially those related to the engineering and architectural professions. With projects becoming more and more complex and time frames shorter and shorter, implied warranty and severe professional liability issues may arise.

Constructability is a project management technique for reviewing construction processes from start to finish during the pre-construction phrase. It will identify obstacles before a project is actually built to reduce or prevent error, delays and cost overruns. It is referred to as:

- The extent to which the design of the building facilitates ease of construction, subject to the overall requirements for the completed building.
- A system for achieving optimum integration of construction knowledge and experience in planning, engineering, procurement and field operations in the building process, and balancing the various project and environmental constraints to achieve overall objectives.

- A system for achieving optimum integration of construction knowledge in the building process and balancing the various project and environmental constraints to maximize achievement of project goals and minimize building performance barriers to improvingconstructability.

Constructability issues not only involve issues of buildability, but also the sequence of construction and integration of systems in a logical sequence using standard substructures.

Building design has a significant impact on construction productivity and quality. Design professionals need to be aware of the potential issues and claims implied by a design's constructability or buildability profile. When a project has inherent constructability issues, resulting **litigation** can involve delay claims, change order issues and disputes, and owner's dissatisfaction with delivery.

In extreme situations, direct claims may be made against the design principal for poor plans, specifications or estimates, or schedules that have made the project difficult to build, or more costly or time consuming than anticipated.

Ligation usually involves the claims which clearly include issues relating to constructability. The constructability claims arise because almost all of these factors relate to inadequate communication, lack of coordination, and inexperienced project teams.

Constructability Review Objectives

The main objective of a constructability review should be to minimise or eliminate potential change orders and schedule delays during construction by ensuring that the construction documents are fully coordinated, complete and buildable. A constructability review should also seek to eliminate redundancy in quality control reviews performed by different entities involved in the project, such as architects, peer reviewers and permitting agencies. The review objectives are as follow:

- Enhance early planning.
- Minimize scope changes.
- Reduce design-related change orders.
- Improve contractors productivity.
- Develop construction-friendly specifications.
- Enhance quality.
- Reduce delays/Meet schedules.
- Improve public image.
- Promote construction safety.
- Reduce conflicts/disputes.
- Decrease construction/maintenance costs.

New Words and Phrases

profitability　盈利能力；收益率，利润率
intersection　交叉；交叉点；十字路口
stakeholder　利益共享者；赌金保管人
constructability　施工能力；可施工性
egress　外出，出去；出口，出路

Unit 10 Model Interoperability in Building Information

essence　本质，实质；本体，实体
aesthetic　美学的；美感的；审美的
prototype　原型；样板；样品
infiltrate　（使）渗入；（使）潜入
litigation　诉讼，打官司；诉讼案件
parametric building modeling　参数化建筑模型
aerial lift　升降机

Notes

[1] Building Information Modeling (BIM) —an innovative new approach to building design, construction, and management introduced by Autodesk in 2002—has changed the way industry professionals worldwide think about how technology can be applied to building design, construction, and management.

建筑信息模型——2002年由Autodesk引入的建筑设计、施工和管理的一种创新型方法——已经改变了全球业内专家看待技术如何应用于建筑设计、施工和管理的方式。

[2] The resulting model, a Building Information Modeling, is a data-rich, object-oriented intelligent and parametric digital representation of the facility, from which views and data appropriate to various users' needs can be extracted and analyzed to generate information, which can be used to make decisions and improve the process of delivering the facility.

作为建模结果的模型，建筑信息模型是一个数据丰富的、面向对象的智能化的和参数化的设施数字表示，可以根据不同用户所需的视图和数据从该数字表示提取、分析并生成信息，该信息可以用于决策和改善项目设施交付的流程。

[3] BIM can help construction professionals create such a model for different interests, including architects, engineers, contractors, subcontractors, fabricators, suppliers and others offering myriad virtual details in the design, construction, and management phases of the building lifecycle, and sort out and work with the problems before hand.

BIM可以帮助建筑专业人士为了不同的兴趣而创建这样一个模型，这些专业人士包括在建筑生命周期的设计、施工和管理阶段提供无数虚拟详细资料的建筑师、工程师、承包商、分包商、装配商、供应商及其他人员，并且预先分类和解决问题。

[4] The 4D model enabled the project team to produce a better set of specifications and design drawings for the construction of the project, resulting in fewer unplanned change orders, a smaller construction team, and a comfortable completion of the project ahead of schedule.

四维模型能够使项目团队为项目的施工提供一套更好的施工设计和设计图，从而以更少的非计划变更指令、更小的施工队伍，愉快地提前完成项目。

[5] In general, BIM is growingly changing the way employers, designers, engineers, contractors, subcontractors and fabricators approach building design, construction and operation.

总体来说，BIM正逐渐改变着雇主、设计师、工程师、承包商、分包商和装配商处理建筑设计、施工及运营的方式。

Exercises

I. Translate the following phrases into English.

1. 建筑信息模型

2. 三维概念设计模式
3. 可视化
4. 参数化建筑模型

II. Translate the following sentences into Chinese.

1. The ability to keep this information up to date and accessible in an integrated digital environment gives architects, engineers, contractors, and employers a clear overall vision of their projects, as well as the ability to make better decisions faster—raising the quality and increasing the profitability of projects.

2. The consequences of proposed or procured products can be studied and understood easily, and the contractor can quickly prepare plans showing site use or renovation phasing for the employer, thereby communicating and minimizing the impact of construction operations on the employer's operations and personnel.

3. Such as an accurately detailed BIM 3D model will give wall and ceiling subcontractor not only the location and interrelation of each wall-and-ceiling item, but also the materials of what exactly comprises each component for an accurate take-off quantity, through visualizing the project contractors make sure all the constructing pieces are included.

4. In the management phase of the building lifecycle, Building Information Modeling makes available concurrent information on the use or performance of the building, its occupants and contents, the life of the building over time, and the financial aspects of the building.

5. The main objective of a constructability review should be to minimise or eliminate potential change orders and schedule delays during construction by ensuring that the construction documents are fully coordinated, complete and buildable.

Introduction about BIM

The design and construction industry is undertaking a significant shift away from the use of **two-dimensional CAD** and paper for design towards three-dimensional, **semantically** rich, digital models. This trend has reached a point where this technology, generally referred to as Building Information Modeling (BIM), is being used in some form by the majority of the industry. A recent survey by McGraw Hill Construction found that in 2008, 45% of architects, engineers, contractors and building owners surveyed used BIM on 30% or more of their projects. Usage of BIM is forecast to continue growing in coming years.

One of the challenges faced by the industry is the use of BIM not only as a tool in the design process, but as the interface for the exchange of information between the different parties involved in projects. A typical construction project will necessitate collaboration and information exchange between a variety of parties, including the client, architects, engineers, estimators and quantity surveyors, contractors and regulators. Traditionally, information was exchanged in the form of drawings and documents. As each of these parties' moves towards the use of BIM tools within their own organization, there is a significant **incentive** to instead use digital design models as the medium for exchanging information. However, these parties frequently use different tools, either from different vendors or specific to their business domain and this diversity of tools poses a challenge for model exchange.

Unit 10 Model Interoperability in Building Information

The **Industry Foundation Classes** (IFC), defined by the building SMART alliance, represents the accepted industry standard for design models. IFC models are semantically rich in that they capture not only the **3-dimensional geometry** of the objects, but **meta data** related to many other aspects of the building. For example, if we consider an instance of a door object, this door will be situated in a wall, on a defined building storey, within the building. It will have attributes associated with it that describe its thermal performance, costing, **fire safety performance**, etc. Which building components need to be accessed to resolve an issue can be determined by tracing system descriptions within the model, for example, the thermal zones system, cost breakdown structure and the fire safety system. The necessary attribute definitions and the system descriptions are derived from **legislative** requirements and analysis software input requirements.

Many of the significant BIM tools currently used by industry support import and export of IFC files. We have used IFC as an **interoperable** format over a number of years, both as a mechanism for exchanging models between tools, and as an input format for software tools that we have built for design analysis and automation. This paper presents our observations of the successes and challenges of IFC as an interoperable standard for building models.

Building Information Modeling is an interdependent network of policies, processes and technologies, which together constitute a "methodology to manage the essential building design and project date in digital format throughout the building's life cycle". BIM tools are being increasingly incorporated into collaborative design and modeling processes, with the promise of **substantive** benefits for the efficiency of the design process.

The construction of a building or group of buildings is a complex endeavor, involving many parties and numerous diverse activities. Even small projects are beyond the scope of any single company to complete in isolation, and larger projects will necessitate the interaction of potentially dozens of organizations including clients, architects, engineers, financiers, builders and subcontractors. The processes can be likened to that of co-design in computing, in which the domain knowledge of hardware and software engineers are distinct and successful completion of the project requires intense cooperation during design, manufacture and maintenance/management of the system.

The information models that are used are also large, complex, and highly interdependent, and includes architectural components, engineering system for structural, electrical, HVAC (heating, **ventilation** and air conditioning), and mechanical services, as well as details of cross cutting concerns such as project management, scheduling and cost planning/estimation.

Traditionally, the dominant medium for exchanging information between parties has been as drawings and other paper documents (e. g. **bill of quantities**, cost plan, **building specification**), and this remains the case for many projects today. Although many organizations use some software tools for the definition of their design models, the models are frequently rendered as 2D drawings when they are sent to other organizations.

The information exchanged serves not only to inform the receiving party, but also as a record of what information was or was not conveyed, so that, in the event of a dispute problem, responsibility for a decision may be clearly determined. Companies are comfortable with the use of paper drawings for this purpose, and are still reluctant to sign off on digital information represented in three dimensions, often with additional information compared to the paper equivalent. For example, architects often associate material types with building objects in order to make the building look right for a client presentation, and not necessarily because that is the material to be used in construction. When the model is then given to the engineer or quantity surveyor, it might be unclear whether the material has been selected **intentionally**, or simply for visual effect. Which parts of the model are definitive, and which are illustrative? This is important from a legal perspective.

Understanding of liability implications is also an important reason why the current use of digital models mainly involves exchange of models as files, as opposed to inspection of and linking to models using service-oriented or distributed object technologies.

Despite these concerns, the use of BIM has reached tipping point in the industry. Use of 3-dimensional CAD tools is commonplace amongst architects, and is also seeing significant uptake in other sectors such as amongst engineers, owners and contractors. In addition to being used in the design process, BIM is also beginning to be used for design analysis, including quantity surveying and cost planning, environmental assessment, **acoustic** and **thermal performance** assessment scheduling and simulation, and checking designs against codes and regulations. As tools for these activities gain popularity, it is going to become more crucial that software packages manipulating the models are able to inter-operate reliably and without necessitating significant human intervention.

New Words and Phrases

semantically   语义地；字义上
incentive   刺激；动机；刺激物
legislative   立法的；有立法权的；有法律规定的
interoperable   可由双方（或多方）共同操作的；能共同使用的
substantive   实质性的；真实的；独立的
ventilation   通风；空气流通；通风设备；通风系统
intentionally   故意的；与目的（或意图）有关的
acoustic   声学的；听觉的；声波的
two-dimensional CAD   二维计算机辅助设计
Industry foundation classes   工业基础类
3-dimensionalgeometry   三维几何体
meta data   元数据
fire safety performance   消防安全性能
bill of quantity   工程量清单
building specification   建筑规范
thermal performance   热工性能

BIM: A Primer

The Value and Potential of BIM Technology

BIM is a revolutionary technology and process that has transformed the way buildings are designed,

Unit 10　Model Interoperability in Building Information

analyzed, constructed, and managed. Currently, an **overwhelming** amount of information is available about BIM, such as theories on where BIM can go, the vast **array** of tools available, and how BIM seems to be the answer to all the problems facing a Construction Manager (CM). Although some of this information is useful, often it **inundates** potential users because the information all seems to **meld** together. BIM has become a proven technology. What it can do and the concepts associated with BIM taken out of context, however, can become misleading and **frustrate** users and owners alike to the point of not wanting to use this technology again on future projects. This not only hurts the future growth of BIM technology, but it inhibits users from getting involved and sharing their experiences with others in the BIM community to further refine lessons learned and best practices. Figure 10-1 shows an example of a building constructed using BIM technology.

Fig 10-1　Sunset Drive office building, a LEED Gold building constructed using BIM technology

While there currently are a number of inefficiencies that will continue to be refined, BIM as a technology is no longer in its infancy and has started to produce results for the AEC/O industry all over the world. The new frontier for BIM and for its users is to define a new process that better enables this new technology. This book identifies a new process and a way of thinking about BIM that is different than previous processes based off older technology.

What is BIM

Informed contractors and **sophisticated** owners have begun to look at the current processes and demand higher interoperability among teams and among software packages, better tools, fewer change orders, and fewer questions in the field. The question then becomes, how? How can building professionals begin to deliver better projects to their owners even as buildings become more and more complex and dependent on new technologies in an ever changing and moving world? One of the loudest answers has been BIM.

BIM is not just software. BIM is a process and software. Many believe that once they have purchased a license for a particular piece of BIM software, they can sit someone in front of the computer and they are now "doing BIM." What many don't realize, though, is that Building Information Modeling means not only using three-dimensional modeling software but also implementing a new way of thinking. It is in essence a new way of not doing the same old thing. In my experience, as a company integrates this technology, it begins to see other processes start to change. Where a certain process might have made perfect sense for a CAD-type technology, now that doesn't seem to be as efficient. As the technology changes, so do the practices and functions of the people using the technology. In other words, don't expect to begin adapting to this new technology and have everything function as it has in the past. Chances are that very few of your practices will remain the same, because when the information is much richer and more robust, the management of this information must change in order to fully utilize its potential. Although it is clear that many BIM technologies continue to grow and develop, it is even more apparent that the "old way of doing things" has a limited future.

So, what are the advantages of BIM? Let's first look at the owner's perspective. According to interoperability in the construction industry, 49 percent of owners are now demanding BIM be used on their projects. Right behind the owners' demand for BIM, 47 percent of construction industry professionals are choosing to use BIM for its "ability to improve communication with clients/others in the design and construction process." Clearly, BIM is being perceived by owners as a tool that can better coordinate and manage building information. Additionally, construction industry professionals are choosing to use BIM to improve the design and construction process. Although the technology is a key, it is perhaps even more critical to define processes that utilize this technology and how to work better with all members involved.

Clarifications of Information

The process of clarifying information with a CM-at-risk delivery is integrated and project focused. Clarification during preconstruction involves direct interaction and input from the general contractor and even subcontractors. The contractor is able to clarify a number of issues, including budget, estimate breakdown, trade coordination, and construct ability. By providing a GMP for the project, the contractor has a vested interest in providing the design team with as accurate of information as possible. Likewise, the architect and engineers have an obligation to the contractor to provide as much information as possible along the process of design development to further refine the scope, budget, and schedule of the project.

During construction, the contractor is typically very **pliable** and, instead of taking an **adversarial** approach to issues that arise, takes on a mediator role. This is because profitability is directly tied to the contractor's performance and project coordination. While bidding to subcontractors, if required, the contractor and design team have it in their best interest to give the subcontractors as much information as possible about the project to improve the accuracy of the estimate and to reduce any large contingencies. Although many of the issues should be resolved prior to construction because of integration and team involvement, there exists the potential for a general contractor to receive an additional bid for a scope of work if they believe the estimate to be too high. BIM fits well into the CM-at-risk method of delivery. The BIM tools available allow for the ability to test and coordinate prior to construction, thus limiting the need for clarifications. Yet if clarifications are needed, BIM provides the ability to quickly find answers, which is critical in a CM-at-risk project where large amounts of data are being frequently moved.

New Words and Phrases

overwhelm　压倒；淹没；受打击
array　数组，阵列；排列，列阵；大批，一系列；衣服
inundate　淹没，使泛滥，使充满；（似洪水般）充满；压倒

meld　合并；混合；使……合并；使……混合
frustrate　挫败；阻挠；使感到灰心
sophisticated　复杂的；精致的；久经世故的；富有经验的
clarification　澄清，说明；净化
pliable　易弯的，柔韧的；易被说服的，顺从的；能适应的
adversarial　敌手的，对手的；敌对的，对立的；相反的，对抗行动（或程序）的

Part II　Speaking

Subletting the Construction Camp

（Mr. Yang from COCC has made an appointment by telephone with Mr. Howell, President of World Shelters, a local company which specializes in **residential buildings**. They are going to talk about the possibility of subletting the construction camp to World Shelters.）

Receptionist: Good morning, sir. Can I help you?

Yang: Good morning. I **have an appointment with** Mr. Howell at 9.

Receptionist: Your name, sir?

Yang: Yang, from COCC, the Hydro.

Receptionist: Ah, yes. Mr. Howell is expecting you in his office. Let me show you in. This way, please.

Yang: Thank you.

（Entering Mr. Howell's office）

Howell: Hello, Mr. Yang. Very pleased to meet you in person.

Yang: Very pleased to meet you, too, Mr. Howell.

Howell: Take a seat, please.

Yang: Thank you.

Howell: Well, how is everything going, Mr. Yang?

Yang: Not too bad. Just busy. We're quite new here, you know.

Howell: What's your first impression of our country?

Yang: It's a beautiful country with plenty of primeval forests. People here are friendly and very easy to **get along with**. It seems to me that most of the people here speak quite different English. It's hard to understand them sometimes.

Howell: You will soon get used to it. Only officials, teachers and businessmen speak standard English.

Yang: So it seems.

Howell: Let's get down to business, Mr. Yang. You asked me on the phone whether we would like to bid for a construction camp to **accommodate** eighty men. Could you put it in more detail, please?

Yang: As you know, the camp will mainly be for the accommodation of about eighty Chinese men who will be working for the Hydro. It includes double occupancy staff units, four man occupancy units for workers and cooks, a kitchen and dining unit, **shower bath units**, office units, a conference room and a **recreation unit**.

Howell: So the camp will accommodate about eighty men. Do you have any specific requirements?

Yang: I would like to hear your recommendation.
Howell: In my opinion, there's a kind of **prefabricated house** which is most suitable for such a camp. It's easy and economical to transport, fast to erect and very convenient to dismantle for either relocation or disposal when the whole project is completed.
Yang: Sounds fine. What's it made of?
Howell: **Light concrete slabs.** They are often imported from a local supplier in El Salvador.
Yang: Good. Would you please give us a quotation for such a camp **on a turn-key basis** as soon as possible?
Howell: All right. Where will the camp be located?
Yang: Somewhere on Arenal Road in Benque Town, Cayo District. I'll let you know right after we finalize it with the Owner.
Howell: Who will be responsible for **leveling the ground** for the camp site?
Yang: We will do that. You will be responsible for the water and power supply. One more thing, this is a **duty-free** project. So everything imported for it is duty-free. Please take it into consideration in your quotation.
Howell: In that case, our quotation will be much lower.
Yang: We really appreciate that.
Howell: When do you want the camp to be completed?
Yang: Within sixty days, starting from our notice to **commence the work**.
Howell: OK. Mr. Yang. I hope we can be given the opportunity to work for you and if so, we will hold ourselves responsible to you and I believe we will surely do a good job.
Yang: I hope so, too.

New Words and Phrases

sublet　分包
accommodate　容纳，提供（居宿）
residential building　住宅楼
have an appointment with　与……有约
get along with　与……相处
shower bath unit　淋浴室
recreation unit　娱乐室
prefabricated house　活动房屋、预制住宅
light concrete slab　轻混凝土板
on a turn-key basis　以交钥匙方式
level the ground　平整场地
duty free　免税的，免关税的；免税地，免关税地
commence the work　开工

Unit 11 Risk Management of Construction Projects

Part I Reading and Translating

Professional Knowledge Guidance

1. 工程项目风险管理：指工程项目管理主体为减少或消除风险对项目目标的不利影响而对风险进行识别、衡量、控制等一系列管理行为的统称。

2. 工程项目风险的管理主体：包括业主、设计单位、监理单位、承包商、材料供货商、银行等工程项目参与主体。

3. 工程项目风险分类：按成因可分为工期风险，费用风险，质量风险，市场风险，信誉风险，人身伤亡、安全、健康及工程或设备的损坏风险，法律责任等。

4. 工程项目风险管理程序：包括风险识别、风险估计与评价、风险处置策略选择和风险计划制定、风险计划实施和监控。

5. 工程项目风险识别方法：包括专家调查法、初始风险清单法、风险分解法、图形技术法、财务报表法、情景分析法。

Construction Risk Management

Introduction

The management of risks is extremely critical for project success. Risk management has been widely applied in various fields such as economics, insurance, industries, and so on. While the word "risk" means that uncertainty can be expressed through probability, risk management is a structured process for the management of uncertainty through risk assessment. All risks must be evaluated in terms of two distinct elements: the likelihood that the event is going to occur as well as the consequences, or effect, of its occurrence. Risk and opportunity are mirror opposites of each other. Opportunity emerges from favorable project circumstances and risk emerges from unfavorable events.

The inherent uncertainties are generally not only from the unique nature of the construction project, but also from the diversity of resources and activities. Moreover, risks are not always independent and static in construction projects. The effect of two events is not necessarily the sum of their individual effects. For example, one-day delay due to snow storm and the same day delay due to a **design change** are two independent events, but in combination they have the same consequence—no work can be done that day. Accordingly, risks are usually dynamic, that is, their characteristic, probability and impact can change during the project process.

Risk management refers to the art of identifying, analyzing, responding to and controlling project risk factors in a manner which best achieves the objectives of all participants. Additionally, effective risk management typically generates positive results on a project by **improving project performance**, increasing cost effectiveness and creating a good working relationship between **contracting parties**. [1]

Risks in Construction

Construction project success is usually measured by its schedule, budget and quality which conflict is inherent. Broadly, various risks can affect these three basic factors against the success of a project. [2] In general, the project scale and complexity have close relation to the schedule of the project; and at the same time those two aspects have relations with the impact or **severity** of risk, that is, in many circumstances, the larger and more complex the project is, the longer the time is required to complete the project, and more severely it will be affected by project uncertainties and risks. Thus, in large and complex projects, the potential risks in construction projects are many and varied; **budget overruns** and schedule **slippages** have been common and scope changes are inevitable as well. The main risks in construction projects can be classified into physical technical (construction, design), political, financial, **legal-contractual** and environmental risks.

Contractor's Risk in International Market

The contractor faces a multitude of risks in international market. From **tendering stage**, the contractor needs to be able to identify the risks in the contract in order to prepare the tender. Among them are inflation, bad weather, strikes and other labour problems, shortage of materials, unforeseen conditions at the construction site, accidents (whether by fire, flood or carelessness), and innovative design that does not work or proves impossible to construct, and the interaction between liability for defective workmanship and for faults in design, because lack of coordination between design and construction is a common source of dispute. [3] Many of the risks posed by **archaeological finds**, environmental or other citizen opposition are shared by the contractor. **Work stoppage** can affect contractors' allocation of men and materials or preven contractor from bidding other work. Ultimately, the contractor faces the possibility of losing a great deal of money or of **being forced out of the business**.

Risk of Changed Conditions

Historically, unforeseen site conditions have caused many **construction claims** and have driven more than some contractors into default. This important provision, sometimes referred to as a "differing site conditions" clause, is now part of the international standard documents, as well as the ALA and FIDIC documents. Some changed conditions or unforeseen site conditions might affect the cost of work. For example, those unforeseen ground conditions can necessitate the driving of longer piles or the use of more support steel than was first planned foundation work. Both operations might disrupt and delay work, throw schedule out of kilter, and cost significantly more than a contractor could reasonably expected. Although the contractor denotes acceptance of the risk, when he is **signing the contract documents**, however, some contractors are still gamblers at heart and prefer to take the risks, and along with that risk potential for a windfall profit. In the presence of a changed condition, the employer should provide an **equitable** means of paying the contractor for overcoming conditions that neither he nor the employer could have expected from the information available at the time the contract was prepared, but it always is not the case. Changed conditions or unforeseen site conditions are not a rare case in international construction market.

Factors such as these can result in contractors experiencing significant increases in the cost of the works, as well as delay. The key questions for the contractor are accordingly whether the additional costs can be recovered from the employer, and whether an extension of time to completion and relief from delay damages can be obtained.

International Project Risks

International project risks are sometimes overlooked or assessed haphazardly by some contactors; such cases have incurred **colossal financial damages**. For international construction, the purpose of risk management is to mitigate risks by planning for factors that can be **detrimental** to project objectives and deliverables. Although risk management is a relatively known and practiced process, few contractors have conquered its successful implementation. Much of what is practiced is based on intuition, personal judgment. Such risks include war, civil war, terrorism, and **expropriation**, inability to transfer currency **across borders**, and **trade credit defaults** by foreign customers.

Although risks such as **civil unrest** and economic unstability are typically outside the scope of normal business, understanding and dealing with these risks are critical for companies working internationally. Study discovered that only few of companies had in place systematic and consistent methodologies to assess political risks. Working in an **international setting** often requires a much wider view of the project's context than with domestic project.

Risk Management

Risk management requires a systematic and practical method of dealing with both the predictable and unpredictable risks inherent in the construction market. Contractors must acquaint themselves with the risks, and they should manage and **develop specific risk minimization strategies**. Project risk management must be comprised of the feedback used to regulate the risk management performance. Risk management typically involves the following four distinct functions:

Risk Identification

The initial step is to identify of the risks associated with a proposed construction project or contract at the early stages of the project's life. The identification process will form the basis hereby risks, uncertainties, constraints, policies and strategies for the control and allocation of risk are established. The **formulation** of construction risk management is to allocate risk among the employer, the contractor, and the architect.

Risk identification is the process of determining the specific risk factors that can reasonably be expected to affect the project. Risk identification is the essential step for a successful project. **Prior to negotiation**, contractor should assign at least one experienced person to identify contractual and **extra-contractual risks**. Identification of risk factors is fundamental requirement. Risk identification can be done by approaches such as **standard checklists**, **expert interviews**, **Delphi technique**, comparing to other projects and facilitated **brainstorming sessions**.

Impact Analysis

Analysis of probability and consequences—the potential impact of these risk factors, is determined by how likely they are to occur and the effect they would have on the project if they did occur. Since risks influence all aspects of a project, each party should quantify the impact a risk will have on the project cost, schedule, quality and/or profit. Contactor must evaluate risk factors or characteristics of a risk such as the risk event, its probability of occurrence, and the amount of potential loss or gain, and analyze every possible issue or event causing or that may cause harm to the project. [4] So the impact of possible risks can be controlled to the extent where the risks are effectively identified and managed.

Response System

There are some actions which needed to be taken responding to **residual** risk coming in the risk response. Sometimes reevaluation is needed. The uncertainty of a risk event as well as the probability of occurence or potential impact should decrease by selecting the **appropriate risk mitigation strategy** or avoiding of the risk factors. Uncertainty is reduced by using more data and information. Risk mitigation strategies are steps taken to minimize the potential impact of those risk factors deemed sufficiently threatening to the project. Those mitigation strategies are the most common risk management and handling techniques. Four mitigation strategy categories commonly used are:

- Avoidance—when a risk is not accepted and other lower risk choices are available from several alternatives. In case of intolerable risk and no way for mitigation of damages, the project is aborted.
- Retention/Acceptance—when a conscious decision is made to accept the consequences should be the event occur.
- Control/Reduction—when a process of continually monitoring and correcting the condition on the project is used. This process involves the development of a risk reduction plan and then tracking the plan.
- Deflecting/Transferring—deflecting or transferring risks by contract is a common response ranging from total allocation of risk to another party or risk-sharing between two or more parties. [5] Forms of sharing the risk with others include contractual shifting, performance incentives, insurance, **warranties**, **bonds** etc. The risk elements are transferred by contracting out the affected work. Project managers should be educated regarding how risks can be managed by negotiating and drafting carefully considered and project specific contract provisions. Some basic risk management concepts are:
  - Public work—transfer risk to others.
  - Private work—some employers are uninterested, uninformed or naïve.
  - **Reciprocal** contract provisions—minimize exposure to the risks assumed.

- Mitigate risks by requiring and enforcing compliance with insurance provisions.
- Effective risk management requires project management's attention not only during the negotiating/contracting phase but throughout the entire project.

Risk Register

In the past decades or so the use of the risk register as a key control document has gained acceptance with most clients. The risk register lists all the identified risks and the results of their analysis, evaluation and information on the status of the risk. The risk register should be continuously updated and reviewed throughout the course of the project.

The risk register should contain the following information: risk number (unique within register); risk type; author (who raised it); date last updated, description; likelihood; interdependencies with other sources of risk; expected impact; bearer of risk; countermeasures; and risk status and risk action status. All the risks, including potential variations, were subject to continuous review and modification.

The risk register is important for the following five reasons:
- Monitoring and, if necessary, correcting progress on risk mitigation measures.
- Identifying new risks.
- Closing down **expired** risks.
- Amending risk assessment for existing risks.
- Approving the **drawdown** of project contingencies by the client when required.

New Words and Phrases

severity   严重；严格；猛烈
slippage   滑动，滑移；下降
legal-contractual   法律合同的
equitable   公平的，公正的；平衡法的巨大的经济损失
detrimental   不利的；有害的
expropriation   没收；征收，征用
formulation   构想，规划；公式化；简化
residual   残渣，剩余；剩余的，残留的
mitigation   减轻，缓和，平静
warrant   担保
bond   债券
reciprocal   互惠的，相互的；互相起作用的事物；倒数的
expired   过期的，失效的；期满
drawdown   减少；水位降低
construction risk management   建设风险管理
design change   设计变更
improving project performance   提高工程项目性能
contracting party   缔约方
budget overrun   预算超支
tendering stage   投标阶段
archaeological find   考古发现

work stoppage　停工
be forced out of the business　置身局外
construction claims　施工索赔
signing of the contract documents　签订合同文件
colossal financial damage　巨大经济损失
across border　跨境，跨越国界
trade credit default　贸易赤字
civil unrest　社会动荡
international setting　国际环境
develop specific risk minimization strategy　制定风险最小化的具体策略
prior to negotiation　谈判前
extra-contractual risk　合同之外的风险
standard checklist　标准清单
expert interview　专家访谈法
Delphi technique　德尔菲法技术
brainstorming session　头脑风暴会议
appropriate risk mitigation strategy　合适的风险缓解政策

Notes

[1] Risk management refers to the art of identifying, analyzing, responding to and controlling project risk factors in a manner which best achieves the objectives of all participants. Additionally, effective risk management typically generates positive results on a project by improving project performance, increasing cost effectiveness and creating a good working relationship between contracting parties.

风险管理指在一定方式上识别、分析、响应和控制项目风险因素的行为，它能最好地实现所有参与方的目标。同时，通过改善项目实施、增加成本效益和创造合同缔约各方之间的良好工作关系，有效的风险管理往往能对项目产生积极的结果。

[2] Construction project success is usually measured by its schedule, budget and quality which conflict is inherent. Broadly, various risks can affect these three basic factors against the success of a project.

建设项目的成功通常由存在内存矛盾的进度、预算和质量来衡量，大体上讲，各种风险都能影响到这三种对项目成功不利的基本因素。

[3] Among them are inflation, bad weather, strikes and other labour problems, shortage of materials, unforeseen conditions at the construction site, accidents (whether by fire, flood or carelessness), and innovative design that does not work or proves impossible to construct, and the interaction between liability for defective workmanship and for faults in design, because lack of coordination between design and construction is a common source of dispute.

这些风险有通货膨胀、恶劣天气、罢工和其他劳工问题、材料短缺、施工现场不可预见的情况、意外事故（由火灾、洪水或粗心大意引起的），不能实施或证明不可能施工的革新设计，以及有缺陷工艺责任和设计失误责任之间的相互影响等，因为设计和施工之间缺乏协调是争执的普遍源头。

[4] Contactor must evaluate risk factors or characteristics of a risk such as the risk event, its probability of occurrence, and the amount of potential loss or gain, and analyze every possible issue or event causing or that may cause harm to the project.

承包商必须评估风险因素或风险特征,如风险事件、其发生的可能性以及潜在损失量或收益量,且必须分析每个正在出现或可能对项目产生危害的问题或事件。

[5] Deflecting/Transferring—deflecting or transferring risks by contract is a common response ranging from total allocation of risk to another party or risk-sharing between two or more parties.

风险转向/转移——通过合同来转向或转移风险是通用的风险对策,该对策可以将风险全部转给另外的项目参与方,或者在两个或更多参与方之间分担风险。

Exercises

I. Translate the following phrases into English.
1. 提高工程项目建设的性能
2. 签署法律合同文件
3. 制定风险最小化的具体策略
4. 专家访谈法,德尔菲法与头脑风暴会议法
5. 建设项目合同具体条款
6. 建筑工程承包合同
7. 合同工程保险、公共责任保险与财产保险

II. Translate the following sentences into Chinese.

1. All risks must be evaluated in terms of two distinct elements: the likelihood that the event is going to occur as well as the consequences, or effect of its occurrence.

2. A changed conditions or unforeseen site conditions might affect the cost of work. For example, such unforeseen ground conditions can necessitate the driving of longer piles or use of more support steel than was first planned foundation work.

3. In the presence of a changed condition, the employer should provide an equitable means paying the contractor for overcoming conditions that neither he nor the employer could have expected from the information available at the time the contract was prepared, but it always is not the case.

4. There are some actions which needed to be taken responding to residual risk comes in the risk response.

Construction Risks and Insurance

Risk management may be defined as a comprehensive approach to handing exposures to loss. Any peril that can cause **financial impairment** to the business enterprise is subject of risk management. The following are four steps that a contracting firm can follow in applying risk management to its business:

1) Recognize and identify the varied risks that apply to the construction process. These may arise as a consequence of contract provisions, the nature of the work, site conditions, or the operation of law.

2) Measure the degree of exposure presented by the risks identified. This involves establishing the frequency of losses and the potential severity of the losses that may occur.

3) Decide how to protect against those risks that have been identified. If the risk cannot be eliminated

by an alternative procedure or by contractual transfer to another party, the choice may be to purchase commercial insurance, or assume the risk, etc.

4) Conduct a company-wide program of loss control and prevention.

In devising the best risk-handling program, commercial insurance is the keystone to adequate financial protection. Insurance does not eliminate the risks involved in construction contracting, but it does shift most of the financial threat to a professional risk-bearer. In addition to paying losses, insurance companies offer valuable services to contractor in the areas of safety, loss prevention, educational and training programs, site inspections, and others.

Construction Risks

Construction work by nature is hazardous, and accidents are frequent and often severe. The annual toll of deaths, bodily injuries, and property damage in the construction industry is extremely high. The potential severity of accidents and the frequency with which they occur require that the contractor protect itself with a variety of complex and expensive insurance **coverages**. Without adequate insurance protection, the contractor would be continuously faced with the possibility of serious or even ruinous financial loss.

Construction projects usually have in force several simultaneous contractual arrangements: between the owner and architect-engineer, between the owner and general contractor, and between the general contractor and its several subcontractors. Contracts that provide for the design-construct and construction management services and the use of separate prime contracts introduce additional features. Construed as a whole, these contracts establish a complicated structure of responsibilities for damages arising out of construction operations. Liability for accidents can **devolve** to the owner or architect-engineer, as well as to the prime contractor and subcontractors whose equipment and employees perform the actual work. Construction contracts typically require the contractor to assume the owner's and architect-engineer's legal liability for construction accidents or to provide insurance for the owner's direct protection. Consequently, a contractor's insurance program normally includes coverages to protect persons other than itself and to protect it from liabilities not legally its own.

The matter of risk and insurance for the construction contractor is rendered even more difficult on large projects by confusion as to which party is responsible for a given loss or liability. The matter of how the responsibility should be divided among owner, architect-engineer, fabricators, general contractor, subcontractors, and construction manager has become a tangled and extremely complex legal matter. Modern conditions of fast-tracking, alternate designs, shop drawings, design-construct, and construction management have blurred the lines that divide the multiple participants involved with today's construction projects. The division of responsibility in such cases can be very imprecise.

The Insurance Policy

An insurance policy is a contract, under which the insurer promises, for a consideration, to assume financial responsibility for a specified loss or liability. The policy contains many provisions pertaining to the loss against which it affords protection. Fundamentally, the law of insurance is identical with the law of contracts. However, because of its intimate association with the public welfare, the insurance field is controlled and regulated by federal and state statutes. Each state has an insurance regulatory agency that administers that state's insurance code, a set of statutory provisions that imposes regulations on insurance companies concerning investments, reserves, annual financial statements, and periodic examinations. Insurance companies are controlled as to their organizational structure, financial affairs, and business methods. In most states insurance policies must conform to statutory requirements as to form and content.

A loss suffered by a contracting firm as a result of its own deliberate action cannot be recovered under an insurance policy. However, **negligence** or **oversight** on the part of the contractor will not generally **invalidate** the insurance contract. The contractor will not generally invalidate the insurance contract. The contractor must pay a premium as the consideration for the insurance company's promise of protection against the designated loss. Most types of insurance require that the premium be paid in advance before the policy becomes effective. In the event of a loss covered by an insurance policy, the contractor cannot recover more than the loss; that is, a profit cannot be made at expense of the insurance company.

Contract Requirements

With the many hazards that confront a construction business and the **plethora** of insurance types that can be purchased, one might wonder how a contractor decides just what insurance is really needed. In reality however, the contractor quite often has no choice. For example, it is standard practice that construction contracts require the contractor to provide certain insurance coverages.

Construction contracts typically make the contractor responsible for obtaining coverages such as workers' compensation insurance, employer's liability insurance, and comprehensive general liability insurance. Property insurance to protect the project and liability insurance to protect the owner may be made the responsibility of either the owner or the contractor, depending on the contract. When the contract delegates specific responsibility to the contracting firm for obtaining certain insurance, it is customary that insurance certificates must be submitted to the owner or the architect-engineer as proof that the coverage stipulated has, in fact, been provided.

Construction contracts frequently require the contractor to hold the owner and architect-engineer harmless by accepting any liability that either of them may incur because of operations performed under the contract. Most contract documents that contain such indemnity clauses are explicit in requiring the contractor to procure appropriate contractual liability insurance.

With regard to project insurance requirements, it is always good practice for a contractor to submit a copy of the contract documents to its insurance company before construction operations commence. The contracting firm is not an insurance expert and is not really competent to evaluate the risks and liabilities placed on it by the contract. Its insurance agents or **brokers** are qualified to comb the documents and advise the firm concerning the insurance needs dictate by the language and requirements of a given construction contract.

Legal Requirements

Certain kinds insurance are required by law, and the contractor must provide them whether or not they are called for by the contract. Workers' compensation, automobile, unemployment, and social security are examples of coverages required by statute. It can be argued that unemployment and social security payments made by the contractor are more in the nature of a tax than of insurance premiums in the usual sense. Nevertheless, both unemployment and social security are treated as forms of insurance for the purpose of discussion in this lesson.

The law makes the independent contractor liable for damages caused by its own acts of **omission** or **commission**. In addition, the prime contractor has a **contingent** liability for he actions of its subcontractors. Therefore, whether or not the law is specific concerning certain types of insurance, the contractor as a practical fact must procure several different categories of liability insurance to protect itself from liability for damages caused by its own construction operations as well as those of its subcontractors.

Analysis of Insurable risks

Aside from coverages required by law and the construction contract, it is the contractor's **prerogative** to decide what insurance it shall all carry. Such elective coverages pertain principally to the contractor's own property or to property for which it is responsible. It is not economically possible for the contractor to carry all the insurance coverages available to it. If it purchased insurance protection against every risk that is insurable, the cost of the resulting premiums would impose an impossible financial burden on its business. The extent and magnitude of a contractor's insurance program can be decided only after careful study and consideration. If a risk is insurable, the cost of the premiums must be balanced against the possible loss and the probability of its occurrence. There are, of course, risks that are not insurable or for which insurance is not economically practicable. Associate losses must be regarded simply as ordinary business expenses.

At times, careful planning and meticulous construction procedures can minimize a risk at less cost than the premium of a covering insurance policy. Thus the contractor may choose to assume a calculated risk rather than pay a high insurance premium. A common example of assuming such a risk involves construction that is to be erected immediately adjacent to an existing structure. If the nature of the new construction is such that the existing structure may be endangered by settlement or collapse, the contractor has two courses of action open to it. As one alternative it can include in its estimate the premium for a collapse policy. Such protection is high in cost and is generally available only with substantial **deductible** amounts. Instead, the contractor can assume the risk without insurance protection, choosing to rely on skill and extraordinary precautions in construction procedures to get the job done without mishap. Many analogous cases can be cited with respect to pole driving, **blasting**, water damage, and others.

Construction Insurance Checklist

Insurance coverages are complex, and each new construction contract presents its own problems. The contractor should select a competent insurance agent or broker who is experienced in construction work and familiar with contractors' insurance problems. Without competent advice, the contractor may either incur the needless expense of overlapping protection or expose itself to the danger of vital gaps in insurance coverage. The contractor can often reduce insurance costs by keeping its agent or broker advised in detail as to the nature and conduct of its construction operations.

In the long list of possible construction insurance coverages, not every policy applicable to a given firm's operations. The following checklist is not represented as being complete, but it does contain insurance coverages typical of the the construction industry.

Property Insurance on Project

All Risk Builder's Risk Insurance

This insurance protects against all risks of direct physical loss or damage to the project or to associated materials caused by any external effect, with noted exclusions.

Named-Peril Builder's Risk Insurance

The basic policy provides protection for the project, including stored materials, against direct loss by fire or lighting. A number of separate endorsements to this policy are available that add coverage for specific losses.

1) Extended coverage endorsement. This covers property against all direct loss cause by windstorm, hail, explosion, riot, civil commotion, aircraft, vehicles, and smoke.

2) **Vandalism** and malicious mischief **endorsement**.

3) Water damage endorsement. Insurance of this type indemnifies for loss or damage caused by accidental discharge, leakage, or overflow of water or steam. Included are defective pipes, roots, and water tanks. This does not include damage caused by sprinkler leakage, floods, or high water.

4) Sprinkler leakage endorsement. This provides protection against all direct loss to a building project as a result of leakage, freezing, or breaking of sprinkler installations.

Earthquake Insurance

This coverage may be provided by an endorsement to the builder's risk policy in some states. Elsewhere a separate policy must be issued.

Bridge Insurance

This insurance is of the inland marine type and is often termed the "bridge builder's risk policy". It affords protection during construction against damage that may be caused by fire, lightning, flood, ice, collision, explosion, riot, vandalism, wind, tornado, and earthquake.

Steam Boiler and Machinery Insurance

A contractor or owner may purchase this form of insurance when the boiler of a building under construction is being tested and balanced or when being used to heat the structure for plastering, floor lying, or other purposes. Unlike other property insurances listed here, this type includes some liability coverage. This policy covers any injury or damage that occurs to or be caused by the boiler during its use by the contractor.

Installation Floater Policy

Insurance of this type provides named-peril or all-risk protection for property of various kinds such as project machinery (heating and air conditioning systems, for example) from the time that it leaves the place of shipment until it is installed on the project and tested. Coverage terminates when the insured's interest in the property ceases, when the property is accepted, of when it is taken over by the owner.

Property Insurance on Contractor's Own Property

Fire Insurance on Contractor's Own Buildings
This coverage affords protection for offices, sheds, warehouses, and store contents. Endorsements for extended coverage and for vandalism and malicious mischief are also available.

Contractor's Equipment Insurance
This type of policy, often termed a "floater", insures a contractor's construction equipment regardless of its location.

MotorTruck Cargo Policy
This insurance covers loss by named hazards to materials or equipment carried on the contractor's own trucks from supplier to warehouse or building site.

Transportation Floater
Insurance of this type provides coverage against damage to property belonging to the contractor or others while it is being transported. It may be obtained on a per-trip, project of annual basis.

Burglary, Robbery and Theft Insurance
This form of insurance protects the contractor against the loss of money, securities, office equipment, and similar valuables through burglary, destruction, disappearance, or wrongful abstraction.

Fidelity Bond
This surety bond affords the contractor protection against loss caused by dishonesty of its own employees.

Dishonesty, Destruction, and Disappearance Policy
A comprehensive policy of this form protects against the loss of money and securities, on and off the premises, caused by dishonesty, mysterious disappearance, or destruction. It insures against dishonesty of employees, loss of money and securities, loss of securities in safety deposit, and forgery.

Valuable Papers Destruction Insurance
This policy protects the contractor against the loss, damage, or destruction of valuable papers such as books, records, maps, drawings, abstracts, deeds, mortgages, contracts, and documents. It does not cover loss by misplacement, unexplained disappearance, **wear and tear**, deterioration, vermin, or war.

Liability Insurance
Employer's Liability Insurance
This insurance is customarily written in combination with workers' compensation insurance. It affords the contractor broad coverage for the bodily injury of death of an employee in the course of his employment, but outside of and distinct from any claims under workers' compensation laws.

Contractor's Protective Public and Property Damage Insurance
This insurance protects the contractor from its legal liability for injuries to persons not in its employ and for damage to the property of control, when such injuries or damages rise out of the operations of the contractor.

Contractor's Protective Public and Property Damage Liability Insurance
This protects the contractor against its liability imposed by law arising out of acts or omissions of its subcontractors.

Contractual Liability Insurance
This form of insurance is required when one party to a contract, by terms of that contract, assumes

certain legal liabilities of the other party. The usual forms of liability do not afford this coverage.

Owner's Protective Liability Insurance

This insurance protects the owner from its contingent liability for damages arising on the operations of the prime contractor or its subcontractors.

Completed-Operation Liability Insurance

This form of insurance protects the contractor from damage claims stemming from its faulty performance on projects already completed and handed over to the owner. The usual forms of liability insurance provide protection only while the contractor is performing the work and not after it has been completed by the owner.

Professional Liability Insurance

This insurance protects the contractor against damage claims arising out of design and other professional services rendered by the contractor to the owner.

Employee Insurance

Worker's Compensation Insurance

This insurance provides all benefits required by law to employees killed or injured in the course of their employment.

Social Security

This all-federal insurance system operated by the U. S. government provides retirement benefits to his family when the worker dies, disability benefits, hospitalization benefits, and medical insurance.

Unemployment Insurance

This federal-state insurance plan provides workers with a weekly income during periods of unemployment between jobs.

Disability Insurance

This insurance, required by some states, provides benefits to employees for disabilities caused by nonoccupational accidents and disease.

Automobile Insurance

Various forms of insurance are available in connection with the ownership and use of motor vehicles. Liability coverages protect the contractor against third-party claims of bodily injury or property damage involving the contractor's vehicles of non-owned vehicles that are used in its interest. Collision insurance, together with comprehensive fire and theft coverage, indemnifies the contractor for damage to its own vehicles.

Business, Accident and life Insurance

Business Interruption Insurance

This insurance is designed to reimburse the owner for losses suffered because of an interruption of its business.

Sole Proprietorship Insurance

A policy of type provides cash to assist heirs in continuing or disposing of the business without sacrifice in the event of death of the owner.

Key Person Life Insurance

This insurance reimburses the businessfor financial loss resulting from the death of a key person in the business. It also builds up a sinking fund to be available on retirement.

Group Life Insurance

Contractors often purchase life insurance for their employees. This affords protection for each participant at a low group cost, the premium for which may be paid wholly or partly by the contractor. Additional amounts can often be purchased by the employees at their own expense.

Major Medical Insurance

Such insurance covers hospitalization and medical expenses incurred by covered employees. A portion of the premium may be paid by the employer and the balance by the individuals insured.

Disability Insurance

This insurance can provide benefits to employees for death of **dismemberment** caused by accident.

Accidental Death and Dismemberment

Insuranceof this type provides benefits for death or dismemberment caused by accident.

Corporate Continuity Insurance

In the event of a stockholder's death, this insurance furnishes cash for the purchase of his corporate stock. This provides liquidity for the decedent's estate and prevents corporate stock from falling into undesirable hands.

New Words and Phrases

coverage 覆盖，覆盖范围
devolve 转移；移交；使滚下；衰落
negligence 疏忽；忽视；粗心大意
oversight 监督，照管；疏忽
invalidate 使无效；使作废
plethora 过多；过剩
broker 经纪人
omission 疏忽，遗漏；省略；冗长
commission 委员会；佣金；委任；委任状
contingent 附带的；偶然发生的
prerogative 特权
deductible 可扣除的；可减免的
blasting 爆破
vandalism 恶意破坏
endorsement 认可，支持；背书；签注（文件）
floater （特指流动财产的）保险
burglary 盗窃行为，盗窃
dismemberment 伤残，肢解；分割
financial impairment 财务减值
wear and tear 磨损，耗损

Basics of Managing Risks

So you have been asked to put together a project risk management plan. No idea where to start. Here is a brief guide to putting together a risk management plan.

Project Risk Management

A risk is something that may happen and if it does, will have an **adverse** impact on the project. A few points here, "That may happen" implies a probability of less then 100%. If it has a probability of 100 % - in other words it will happen-it is an issue. An issue is managed differently to a risk. A risk must also have a probability something above 0 %. It must be a chance to happen or it is not a risk. The second thing to consider from the definition is "will have an adverse impact". If it will not have an adverse impact, it is not a risk. Suppose we said a risk was that we would find the project less complicated than we thought, and could finish early. Unless finishing early has an adverse effect on the project, it is not a risk.

Risk Management Plan

There are four stages to risk management planning. They are **risk identification, risks quantification, risk response, risk monitoring and control**.

Risk Identification

In this stage, we identify and name the risks. The best approach is a workshop with business and IT people to carry out the identification. Use a combination of brainstorming and reviewing of standard risk lists. There are different sorts of risks and we need to decide on a project by project basis what to do about each type.

Business risks are ongoing risks that are best handled by the business. An example is that if the project cannot meet end of financial year deadline, the business area may need to retain their existing accounting system for another year. The response is likely to be a contingency plan developed by the business, to use the existing system for another year. Generic risks are risks to all projects, for example, the risk that business users might not be available and requirements may be incomplete. Each organization will develop standard responses to generic risks.

Risks should be defined in two parts. The first is the cause of the situation (vendor not meeting deadline, business users not available, etc.). The second part is the impact (budget will be exceeded, milestones not achieved, etc.). Hence a risk might be defined as "the vendor not meeting deadline will mean that budget will be exceeded". If this format is used, it is easy to remove duplicates, and understand the risk.

Risk Quantification

Risk need to be quantified in two dimensions, the impact of the risk needs to be assessed, the probability of the risk occurring needs to be assessed (Figure 11-1). For simplicity, rate each on a 1 to 4 scale. The larger the number, the larger the impact or probability. By using a matrix, a priority can be established.

Note that if probability is high, and impact is low, it is a medium risk. On the other hand if impact is high, and probability low, it is high priority. A remote chance of a catastrophe warrants more attention than a high chance of a hiccup.

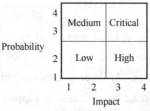

Figure 11-1　Risk Quantification

Risk Response

There are four things you can do about a risk. The strategies are:
- Avoid the risk. Do something to remove it. Use another supplier for example.
- Transfer the risk. Make someone else responsible, Perhaps a vendor can be made responsible for a particularly risky part of the project.
- **Mitigate** the risk. Take actions to lessen the impact or chance of the risk occurring. If the risk relates to availability of resources, draw up an agreement and get sign-off for the resource to be available.
- Accept the risk. The risk might be so small the effort to do anything is not worth while.

A risk response plan should include the strategy and action items to address the strategy. The actions should include what needs to be done, who is doing it, and when it should be completed.

Risk Control

The final step is to continually monitor risks to identify any change in the status, or if they turn into an issue. It is best to hold regular risk reviews to identify actions outstanding, risk probability and impact, remove risks that have passed, and identify new risks.

Summary

Risk management is not a complex task. If you follow the four steps, you can put together a risk management plan for a project in a short space of time, without a plan, the success of the project, and your reputation as a project manager, are on the line. Follow these steps and you will increase your chances of success.

Unit 11 Risk Management of Construction Projects

New Words and Phrases

adverse　不利的；相反的；敌对的
mitigate　使缓和，使减轻
risk identification　风险辨识
risk quantification　风险量化（评估）
risk response　风险应对
risk monitoring and control　风险监控

Part II Speaking

Completion and Handing-Over

B: A month ago we submitted our plan for taking over the works along with a timetable, Two weeks ago a combined inspection group composed of the employer, the relevant government departments and you inspected the facilities in our contract and had a trial run of all the systems. We wonder if we can obtain the **take-over** certificate now. The early issuing of the certificate will be greatly appreciated.

A: In my opinion it is too early to issue the take-over certificate for the plant.

B: I'm afraid I can't agree with you on this point. In accordance with Clause 60. 3 of Conditions of the Contract: "A take-over certificate will be issued at the stage when the plant is substantially completed and functioning normally." We should be given the take-over certificate since the works has been substantially completed, this has been confirmed by the engineer and the relevant government departments.

A: From our point of view, there're still a lot of items of works not yet finished and some works need to be corrected. For example, the paint spilled on the floor, the missing drainage grid, and the pipes need to be repainted. Meanwhile, there're still some **outstanding works**. They are all in the **punch list** transmitted to you last week.

B: It's true that a few minor defects remain to be rectified and some items of the works to be completed. But they do not affect the normal operation of the whole works, as you can see from all the functioning tests. This means, according to the contract, that **substantial completion** has been achieved; therefore we should receive a take-over certificate from you. Here is our written undertaking that we will finish the outstanding works and making good the defects with due speed in the **defects liability period**.

A: (studying it) Well done. We shall issue the certificate to you as soon as possible. By the way, are all the construction completion files ready for delivery?

B: Yes. All the **as-built drawings**, **QA/QC inspection forms**, **survey records**, and **execution-tracing files** shall be submitted in one day.

A: Good. Once we receive all your construction files, we will issue the take-over certificate to you.

B: Does the maintenance period start on the date when your take-over certificate is issued?

A: Certainly.

B: May I remind you that it is also time to release the first half of the retention money to us?

A: I will arrange for its release soon.

New Words and Phrases

handing-over　（工程）交付
take-over　（工程）接收
outstanding work　未完工程
punch list　遗留问题清单
substantial completion　实质性竣工
defects liability period　保修期
as-built drawings　竣工图
QA/QC inspection form　质量保证/质量控制检查表格
survey record　测量记录
execution-tracing file　隐蔽工程记录

Unit 12 Construction Claims

Part I　Reading and Translating

Professional Knowledge Guidance

1. 建设工程索赔：是指在工程合同履行过程中，合同当事人一方因对方不履行或未能正确履行合同或者由于其他非自身因素而受到经济损失或权利损害，通过合同规定的程序向对方提出经济或时间补偿要求的行为。

索赔一词来源于英语"claim"，其原意表示"有权要求"，法律上叫"权利主张"，并没有赔偿的意思。在国际工程承包市场上，工程索赔是承包人和发包人保护自身正当权益、弥补工程损失的重要而有效的手段。

2. 索赔目的分类：包括工期索赔和经济索赔。工期索赔是承包商向业主要求延长施工的时间，是原定的工程竣工日期顺延一段合理时间。经济索赔：经济索赔就是承包商向业主要求补偿不应该由承包商自己承担的经济损失或额外开支，也就是取得合理的经济补偿。

3. 工期索赔计算：有直接法、比例分析法、网络分析法三种。

1）**直接法**：如某干扰事件直接发生在关键线路上，造成总工期的延误，可以直接将该干扰事件的实际干扰时间（延误时间）作为工期索赔值。

2）**比例分析法**：通过分析增加或减少的单项工程量（工程造价）与合同总量（合同总造价）的比值，推断出增加或减少的工期。

3）**网络分析法**：通过分析延误前后的施工网络计划，比较两种计算结果，计算出工程应顺延的工期。

Construction Claims

Construction Claims Calculation

One of the most **contentious** areas in construction claims is the calculation or estimation of lost productivity.

Therefore, all direct costs of labor, equipment, materials and other costs should be captured and associated with the work according to the contract. There are two typical methods of claim calculation on whether the claim is being priced on a pre-performance basis or on an after-the-fact basis. Other direct costs associated with the claim such as field overhead, bond costs, insurance, interest and profit should also be noted on the forms.[1]

Direct costs as defined in this section include only the costs of labor, equipment and materials needed to perform the actual work within the scope of the change. It does not include the **consequential** effect of changes such as costs for the disruption and inefficiency created by change orders; costs of acceleration of work; and costs as a result of project extensions.

Direct Labor Costs

Direct labor costs should be based on actual or anticipated increased costs of the various craftsmen, operating engineers, laborers, etc. Rates of pay may be dictated by contract terms (such as day work schedules), or if not in the contract may be supported by various union wage scales or other supportable bases. Costs of supervision should also be calculated and noted. Regular time and overtime work should be noted, and if overtime rates are requested they should be justified on the basis that the work could not be completed on regular time, that no time extension was granted, or other appropriate basis. Documents to support labor charges include **payroll** records, invoices, estimates, bid **takeoffs**, job diaries, and other daily project reports.

Labor issues, including contract negotiations, walkouts, slowdowns, and strikes, may delay completion of a project. Depending on the nature and duration of the labor issue, the contractor may need to work overtime or double shifts to make up for time lost during a labor dispute. This significantly increases the contractor's labor cost. An extension of the contract time results in increased overhead costs and may reduce a contractor's ability to begin or continue work on other projects.

Direct Equipment and Material Costs

Equipment costs may be increased due to additional equipment needed to perform the work. Charges for equipment usage may be based on contract terms, or if not specified in the contract may be based on rental invoices or hourly rates.[2] The appropriate price to charge is the substantiate, increased time-related costs associated with owning or providing equipment on the site to perform the work within the change. Payroll reports for operating engineers may provide evidence of when equipment was used. For contractor owned equipment, internal rates may have been developed based on the total costs of owning the equipment spread out over the useful life of the equipment. Costs such as depreciation, insurance, taxes, storage and administrative costs should be included in the rate. The rate is usually expressed in hourly, daily or weekly costs of operation. However, only excess costs incurred as a result of the change should be included.

Project Site Overhead

Site overhead is frequently referred to as **preliminary** and general in contract conditions or BOQ. These costs include costs of on-site project management and administration, plants rentals, storage charges, utilities, etc. Contracts usually provide for percentage mark-ups on labor and other direct costs to account for site overhead. If need be, the contractor can support its claim by reference to bid documents and estimates, or international practice. Further support can be shown by actual costs for additional time and effort spent on meetings and discussions regarding estimating and engineering with respect to the change. Unanticipated additional manpower needed to perform work may also result in additional expenditures for small tools, supplies, consumables or other miscellaneous items that were carried as general conditions. [3]

Interest Claims

The financing of **unreimbursed** project costs as a result of changes can have a significant impact. Interest charges may be appropriate to **recoup** financing costs or the lost opportunity to utilize internal funds in a manner other than as planned. The key factors to quantifying a claim for interest is to determine the period over which the interest is computed, and the rate or cost of money.

These factors may be set forth in the contract documents or by applicable local or legal regulations.

Profit

In addition to being entitled to recover excess costs attributable to a party's breach of contract, FIDIC allows an injured contractor to recover the profit anticipated under the contract if the evidence is sufficiently certain and definite to afford a basis on which to estimate its extent. There are at least some exceptions.

Construction Claims Documentation

Once a potential claim or dispute has been identified, the value of developing and reserving supporting documentation cannot be **overstated**. It is very crucial that the contractor prepare an effective document present accurate estimated damage amounts at the complaint stage. Disputes are often won or lost on the strength of a contractor's documentation. Even before a claim is identified, it is important that the contractor keep good records of its activity on the project.

Components of Claim

A construction claim consists of two major parts: the entitlement section, which usually includes a detailed description of the actions or in actions of the party from whom relief is sought, entitling the claimant to compensation; and the damages section, which sets forth the calculations and support for the compensation claimed.

Claim Analysis

Construction claims analysis, rather than coming at the end of the claim process, should proceed concurrently with the entitlement analysis. When filing a construction claim, performing damage analyses early can result in finding alternative explanation for increased costs by presenting the contractor's own convincing records.

Delay Analysis

Construction delays are very costly. Delay analysis involves a thorough examination of the various activities of the project, **pinpointing** deviations from planned performance, and then quantifying the delay. Delay impact analysis requires first that the contractor review project drawings, specifications and other contract documents as well as schedules, progress logs, and similar records. Next, planned and actual performance are compared in the form of CPM network schedules to identify critical deviations. Extended costs for delays are a common and hotly contested element in pricing. Quantification of delay damages requires an analysis to determine the type of delay, time analysis of the delay period, an analysis of the cause and liability for the delay, and an analysis to determine the costs related to the delay.

1) Schedule analysis. A scheduling analysis representing the project is generally prepared using a computer program that plots the sequence and interdependencies of the project's significant activities. This analysis will reveal the activities' most logical sequence. Many contracts, particularly for large projects,

require identification of a critical path.

2) Activity analysis. An analysis is required of three basic types of CPM schedules. The contractor reviews the following schedules:

"As-planned" schedule. This schedule represents the planned sequence and timing of original contract work. It is important that this schedule be reviewed for reasonableness, and determined to be a realistic, achievable plan.

"As-built" schedule. This schedule sets forth the various project activities as they were actually performed, reflecting the actual sequence and duration of each activities, and the actual interrelationships among activities.

As the "as-planned" and "as-built" schedules are compared, deviations are identified. These deviations represent changes in the planned performance. As each impact is identified, the "as-planned" schedule is revised to reflect the impact, yielding an "as-adjusted", which will then be compared to the "as-built" to identify further impacts and determine the overall magnitude of the project delay and to identify major discrepancies.

After specific activities and time periods have been pinpointed through the network analysts, project records and interviews can be utilized to determine why these delays occurred and who bears the responsibility of the time extension.

3) Costs of delay. The object of pricing an extension claim is to quantify the increased costs that were incurred only as a result of actions by the responsible party that caused a longer than planned period of performance. There typically are four types of damages associated with delay: extended project costs, escalation, inefficiency, and unabsorbed overhead.

Delays in product fabrication or delivery create challenges to project completion. If products can bot be fabricated because of the unavailability of a certain material, an alternate product may need to be considered. Product substitutions increase the risk that an inferior product may be furnished in lieu of the product originally specified or selected, and increases the potential for installation conflicts when other contractor proceeds with related work based on the originally selected product. When delivery dates are not met, expedited shipping may be required to keep the project on schedule. In addition to increased shipping costs, delivery delays may adversely impact the performance of related work. Proper sequencing of the work may again be affected.

Claims Documents Backup and Record

Certain records, such as daily poet logs, can constitute critical evidence in establishing entitlement to a claim. A detailed project log can document levels of manpower, the progress of the work on a particular date, and any problems that the contractor may encounter.[4] Obviously, a project log prepared contemporaneously with the work performed will have greater weight as evidence than the verbal testimony of a project manager or foreman months or even years after the events in question. Moreover, if the claim is being presented to a fact finder from the construction industry, it is likely that the contractor's credibility will be enhanced if it maintains detailed and accurate records, particularly if the opposing party's documentation is weak. Of course, the above factors apply to all documentation that might be used to support a claim, such as cost accounting records, project correspondence, site meeting minutes, notes of conversations, internal memos and project schedule.

Large construction projects generate thousands of pages of documents. Some of those documents create the legal relationships between the parties who were actively involved in the construction process. Others vividly demonstrate how the parties dealt with issues as they came up during the course of construction.

Consider the **spectrum** of project documents:

- Contract documents (including general conditions, particular conditions, specifications, drawings, soils reports and bonds).
- Drawings (including tender set, issued-for-construction set, as-built set, shop drawings, erection drawings and coordination drawings).
- Bar chart and electronic schedules (engineer approved).
- **Contemplated** change notices, site instructions, price quotations and change orders.
- Applications for payment and payment certificates.
- Inspection reports and testing reports.
- Minutes of site meetings.
- Correspondence, inter-office memos and e-mails.
- Handwritten notes of meetings and telephone conversations.
- Site **superintendent** reports (for example, daily reports, diaries and logs).

These documents, for better or worse, complete or deficient, accurate or self-serving, comprise the complete written history of the project. One thing is very clear—the importance of these documents should never be underrated. Most of the documents are automatic and self-explanatory. However, the following items are often overlooked and are therefore worth elaborating.

1) Original records. As noted earlier, for the **prudent** contractor anxious to stay solvent, records are required for estimating future work, and for protecting his contractual rights. Both of these require some form of post-contract review. However, there can be little argument that reliable data cannot be extracted from records created after the fact. Even the best of memories are fallible, and the written record serves to provide the solid reminder. Data may be extracted, analyzed and presented in a different light, but satisfactory records cannot be created later.

2) Instant memos. For example, all verbal directives should be committed to writing immediately and exchanged with the other party. This serves to keep the other party properly informed, clarify understanding if the instructions were not clear, and, of course, to preserve contractual rights.

3) Personal diaries. Diaries can provide a wealth of information. Unfortunately, they tend to be overlooked, either because the pace is so **hectic** that there is not time to keep one current, or alternatively, there seems to be so little of importance going on that it hardly seems worth writing. In any case, what should be recorded are solid facts, such as the make-up of various crews, subcontractors and equipment on site, work reallocation and for what reasons, delivery problems, weather conditions, visitors to the site, discussions, and seemingly innocuous comments about the work. Needless to say, what should be avoided, are personal opinions and **derogatory** remarks.

4) Photograph. For record purposes, these must show what is actually going on at the time with the location and view point identified, as well as the date and photographer's name. A camera which prints the date on the negative/memory is a great start and well worth the expense. Also the photographer should realize that it is the content, and not the artistic effect, that is the most important.

5) Computer application. As we have seen, the road to contract documentation is long and **arduous**. The worst part is trying to find that vital piece of information amongst the **morass** of paper, which is now so

urgently required. Computer is so powerful that it seems impossible to do without them. However, the secret is to get data organized as early in the project as possible, and then commit to consistent maintenance, regular backup and of-site storage. If this is done meticulously, the subsequent saving in time through search and find, or through spread sheet and database design and use, can be invaluable.

6) Managing the records. As well as managing the files, the records themselves also need managing. Some simple rules can help as follows:

- Determine what records are to be kept, and how. Establish logs of the records, so that they can be found, referred to and/of followed up as required. Well organized contractors establish standard reference lists and code for all their contracts. This greatly facilitates managing, analyzing and comparing contracts.

- Once the records have been identified, ensure that they are in fact set up, maintained and used for managing the job.

- Review the record keeping system from time to time, because records have a habit of growing in unexpected ways-like half the correspondence showing up under miscellaneous, and the other half under general. In addition, some records may become **obsolete** or **redundant**, and should be discontinued. Unnecessary record keeping can waste a lot of time and money.

- Records also take up space and equipment. Determine the useful life of the different components, and take a systematic approach to record disposal.

- Take steps to ensure accuracy, reliability and hence credibility. Unreliable records can be quite useless, as well as a waste of money, and possibly even **detrimental**.

Advice for Contractor's Misapprehensions on Variation/Change

Finally, some advice, contractors should be aware of certain pitfalls of claims. Contractors generally suffer from the following misapprehensions **pertaining** to variation claims:

- That the employer is bound to pay for any change or additional work whatsoever undertaken by the contractor whether expressly directed or not.

- Where the scope of work is unclear or if there should be a discrepancy in the contract documents, the contractor is automatically entitled to extras.

- In the event work is omitted, the contractor is automatically entitled as of right to loss of profit.

- Prior to ordering extras, the employer must obtain the contractor's agreement to the rates for valuing the varied work.

- The contractor has a right to refuse to undertake varied work if he so desires in particular if there is disagreement as to the rates and time extension sought.

- In the situation where varied work has been undertaken, measured and valued by the quantity surveyor but payment is not effected, the contractor is automatically entitled to interest on the amount due.

- The employer has no right to order and the contractor is not obliged to carry out varied work in the defect liability period.

- The contractor has a right to call for a review of measured and valued work involving variations even alter the final account has been prepared the final certificate issued.

- The contractor has, in addition to the monetary claim for the varied work, a **parallel** right to claim for extension of time and direct loss and expense.

New Words and Expressions

contentious 诉讼的；有异议的，引起争论的；爱争论的
consequential 间接的；结果的；重要的
payroll 工资单；工资名单
takeoff 起飞；开始；起跳
preliminary 初步的；开始的；预备的
reimburse 偿还；赔偿
recoup 收回；恢复；偿还；扣除
overstate 夸张；夸大的叙述
pinpoint 查明；精确地找到；准确描述
spectrum 光谱；频谱；范围；余象
contemplate 沉思；注视；思忖；预期
superintendent 监督人；负责人；主管；指挥者
prudent 谨慎的；精明的；节俭的
hectic 忙碌的
derogatory 贬损的；不敬的
arduous 努力的；费力的；险峻的
morass 沼泽；困境；乱糟糟的一堆
obsolete 废弃的；老式的
redundant 多余的；累赘的
detrimental 不利的；有害的
pertain 关于；适合
parallel 平行的；类似的，相同的
direct labor costs 直接劳工成本
direct equipment and material costs 直接设备和材料成本
interest claims 利息索赔
construction claims documentation 施工索赔证明材料
costs of delay 误期成本
claims documents backup and record 索赔文件证据及记录

Notes

[1] There are two typical methods of claim calculation on whether the claim is being priced on a pre-performance basis or on an after-the-fact basis. Other direct costs associated with the claim such as field overhead, bond costs, insurance, interest and profit should also be noted on the forms.

有两种典型的索赔计算方式，索赔是在以工程实施之前的定价基础上，或是在以工程实施后的基础上。其他与诸如工地管理费用、保函成本、保险、利息和利润有关的直接成本也应当在索赔表格中注明。

[2] Charges for equipment usage may be based on contract terms, or if not specified in the contract may be based on rental invoices or hourly rates.

设备使用费用可能以合同条款为基础，或者如果没有在合同中规定，则可能以租金发票或者

计时工资为基础。

[3] Further support can be shown by actual costs for additional time and effort spent on meetings and discussions regarding estimating and engineering with respect to the change. Unanticipated additional manpower needed to perform work may also result in additional expenditures for small tools, supplies, consumables or other miscellaneous items that were carried as general conditions.

进一步的证据可以根据就变更工程的估价和工程设计而进行会议和讨论所增加的额外时间和精力的实际成本来支持。未曾料到的其他的为完成工程所需的人工也可以通过小工具、日用品、消耗品或者其他混杂事项的额外支出计入通用费内。

[4] Certain records, such as daily poet logs, can constitute critical evidence in establishing entitlement to a claim. A detailed project log can document levels of manpower, the progress of the work on a particular date, and any problems that the contractor may encounter.

某些记录，如每日项目日志，可能构成索赔资格确立的决定性证据。一份详细的项目日志可以证明劳动力等级、在特殊日期的工程进展，以及承包商可能遭遇的任何问题。

Exercises

I. Translate the following phrases into English.

1. 关键路径法
2. 项目成本增加
3. 横道图表和电子进度表
4. 施工安装图
5. 成本会计记录

II. Translate the following sentences into Chinese.

1. A project log prepared contemporaneously with the work performed will have greater weight as evidence than the verbal testimony of a project manager or foreman months or even years after the events in question.

2. Needless to say, what should be avoided, are personal opinions and derogatory remarks.

3. If this is done meticulously, the subsequent saving in time through search and find, or through spread sheet and database design and use, can be invaluable.

4. Where the scope of work is unclear or should there be a discrepancy in the contract documents, the contractor is automatically entitled to extras.

Claims

Claims play an important part in the everyday life of many engineers. Claims mean different things in different cultures, and attitudes to claims vary widely.

In some environments, a claim is a very natural thing. In those cultures the monthly request for ordinary payment is sometimes referred to as a "claim".

In other cultures a claim is regarded as a declaration of war. It is something that signals a serious dispute. In some cultures you won't submit a claim unless your intention is to **cut off** friendly relations with the receiver.

In this article we use the word "claim" in the most common European sense. It then means a request for additional payment, for whatever reason. Because it is additional, it may be **disputatious**. Most disputes and contractual conflicts are started, or made known, by a claim. But most claims don't lead to disputes. They are settled by **negotiation** between the parties.

In this article the concentration is on disputatious claims, and the claim situation is seen chiefly from the seller's **perspective**.

The **sequence** which this article follows is always claim, claim all you can, **marshal** (arrange) the arguments, and timing.

Always Claim

It is easy to find excuses for not making claims. It is easy to go broke by being **charitable**.

Buyers and consulting engineers dislike claims instinctively. In their opinion sellers always make too many claims and the claims are almost always without merit.

Most of my experience is from the seller side and my opinion is different. I have found that site agents are normally reluctant to submit claims, to the extent that they avoid them at almost any cost. The reasons they give are typically:

- We have such a good climate on site; we won't destroy it by claiming.
- It's such a small claim anyway; it's not worth risking my relationship with the RE.
- The fact is that we are not without blame ourselves; if we claim, they can **hit** us **back** with these arguments.

The above confirms that in the contract administration phase the climate is most important to the buyer. By maintaining a good climate he avoids claims, because the seller wants to maintain the good climate. The seller's reaction is unnecessary, however. In a good climate it's always possible to submit defensible claims without risking the climate.

For the buyer, it may be wise to keep the climate constructive through the whole contract period, including the claims negotiations. This is because claims negotiated in a constructive climate are likely to cost less than if the seller negotiates aggressively. Still, it is quite common for buyers to have started the earlier contract negotiations in an aggressive climate, which always induces a host of claims at a later stage. Then, when the works get near to completion, the buyer realizes that he needs the cooperation of the seller to get a proper result—you cannot force anybody to do his best—and tries to change his mode into constructive.

Sellers often make the opposite mistake. In the beginning the seller needs cooperation more than the buyer. But the nice and constructive contracts negotiator, who can establish the best climate for the contract, cannot be expected to be the fighter that gets the most out of claims in the end.

A claims negotiation concerns compensation for something unexpected that has happened or for extra work. It is a typical case for aggressive negotiation—the profit of one party is the loss of the other.

Thus, it should be noted that different skills are required for a successful contracts negotiator and a successful claims negotiator. This is a **dilemma** (difficult for both parties), because very often the same persons are involved in both situations. And it is a fact that most people are either naturally constructive or naturally aggressive negotiators.

By education, such as reading good books on the subject of negotiations, and by training, most people can however improve their skills as negotiators in all styles.

Let's return to the subject of claims with an example of how it pays to claim all you can.

I was involved at a late stage in a bad contract. We were losing heavily and put in claims which were weak in many cases. We originally hoped for about 10% and ended up with 85%.

Claim All You Can

In another example, in Eastern Europe, the most obvious cause of delay was that the buyer didn't make the site available. So we claimed for extension of time and the buyer had to admit that it was their fault.

This was an industrial plant and it was important to the buyer that the original completion date was kept. So we agreed to accelerate the work to reach the original completion date in spite of the delay of several months. The buyer agreed to pay a compensation for the acceleration.

When the work **got into full swing**, we found that we could accelerate even more. In fact, we were able to complete the works several months before even the original contractual completion date. That made us **eligible** for a bonus for early completion under the contract.

The contract also had an inflation clause. It provided for adjustment of the price in relation to an official index. The wording of the clause based the adjustment on the original contract period, plus any extension of time allowed under the contract. If the seller would delay the work, no compensation would be payable for the inflation during that delay. This clause gave us the opportunity to claim an adjustment of the contract price, based on the change in the index up to the date of the allowed extension. That date was in fact almost a year later than the actual completion date, but that was what the contract stipulated.

So we claimed for extension of time, acceleration, bonus for early completion, and compensation for inflation including the period of extension.

The other party accepted the first three. When it came to the inflation clause the buyer's representative said, "I understand you've got a claim, but I won't **stick my neck out** and sign it. We'll have to take this one to the arbitration court." It was smooth riding through the arbitration.

It might seem unreasonable to the **layman** (the man who does not know) that you should be compensated for inflation in a period after you have finished the work. But the contract said so, and the arbitrators could not award otherwise.

Marshal the Arguments

The first essential is to have the arguments, such as records, diaries, photographs, minutes, letters. Unless there has been diligence (hard job) in keeping records throughout the negotiations before and during the contract, the negotiator will be thrust naked into the **fray** (dispute) after the contract, He needs all the evidence he can secure.

We had a project manager who was an **inveterate** (used to) note-taker. Notes during every meeting who was there, what was discussed, who said what. Notes during every telephone conversation with whom, what discussed. Notes of his own decisions and the reasons for them.

In this case we were subcontractors and a key question was whether we would be entitled to a completion certificate when we finished our work, or only when everybody had completed. The key person on the other side had died and our project manager was on another project half way around the world.

The mood between the parties had become **acrimonious** (bad situation).

The buyer claimed that the matter had never been discussed, but we were able to produce our man's notes of relevant discussions.

It was an example of the importance of keeping records.

Then marshal the facts. As ever, it pays to concentrate on the few arguments which are **irrefutable** (difficult to be answered). Do not be tempted also to offer your weak **planks** (points) —the other side will quickly detect the weakest and start hammering holes.

Presenting the arguments demands a great deal of skill.

If we work out that they owe us 100, we can so easily go into a negotiation thinking of little but that 100. Quickly we find that they are talking only of 20 and that only as a gesture because really we don't need to give you anything the scene is soon set for **strife**. It's going to be an aggressive negotiation, the parties are likely to be **intransigent** (not compromised) long before a solution is reached. We're set for impasse and escalation (hard and bad situation).

A more constructive approach is still capable of yielding higher dividends (profit). Try to do some exploration before getting into heavy bidding and bargaining.

Try in that exploration to have the present issue set in a larger and more positive context—the helicopter view.

Let me say to start with how glad we are that this project has been so successfully completed. Great credit to our respective people and to the way we have cooperated. Anxious to get the present issue out of the way today—important to preserve goodwill—it's a small issue in the context of ten thousand. And so on, leading into a constructive bargaining phase—unless the other party is proving **adamantly** (strongly) aggressive. Marshal the arguments and present them appropriately—preferably in a constructive style.

Timing

Timing applies to the time at which claims are submitted and to the timeliness with which they are defended.

It is never too early to submit a claim.

At an early stage of a contract, the seller is most anxious to be cooperative. This often **manifests** itself in a reluctance (not willing) to make claims. "A claim may ruin the climate". In fact it seldom does. If a claim is defendable, it should be made. It will not affect the climate. If the claim cannot be defended, don't make it.

Substantial claims should be presented as quickly as possible. And a timely and adequate response serves to strengthen the defence.

Small claims are another matter. We can all handle substantial and difficult problems but daily pin-pricks become very irritating (bad). There is a strong case for **holding back** small claims and **bunching** them so that they are only sent say every couple of months.

There is another advantage. The other side is doubtless recognizing claims on us. If each of us waits until we have a parcel of small ones, there is chance to do a deal on the parcels rather than the constant **pitting** of wits over the scraps.

I know a number of cases where claims were submitted very late, at the end of the contract period, but in no case has the buyer refused to answer the claim on formal grounds. In some of these cases every reasonable period after the event giving rise to the claim had expired, but the buyer still agreed to discuss claims, of course, but only because he considered the foundations invalid. It has even happened that (in a FIDIC-type contract) the engineer has refused to consider a claim because of late submission, but the buyer has requested him to disregard **formalities**. This is a good illustration of the fact that the buyer needs a co-operative climate towards the completion of works, more than the seller needs it at that time.

New Words and Phrases

disputatious　爱争论（争辩）的；易引起争论（争辩）的
negotiation　谈判；磋商
perspective　观点；看法
sequence　次序；顺序
marshal　安排；整理
charitable　慈善的；宽厚的
dilemma　（进退两难的）困境；进退维谷
eligible　合格的；符合条件的
layman　外行
fray　争论；辩论；冲突
inveterate　长期形成的；积习很深的
acrimonious　（语言、态度等）刻毒的；讥讽的；苛刻的
irrefutable　无可辩驳的；驳不倒的
plank　板；支持物；基础
strife　冲突；争吵
intransigent　不妥协的；不让步的
adamantly　不动摇地；坚强不屈地
manifest　（事物、现象等）出现；显露
bunch　使成一簇（或一捆）
pit　使相斗；使竞争
formality　礼节；俗套
cut off　中断；中止；切断
hit back　还击
get into full swing　（工作等）全面开展
stick one's neck out　冒风险；招麻烦
hold back　阻止；抑制；扣住；隐瞒

Contractor's Claims

If the contractor considers himself to be entitled to any **extension** of the time for completion and/or any additional payment, under any clause of these conditions or otherwise in connection with the contract, the contractor shall give notice to the engineer, describing the event or circumstance giving rise to the claim. The notice shall be given as soon as practicable, and not later than 28 days after the contractor became aware, or should have become aware, of the event or circumstance.

If the contractor fails to give notice of a claim within such a period of 28 days, the time for completion shall not be extended, the contractor shall not be entitled to **additional payment**, and the employer shall be discharged from all liability in connection with the claim. Otherwise, the following provisions of this **subclause** shall apply.

The contractor shall also submit any other notices which are required by the contract, and supporting particulars for the claim, all as relevant to such event or circumstance.

The contractor shall keep such **contemporary** records as may be necessary to **substantiate** any claim, either on the site or at another location acceptable to the engineer. Without admitting the employer's liability, the engineer may, after receiving any notice under this subclause, monitor the record keeping and/ or instruct the contractor to keep further contemporary records. The contractor shall permit the engineer to inspect all these records, and shall (if instructed) submit copies to the engineer.

Within 42 days after the contractor became aware (or should have become aware) of the event or circumstance giving rise to the claim, or within such other period as may be proposed by the contractor and approved by the engineer, the contractor shall send to the engineer a fully detailed claim which includes full supporting particulars of the basis of the claim and of the extension of time and/or additional payment claimed.

If the event or circumstance giving rise to the claim has a continuing effect:
- This fully detailed claim shall be considered as **interim**.
- The contractor shall send further interim claims at monthly intervals, giving the accumulated delay and/or amount claimed, and such further particulars as the engineer may reasonably requires.
- The contractor shall send a final claim within 28 days after the end of the effects resulting from the event or circumstance, or within such other period as may be proposed by the contractor and approved by the Engineer.

Within 42 days after receiving a claim or any further particulars supporting a previous claim, or within such other period as may be proposed by the engineer and approved by the contractor, the engineer shall respond with approval, or with disproval and detailed comments. He may also request any necessary further particulars, but shall nevertheless give his response on the principles of the claim within such time.

Each payment certificate shall include such amounts for any claim as have been reasonably substantiated as due under the relevant provision of the contract. Unless and until the particulars supplied are sufficient to substantiate the whole of the claim, the contractor shall only be entitled to payment for such part of the claim as he has been able to substantiate.

The engineer shall proceed to agree or determine the extension (if any) of the time for completion (before or after its **expiry**), and/or the additional payment (if any) to which the contractor is entitled under the contract.

The requirements of this subclause are in addition to those of any other subclause which may apply to a claim. If the contractor fails to comply with this or another subclause in relation to any claim, any extension of time and/or additional payment shall take account to the extent (if any) to which the failure has prevented or **prejudiced** proper investigation of the claim, unless the claim is excluded under the second paragraph of this subclause.

New Words and Phrases

extension 延长；延期；扩大；伸展；电话分机
subclause 副条款；分条款
contemporary 同时代的人；同时期的东西
substantiate 证实；使实体化
interim 临时的，暂时的；中间的；间歇的
expiry 满期，逾期；呼气；终结
prejudice 损害；使有偏见
additional payment 附加费用

Part II   Speaking

A: From the commencement of the work until now, we have received 6 claims from you. Today I'd like to hear more explanation on your claims.

B: Firstly, thank you for offering this opportunity to discuss the claim issues. Generally speaking, 3 claims are raised for 25 days of time extension. According to the contract, we should have taken possession of the site on April 10, but in fact we couldn't do so until April 17. One week delay was caused by your failure in **requisitioning the land** for the site area on time.

A: I agree. How about the additional 18 days time extension?

B: Because you delayed issuing your revised layout for the production building for 10 days, our earthwork was held up accordingly. Furthermore, in accordance with the contract, you're required to review and approve our proposal for equipment substitution within 2 weeks. But we received your confirmation on May 2, 22 days after our submission of substitution proposal. It caused 8 days delay of our equipment procurement. You can see that delay of the works was not under our control. It's unfair for us to suffer liquidated damages for 20 days.

A: Do you have **contemporary records** or sufficient evidence to support your claims?

B: Sure. Here are all the necessary documents.

A: Well, I accept these claims and withdraw our **back-charge notice** for liquidated damages then.

B: Thank you for your kind understanding.
A: What's the next claim for?
B: It's for the additional pumps in the boiler house. It should be regarded as a **variation item**, it's not shown in the construction drawings and Bill of Quantities. You have certified the quantities of the installation of the pumps. But concerning the cost of the pumps, we can't agree with each other.
A: I'm sorry to tell you that this claim is not effective because it has already expired. It's mentioned in the Conditions of Contract that the contractor must submit the notice of claim to the engineer within 28 days after the event of the claim arising. But your claim 4 was raised to us 3 days later than the valid time for claims.
B: It's unbelievable.
A: I can do nothing about it. What do the remaining 2 claims refer to?
B: They're about the additional cost for the remedial works resulted from your inappropriate activities in the maintenance period.
A: Oh yes, I remember you have repaired them all. OK, I accept them.

New Words and Phrases

requisition the land   征用土地
contemporary record   同期记录
back-charge notice   扣款通知
variation item   变更项目

Unit 13 Contract Disputes and Arbitration

Part I Reading and Translating

Professional Knowledge Guidance

1. 仲裁（Arbitration）：由于诉讼在解决工程承包合同争议方面存在明显的缺陷，国际工程承包合同的争议，尤其是较大规模项目的施工承包合同争议，双方即使协商和调解不成功，也很少采用诉讼的方式解决。当协商和调解不成时，仲裁是国际工程承包合同争议解决的常用方式。

2. 国际工程承包合同争议解决的仲裁地点，通常有以下三种选择：

1）在工程所在国仲裁，这是比较常见的选择。有些国家规定，承包合同在本国实施，则只准使用本国法律，在本国仲裁，裁决结果要符合本国法律，拒绝其他第三国或国际仲裁机构裁决，这对外国承包商很不利。

2）在被诉方所在国仲裁。

3）在合同中约定的第三国仲裁。

Text

Contract Disputes and Arbitration

Arbitration can be an expeditious and inexpensive method for resolving most disputes arising in the construction industry, but, surprisingly, arbitration is a relatively unfamiliar process to most contractors. An insight into the procedures and techniques of arbitration as well as its relative advantages and disadvantages can be helpful in choosing a **remedy** for a dispute. Though arbitration is not always the best **forum** in which to resolve a dispute, it certainly is one alternative that the contractor should consider.

Arbitration is a simple proceeding voluntarily chosen by parties who want a contract dispute determined by an impartial judge of their own mutual selection, whose decision, based on the merits of the case, they agree in advance to accept as final and binding. [1]

The Agreement to Arbitrate

The first step in any arbitration procedure is the agreement to arbitrate.

This agreement may come in the form of a provision within a construction contractor it may be reached after the dispute arises.

When the construction contract provides for arbitration, the first threshold question is whether the agreement is enforceable. In the over-whelming majority of states agreements to arbitrate future disputes are **enforceable**. However, under certain state laws, agreements to arbitrate all future disputes arising under a construction contract are not enforceable. In such states, if one of the parties to the contract doesn't wish to arbitrate, he may be able to defeat any attempt to arbitrate.

It should be noted that these minority state laws only prevent enforcement of arbitration clauses against unwilling parties: should both parties agree and proceed to arbitrate, all states will uphold and enforce the arbitration decision.

Arbitrate Procedure

The procedures for arbitration may be as varied as the imaginations of the participants. Probably the most frequently used procedure is that set out by the American Arbitration Association (AAA). The AAA is a public service, nonprofit organization whose sole function is to resolve disputes through the use of arbitration. The rules of the Association for the settlement of disputes in the construction industry are particular structured for settlement of disputes in the construction industry. [2]

When an aggrieved party initiates arbitration, he should first give wrote notice to the other party of an intention to arbitrate. The notice should **set forth** a statement of the nature of the dispute and the remedy sought. Simultaneously, the initiating party should file with the regional office of the AAA three copies of the notice to arbitrate, together with a copy of the contract or agreement containing the arbitration provision.

When the regional office of the AAA receives the claim, a panel of arbitrators is selected by the AAA and their names are forwarded to each party. This list will usually consist of 7 to 15 prospective arbitrators. Together with the list, the AAA **forwards** instructions to each party requesting each party to **strike** the names of those arbitrators listed who are for some reason unsatisfactory. No reasons need to be given for striking the name of any arbitrator. Each party is instructed further to list in order of preference those arbitrators who have not been stricken and to return the list to the AAA within 7 days. The respective parties do not exchange their list of preferred arbitrators; instead, the AAA receives the respective lists prepared by the opposing parties. If either party fails to submit his preference as to arbitrators, it is deemed that all members of the panel are acceptable to the party failing to respond. Should any party strike the names of all the arbitrators on the panel, the AAA will request each party to select one name from the panel of arbitrators and submit it to the AAA. Then the AAA will select a third panel member to serve.

Simultaneously with the selection of arbitrators, the AAA requests each party to advise when they will be available to arbitrate the dispute. From the dates commonly preferred by both parties, the AAA selects the arbitration date.

As in courts, parties have the right to conduct discovery as **depositions** or written **interrogatories**. If the opposing party refuses to respond, a court order can be obtained to enforce a response or deposition from the opposing party.

The hearing itself resembles a court proceeding. <u>Witnesses are usually, though not always, requested to swear, and the arbitrators sit as judges.</u> [3] Unlike courts of law, the rules of evidence are relaxed: the panel of arbitrators have broad discretion to allow any testimony they believe relevant or of probative value, including hearsay. The moving party first presents its case and is followed by the opposing party. At the end of the proceeding, each party is allowed a closing statement, which resembles the closing argument in a court of law. The arbitrators will frequently request that the closing argument be made in written form. This procedure allows each party to argue both the facts presented as well as the law each party contends to be applicable. After the hearing has been completed, the arbitrators commonly announce that the record will remain open for a definite period of time to allow either party to submit additional evidence or briefs.

The closing briefs mentioned are very important **in that** they must educate the panel or arbitrators as to the pertinent law. <u>The closing argument in an arbitration is considerably more important to present the applicable law than in a court proceeding where a judge has a working knowledge of the applicable law.</u> [4] Most commonly, the arbitrators sitting on the panel may have little or no understanding of the technical rules of law applicable to the situation.

After all closing arguments, oral or written, are submitted and the record is closed, the arbitrators enter their decision. Under the rules of the AAA, the decision must be entered within 30 days of the closing of the record. The decision of the arbitrators is binding and has the effect of a judgment in a court of law. Should the losing party fail or refuse to comply with the arbitrators' decision, the prevailing party may obtain a court order forcing the losing party to carry out its obligations.

A Comparison with Litigation

Arbitration has the particular advantages and disadvantages when compared with litigation. An important advantage to arbitration is that it can be fast and relatively inexpensive, and the arbitrators can use any type of remedy a court could use. From the time the demand for arbitration is filed until a final decision is rendered, it may take no longer than 5 to 6 months. In comparison, litigation can seldom be completed in a period shorter than 12 months. Another advantage to arbitration is that the expenses of arbitration are relatively small. The initial filing fee for an arbitration claim is $50, and for most claims under $10,000 the total expense will not exceed $400, excluding any private attorney's fees.

Another important consideration is the fact that the arbitrators for construction disputes have technical expertise in the field at issue. As indicated previously, it is common that contractors or architects or engineers will sit on the panel deciding the ease, and certainly in technical construction matters it is helpful to have people with expertise determining the issues. Moreover, in arbitration there is little chance for procedural delays in that there are no court **dockets** to postpone the proceeding. <u>The informality of arbitration is very conducive to getting to the facts of the ease without unnecessary delay or hindrances by technical evidentiary arguments.</u> [5] Conversely, in arbitration, the panel often has little or no legal expertise. As a result, the arbitrators may tend to look to the equitable rather than the legal side of the argument. In short, an individual may be defeated in an arbitration proceeding even though he is **in** technical **compliance with** his legal obligations.

It is impossible to generalize as to whether or not arbitration is preferable to litigation. Certainly, where an expeditious remedy is important, arbitration should be considered. Similarly, where the dispute involves technical issues requiring expertise by the party determining the ease, arbitration has definite advantages. On the other hand, where there are technical rules of law that will determine the issues of the ease, a court of law seems preferable. The contractor should consult his attorney for advice as to whether the contractor is already legally bound to submit disputes to arbitration and as to which alternative is preferable in each individual ease if arbitration is not **mandatory**.

New Words and Phrases

arbitration　仲裁，公断；调停
remedy　补救，救济；赔偿，补偿
forum　论坛，讨论会；法庭
enforceable　可强行的，可强迫的；可实施的
forward　转寄，促进，运送；早的，迅速的，前进的
strike　打，撞击，冲击，罢工，打动；（击打）毁坏，勾销
deposition　罢免，废黜；宣誓作证，证言；存放；沉淀
interrogatory　疑问，质问；（法律）质询（书）；问询的，疑问的
docket　（判决书）摘要，技术表，（待判决的）诉讼事件表
mandatory　强制性的，命令的
set forth　法律上的陈述，阐明，提出
in that　由于，因为
in compliance with　依从……，按照……

Notes

[1] Arbitration is a simple proceeding voluntarily chosen by parties who want a contract dispute determined by an impartial judge of their own mutual selection, whose decision, based on the merits of the case, they agree in advance to accept as final and binding.
依据案件的是非曲直做出裁决，且双方均事先同意接受裁决人的作为最终的和具有约束力的决定。

[2] The rules of the Association for the settlement of disputes in the construction industry are particular structured for settlement of disputes in the construction industry.
仲裁协会解决建设行业争端的规则是特别针对建筑业中的争端而设定的。

[3] Witnesses are usually, though not always, requested to swear, and the arbitrators sit as judges.
通常（虽不总是）要求证人宣誓，且仲裁员像法官一样出席。

[4] The closing argument in an arbitration is considerably more important to present the applicable law than in a court proceeding where a judge has a working knowledge of the applicable law.
仲裁的最后申辩中要提出应当适用的法律，这一点和法庭诉讼程序中也要陈述适用的法律相比，其重要性大得多，因为法庭中的法官由于其职业性，熟知适用的法律。

[5] The informality of arbitration is very conducive to getting to the facts of the ease without un-necessary delay or hindrances by technical evidentiary arguments.
仲裁的非正规性也使它有助于认识到案件的真相，且不会由于法律要求的证据辩论导致不必

要的拖延或阻碍。

Exercises

I. Translate the following phrases into Chinese.

1. contract dispute

2. agreement to arbitrate

3. American Arbitration Association

4. Construction industry

5. panel of arbitrators

II. Translate the following sentences into Chinese.

1. Arbitration can be an expeditious and inexpensive method for resolving most disputes arising in the construction industry, but, surprisingly, arbitration is a relatively unfamiliar process to most contractors.

2. When the construction contract provides for arbitration, the first threshold question is whether the agreement is enforceable. In the over-whelming majority of states agreements to arbitrate future disputes are enforceable.

3. This list will usually consist of 7 to 15 prospective arbitrators. Together with the list, the AAA forwards instructions to each party requesting each party to strike the names of those arbitrators listed who are for some reason unsatisfactory.

4. The initial filing fee for an arbitration claim is $50, and for most claims under $10,000 the total expense will not exceed $400, excluding any private attorney's fees.

5. The contractor should consult his attorney for advice as to whether the contractor is already legally bound to submit disputes to arbitration and as to which alternative is preferable in each individual ease if arbitration is not mandatory.

Resolution of Contract Disputes

Once a contract is reached, a variety of problems may emerge during the course of work. Dispute may arise over quality of work, over responsibility for delays, over appropriate payments due to changed conditions, or a multitude of other considerations. Resolution of contract disputes is an important task for project managers. The mechanism for contract dispute resolution can be specified in the original contract, or less desirably, decided when a dispute arises.

The most **prominent** mechanism for dispute resolution is **adjudication** in a court of law. This process tends to be expensive and time consuming since it involves legal representation and waiting in queues of cases for available court times. Any party to a contract can bring a suit. In adjudication, the dispute is decided by a neutral, the third party with no necessary specialized expertise in the disputed subject. After all, it is not **prerequisite** for judges to be familiar with construction procedures. Legal procedures are highly structured with rigid, formal rules for presentations and fact finding. On the positive side, legal adjudication strives for consistency and predictability of results. The results of previous cases are published and can be used as **precedents** for resolution of new disputes.

Negotiation among the contract parties is a second important **dispute resolution mechanism**. These negotiations can involve the same sorts of concerns and issues as to the original contracts. Negotiation typically doesn't involve third parties such as judges. The negotiation process is usually informal, unstructured and relatively inexpensive. If an agreement is not reached between the parties, then adjudication is a possible remedy.

The third dispute resolution mechanism is the **resort to** arbitration or **mediation** and **conciliation**. In these procedures, the third party serves a central role in the resolution. These outside parties are usually chosen by mutually agreement of the parties involved and well have specialized knowledge of the dispute subject. In arbitration, the third party may make a decision which is **binding** on the participants. In mediation and conciliation, the third party serves only as a facilitator to help the participants reach a mutually acceptable resolution. Like negotiation, these procedures can be informal and unstructured.

Finally, the high cost of adjudication has inspired a series of non-traditional dispute resolution mechanisms that have some of the characteristics of **judicial proceedings**. These mechanisms include:

- Private judging in which the participants hire the third party judge to make a decision.
- Neutral expert fact-finding in which the third party with specialized knowledge makes a recommendation.
- Mini-trial in which legal summaries of the participants' positions are presented to a jury comprised of principles of the affected parties.

Some of these procedures may be court sponsored or required for particular types of disputes.

While these various disputes resolution mechanisms involve varying cost, it is important to note that the most important mechanism for reducing costs and problems in dispute resolution is the reasonableness of the initial contract among the parties as well as the competence of the project manager.

New Words and Phrases

prominent　突起的，凸出的；突出的，显著的，杰出的
adjudication　判决，裁决
prerequisite　先决条件，必要条件，前提
precedent　先例
negotiation　谈判，会谈；磋商，交涉
mediation　调解
conciliation　调和，说服
binding　有约束力的
dispute resolution mechanism　争端解决机制
resort to　诉诸
judicial proceeding　司法程序

Passage B

Construction and Engineering Consultancy

Introduction

Construction and consultancy services play a crucial role in infrastructural development, transfer of technology and achieving socio-economic development objectives. They together constitute one of the largest services sectors of the economy and account for a significant proportion of employment and foreign exchange earnings. In most developed and many developing countries the share of construction in the total GDP (Gross Domestic Product) ranges between 5-7 percent. Trade in construction and consultancy services is primarily through the movement of natural persons (skilled labour and professionals) and commercial presence in the form of FDI (Foreign Direct Investment), joint ventures, etc. With developments in Internet technology and advanced communications systems, there has been an increase in **cross-border trade** in some of these services.

Coverage of Construction and Engineering Consultancy

Construction services encompass a wide range of services including construction work for all types of residential and non-residential buildings; civil engineering, such as construction of highways, railways, power station, bridges and tunnels, waterways and harbours, installation and assembly work of **petrochemical** plants, and all other activities relating to constriction.

Consultancy services related to construction include the preliminary study of a problem, through the development of design concepts, the preparation of a design solution for the preferred option, and the calling and evaluation of tenders, to completion and subsequent maintenance and operation of the above works. The architectural firms provide blueprints and designs for buildings, while engineering firms provide planning, design, construction and management services for building structures, installations, civil engineering works and industrial processes, etc.

Construction, architectural and engineering (consultancy) services are primarily traded through commercial presence, that is, the establishment of foreign affiliates and subsidiaries of foreign companies. International construction services involve movement of unskilled, semi-skilled and skilled workers and professionals to perform a wide range of work, including designing, management and physical construction work. Increasingly, with developments in communication and Internet, cross-border supply is becoming an important component of trade in some of these services.

These include the electronic transmission of designs and blueprints and on-line consulting services. However, given the capital-intensive nature of the services, the requirement of specific skills and technical know-how, which may not be available locally and the strong client-oriented focus of these services, the bulk of trade would continue to take place through commercial presence and the movement of natural persons.

Situation of Global Consultancy

Global trade in engineering consultancy services is highly skill-intensive and depends on a nation's technological capabilities. In the export of consultancy services, many industrialized countries, such as the USA, UK, France, Germany, Denmark, the Netherlands and Japan, have prevalence competition advantages over developing countries. Developed countries are the major exporters of construction, architectural and engineering services, such as overseas expansion of major engineering consulting firms in the United States and Europe, while developing countries provide the major markets. Most consultancy service products and processes are innovated in the developed countries and are licensed by the enterprises based there. The developed countries themselves also specialize in a particular sector; for example, the U. S. firms lead in offshore drilling technologies and power, French firms in nuclear power plant constriction, while Japanese firms in high-speed railroad. Construction services supplied internationally are typically related to large-scale projects, such as airports, harbours and petrochemical plants and are often undertaken by specialized contractors with local subcontracting.

Globally, there is an increasing trend towards integrated engineering and project management services. Construction of manufacturing **turnkey projects** whereby a single company or a **consortium** provides a range of services including design engineering, construction, maintenance, management and financing. The ability to provide a total service package is becoming an important advantage in the international market. This trend has been particularly prominent for highly capital-intensive industries such as oil drilling and refinery, electric power station, high-speed railroad and cement factory etc. where contracts are frequently awarded to engineering contractors on an EPC basis. Most major international companies have the technical, management and financial base to support large turnkey projects. Sometime, project management consultancy engages a contract with client to provide service package for the complex and large project, generally on a "cost plus fee" arrangement.

With liberalization, there has been an increase in privatization and foreign direct investments in infrastructure construction projects. Most of these foreign investments and joint ventures are in the form of **BOO (Build-Operate-Own), BOT (Build-Operate-Transfer), PPP/PFI (Public Private Partnership/ Private Finance Initiative) projects**. Construction and engineering services are primarily traded through commercial presence mainly supplied through FDI in construction projects, joint ventures and foreign presence in the form of BOO, BOT and PPP/PFI operations.

Moreover, global commercial presence depends to a large extent on the ability of the companies to develop financial strength and raise their professional and technological standards to compete with foreign companies from countries. In international market, large construction and infrastructure projects are generally awarded by government and public sector undertakings. Hence, inter-government and **bilateral relations** play an important role in determining the award of the contract.

Developed countries have well-established international banking industry, such as the USA, UK, EU, Australia, Japan and Korea. Black & amp, Veatch Corp, MWH, PB (Parsons Brinckerhoff) and Jacobs are all the leading global engineering, construction and consulting company providing services include scientific and specialty consulting, as well as all aspects of engineering construction, operations and maintenance.

International Consultancy Constraints

Construction, engineering and architectural services are characterized by significant barriers to entry of new firms, especially in the international markets. The selection criteria for consultants and contractors tend to give considerable weight to non-price factors, such as past international experience, size of firms, reputation and affiliations of firms. The selection of consultancy service is usually based on the **expertise**, experience and business relation rather than low price. Many clients have a long-established and satisfactory relationship with their consultants, so they choose those appropriately skilled and experienced consultants to undertake the work. There are many types of project where previous experience can be relied on to establish a fair percentage fee for the required engineering services. Cost estimation may range from use of global historical records and experience. More importantly, most of the decisions which will determine a project's life cycle costs, savings and success are made at the conceptual and design stages. It is therefore important for most clients to select the consultant who will contribute most to the overall success of the project.

Developing countries' firms seemed trapped in **a vicious circle**—many international client reject them for lack of experience; on the other hand, they cannot gain experience if they are not able to secure international contracts. Firms from developed countries are organized on a transnational basis and possess requisite managerial expertise, information systems, and linkages and scale for operating overseas affiliates and joint ventures. Only few enterprises from developing countries are equipped and qualified to do so.

China has been a big international player in the global trade of construction, but architectural and engineering services currently occupies a limited portion of international market share. Chinese companies have also explored the possibilities of joint ventures with foreign construction and engineering consultancy companies whereby Chinese consultants can provide the detailed engineering and development of requisite expertise while the foreign company can provide the conceptual design and process know-how. Chinese construction and engineering companies specialize in specific industries and very few of the companies are currently in a position to undertake all types of engineering and related work, namely, engineering consultancy and turnkey projects.

Engineering Design Offshore Services

With respect to the movement of international professional consultancy, many developed countries are seeking out sources to keep competitive advantages. The outsourcing comprises a wide range of services including design and architecture. Other services that lend themselves to outsourcing continue to be those that are of repetitive and data processing nature, such as Computer Aided Drafting (CAD), mapping and **Geographical Information System (GIS)**.

Engineering design offshore services transfer ideas and designs into functional components that can be manufactured and marketed in a short time period. The common composition of team for engineering design offshore services include design leaders, design engineers, program managers, detailers, technicians, specialist in tooling and die design & manufacturing. The potential manufacturing sectors wherein the offshore consultancy opportunities exist include electronic design automation, automotive and infrastructure.

New Words and Phrases

petrochemical   石化产品；石油化学的，石化制品的
consortium   （为金融活动提供大量资金的）财团；银行团；贷款团
expertise   专门技能，专长；专家意见（或鉴定、评价）；鉴定书
construction and consultancy services   工程咨询服务
cross-border trade   跨境贸易；边境贸易
turnkey project   交钥匙工程；全包工程
BOO（Build-Operate-Own）   建设—拥有—运营
BOT（Build-Operate-Transfer）   建设—运营—移交
PPP/PFI（Public Private Partnership/Private Finance Initiative）project   公私伙伴关系/私人主动融资项目
bilateral relations   双边关系；两国关系
a vicious circle   恶性循环；循环论证
with respect to   至于；关于；就……而言
Geographical Information System（GIS）   地理信息系统

Part II   Speaking

Claim in Request of Flood

(After letters and several **lengthy discussions** related to the claim for floods which occured recently, no agreement has been reached between the site management of the Owner and that of the contractor. As arranged, the owner and the contractor send their respective vice presidents, Mr. Guan, and Mr. Flagg, to the project to **engage in a direct negociation**, to try to **resolve the issue**.)

Flagg: It has been almost a year since I saw you last in Beijing, Mr. Guan. How have you been?

Guan: Pretty busy. Our company has won many contracts all over the world in the past 6 year and I have been flying around to see how the projects are progressing. What about you Mr. Flagg.

Flagg: Busy, just like you. Yet I have been thinking of going to Beijing again. I miss **Beijing Roast Duck**. Ok, coming to our subject today, I hope we can work together to find a solution that is acceptable to both sides.

Guan: That is exactly that I think.

Flagg: I agree that you have **gone through many difficulties** to make this project go smoothly. Personally, I appreciate your effort.

Guan: To be frank with you, we are quite upset by your response. We are really suffered a lot because of two floods experienced on June 12th and 24th—as you can see from our contemporary records and **claim calculations**. I am afraid that if our claim cann't be honoured, it will probably jeopardize the smooth progress of this project.

Flagg: I had studied all the **correspondence** regarding your request for **cost reimbursement** and schedule extension before I came here. It is a fact that you suffered a loss because of the high water level. It is also a fact that the loss is partly due to your inappropriate site activities. I regard what happened. However, you are asking too much.

Guan: I don't think that our request for the cost and time reimbursement is a reasonable one. Anyway, what is your suggestion?

Flagg: Let me talk straight. We allow you two-month schedule extention and a total sum of us 100,000 as compensation for all your losses. This proposal represents our final offer. I believe it is fair and equitable.

Guan: Thank you for your proposal, Mr. Flagg. A two-month schedule extension is acceptable to us; but the cost compensation is far less than the amount claimed, which is based strictly on our actually on your actual loss.

Flagg: Mr. Guan, I have to say we have done our best. To settle this claim, both sides have to make concessions.

Gua: I admit that you have moved a step forward but too small. We have been hoping to have a good working relationship with you. We have been hoping to deliver a successful project to you. We also hope to be rewarded fairly and reasonably. We could, if necessary, pursues this claim **by the way of arbitration**.

Flagg: Well, let me suggest at this point that we increase the compensation to us 150,000. This proposal really dose represent our final offer. If the offer is not acceptable to you, we have no choice but to refer the matter to arbitration.

Guan: **In the spirit of** mutual understanding and our future cooperation, we'll take it, though this amount is far from enough to cover our losses.

Flagg: I support you call for mutual understanding and our future cooperation. I'll draft today's agreement as an **addendum to the contract** and forward it to you for your review and signature.

Guan: Thank you. Your personal presence enabled us to settle this matter. Your cooperation is highly appreciated.

Flagg: With 14 more months available, I believe you have the competence to complete the whole project successfully.

Guan: I also have full confidence that we'll succeed, with your cooperation and assistance. At that time, I will invite you to go to Beijing again.

Flagg: For what?

Guan: Beijing Roast Duck!

New Words and Phrases

correspondence　来往信函
lengthy discussion　长期的谈判
engage in a direct negotiation　进行直接谈判
resolve the issue　解决问题
Beijing Roast Duck　北京烤鸭
go through many difficulties　克服许多的困难
claim calculation　索赔金额
cost reimbursement　成本补偿
by way of arbitration　以仲裁的方式
in the spirit of　本着……的精神
addendum to the contract　合同附属条款

Unit 14
Project Financing

Part I Reading and Translating

Professional Knowledge Guidance

1. 项目融资（Project Financing, PF）：广义是指凡是为了建设一个新项目或者收购一个现有项目及对已有项目进行债务重组所进行的融资，包括传统意义上的公司融资和为大型投资项目而专门组织的项目融资。狭义是一种以项目资产和预期收益为保证的、由项目的各参与方分担风险的、具有无追索权或有限追索权的特殊融资方式。

2. 项目融资模式：

1）BOT（Build—Operate—Transfer）模式，即建设—经营—移交模式，是政府与承包商合作经营工程项目的一种运作模式。该模式是政府将一个基础设施项目的特许权授予承包商，承包商在特许期内负责项目设计、融资、建设和运营，并回收成本、偿还债务、获得盈利，特许期结束后将项目的所有权移交政府。

2）BT（Build—Transfer）模式，即建设—移交模式，是BOT的一种形式。BT模式指政府通过与投资者签订特许协议，引入国外资金或国内民间资金实施专属于政府的基础设施项目建设，项目建成后由政府按协议赎回其项目及有关权利。该模式是由BT项目公司进行融资、投资、设计和施工，竣工验收后交付使用，即业主获得工程使用权，并在一定时间内根据BT合同付清合同款，工程所有权随之转移。

3）PPP（Public—Private Partnership）模式，即公私合营模式，是指政府与私营商签订长期协议，授权私营商代替政府建设、运营或管理公共基础设施并向公众提供公共服务。

Text

Facility Financing

The Financing Problem

Investment in a constructed facility represents a cost in the short term that returns benefits only over the long term use of the facility. Thus, costs occur earlier than the benefits, and owners of facilities must obtain the capital resources to finance the costs of construction. A project cannot proceed without adequate financing, and the cost of providing adequate financing can be quite large. For these reasons, attention to project finance is an important aspect of project management. Finance is also a concern to the other organizations involved in a project such as the general contractor and material suppliers. <u>Unless an owner immediately and completely covers the costs incurred by each participant, these organizations face financing problems of their own.</u>[1]

At a more general level, project finance is only one aspect of the general problem of corporate finance. <u>If numerous projects are considered and financed together, then the net cash flow requirements constitute the corporate financing problem for capital investment.</u>[2] Whether project finance is performed at the project or at the corporate level does not alter the basic financing problem.

In essence, the project finance problem is to obtain funds to bridge the time between making expenditures and obtaining revenues. Based on the conceptual plan, the cost estimate and the construction plan, the cash flow of costs and receipts for a project can be estimated. Normally, this cash flow will involve expenditures in early periods. Covering this negative cash balance in the most beneficial or cost effective fashion is the project finance problem. During planning and design, expenditures of the owner are modest, whereas substantial costs are incurred during construction. Only after the facility is complete do revenues begin. In contrast, a contractor would receive **periodic** payments from the owner as construction proceeds. However, a contractor also may have a negative cash balance due to delays in payment and **retainage** of profits or cost reimbursements on the part of the owner.

Plans considered by owners for facility financing typically have both long and short term aspects. In the long term, sources of **revenue** include sales, grants, and tax revenues. Borrowed funds must be eventually paid back from these other sources. In the short term, a wider variety of financing options exist, including borrowing, grants, corporate investment funds, payment delays and others. Many of these financing options involve the participation of third parties such as banks or **bond underwriters**. For private facilities such as office buildings, it is customary to have completely different financing arrangements during the construction period and during the period of facility use. During the latter period, **mortgage** or loan funds can be secured by the value of the facility itself. Thus, different arrangements of financing options and participants are possible at different stages of a project, so the practice of financial planning is often complicated.

On the other hand, the options for borrowing by contractors to bridge their expenditures and receipts during construction are relatively limited. For small or medium size projects, overdrafts from bank accounts are the most common form of construction financing. Usually, a maximum limit is imposed on an overdraft account by the bank on the basis of expected expenditures and receipts for the duration of construction. <u>Contractors who are engaged in large projects often own substantial assets and can make use of other forms of financing which have lower interest charges than overdraft.</u>[3]

In recent years, there has been growing interest in design-build-operate projects in which owners prescribe functional requirements and a contractor handles financing. Contractors are repaid over a period of time from project revenues or government payments. Eventually, ownership of the facilities is transferred to a government entity. An example of this type of project is the Confederation Bridge to Prince Edward Island in Canada.

We will first consider facility financing from the owner's perspective, with due consideration for its interaction with other organizations involved in a project. Later, we discuss the problems of construction financing which are crucial to the profitability and solvency of construction contractors.

Institutional Arrangements for Facility Financing

Financing arrangements differ sharply by type of owner and by the type of facility construction. As one example, many **municipal** projects are financed in the United States with tax **exempt** bonds for which interest payments to a lender are exempt from income taxes. As a result, tax exempt municipal bonds are available at lower interest charges. Different institutional arrangements have evolved for specific types of facilities and organizations.

A private corporation which plans to undertake large capital projects may use its retained earnings, seek equity partners in the project, issue bonds, offer new stocks in the financial markets, or seek borrowed funds in another fashion. Potential sources of funds would include pension funds, insurance companies, investment trusts, commercial banks and others. Developers who invest in real estate properties for rental purposes have similar sources, plus quasi-governmental corporations such as urban development authorities. Syndicators for investment such as real estate investment trusts (REITs) as well as domestic and foreign pension funds represent relatively new entries to the financial market for building mortgage money. [4]

Public projects may be funded by tax receipts, general revenue bonds, or special bonds with income dedicated to the specified facilities. General revenue bonds would be repaid from general taxes or other revenue sources, while special bonds would be **redeemed** either by special taxes or user fees collected for the project. Grants from higher levels of government are also an important source of funds for state, county, city or other local agencies.

Despite the different sources of borrowed funds, there is a rough equivalence in the actual cost of borrowing money for particular types of projects. Because lenders can participate in many different financial markets, they tend to switch towards loans that return the highest yield for a particular level of risk. As a result, borrowed funds that can be obtained from different sources tend to have very similar costs, including interest charges and issuing costs.

As a general principle, however, the costs of funds for construction will vary inversely with the risk of a loan. Lenders usually require security for a loan represented by a **tangible asset**. If for some reason the borrower cannot repay a loan, then the borrower can take possession of the loan security. To the extent that an asset used as security is of uncertain value, then the lender will demand a greater return and higher interest payments. Loans made for projects under construction represent considerable risk to a financial institution. If a lender acquires an unfinished facility, then it faces the difficult task of reassembling the project team. Moreover, a default on a facility may result if a problem occurs such as foundation problems or anticipated unprofitability of the future facility. As a result of these uncertainties, construction lending for unfinished facilities commands a premium interest charge of several percent compared to mortgage lending for completed facilities. [5]

Financing plans will typically include a reserve amount to cover unforeseen expenses, cost increases or cash flow problems. This reserve can be represented by a special reserve or a contingency amount in the project budget. In the simplest case, this reserve might represent a borrowing agreement with a financial institution to establish a line of credit in case of need. For publicly traded bonds, specific reserve funds administered by a third party may be established. The cost of these reserve funds is the difference between the interest paid to bond holders and the interest received on the reserve funds plus any administrative costs.

Finally, arranging financing may involve a lengthy period of negotiation and review. Particularly for publicly traded bond financing, specific legal requirements in the issue must be met. A typical seven month schedule to issue revenue bonds would include the various steps outlined in Table 14-1. In many cases, the speed in which funds may be obtained will determine a project's financing mechanism.

Table 14-1 Illustrative Process and Timing for Issuing Revenue Bonds

Activities	Time of Activities
Analysis of financial alternatives	Weeks 0-4
Preparation of legal documents	Weeks 1-17
Preparationofdisclosure documents	Weeks 2-20
Forecasts of costs and revenues	Weeks 4-20
Bond Ratings	Weeks 20-23
Bond Marketing	Weeks 21-24
Bond Closing and Receipt of Funds	Weeks 23-26

Example 14-1　Example of financing options

Suppose that you represent a private corporation attempting to arrange financing for a new **headquarters** building. These are several options that might be considered:

(1) **Use corporate equity and retained earnings**. The building could be financed by directly committing corporate resources. In this case, no other institutional parties would be involved in the finance. However, these corporate funds might be too limited to support the full cost of construction.

(2) **Construction loan and long term mortgage**. In this plan, a loan is obtained from a bank or other financial institution to finance the cost of construction. Once the building is complete, a variety of institutions may be approached to supply mortgage or long term funding for the building. This financing plan would involve both short and long term borrowing, and the two periods might involve different lenders. The long term funding would have greater security since the building would then be complete. As a result, more organizations might be interested in providing funds (including pension funds) and the interest charge might be lower. Also, this basic financing plan might be supplemented by other sources such as corporate retained earnings or assistance from a local development agency.

(3) **Lease the building from a third party**. In this option, the corporation would contract to lease space in a headquarters building from a developer. This developer would be responsible for obtaining funding and arranging construction. This plan has the advantage of minimizing the amount of funds borrowed by the corporation. Under terms of the lease contract, the corporation still might have considerable influence over the design of the headquarters building even though the developer was responsible for design and construction.

(4) Initiate a joint venture with local government. In many areas, local governments will help local companies with major new ventures such as a new headquarters. This help might include assistance in assembling property, low interest loans or property tax reductions. In the extreme, local governments may force sale of land through their power of **eminent** domain to assemble necessary plots.

New Words and Phrases

periodic　周期的，定期的

retainage 保留金；暂扣款；定金；尾款
revenue 税收
mortgage 抵押；抵押单，抵押契据；抵押借款，抵押贷款
institutional 制度的，由来已久的
municipal 市政的，市办的；自治城市的
exempt 免除……的责任、义务等；被免除（责任、义务、税收等）的
redeem 赎回，买回；收回，恢复；偿还，付清
headquarter 总部
eminent 杰出的
bound underwriter 债券包销人；债券担保人
tangible asset 有形资产
use corporate equity and retained earning 运用公司权益和留存收益
construction loan and long term mortgage 建设贷款和长期抵押
lease the building from a third party 从第三方租赁建筑物

Notes

[1] Unless an owner immediately and completely covers the costs incurred by each participant, these organizations face financing problems of their own.

除非业主能够及时向各方全额支付所发生的费用，否则项目各参与方也要面对各自的融资问题。

[2] If numerous projects are considered and financed together, then the net cash flow requirements constitute the corporate financing problem for capital investment.

如果同时有多个工程在建，并且都存在融资问题，那么净现金流量需求就构成了资本投资中的融资问题。

[3] Contractors who are engaged in large projects often own substantial assets and can make use of other forms of financing which have lower interest charges than overdraft.

而对于规模较大的项目来说，其承包商通常都拥有相当的资产，并且可以运用其他的融资方式，这些方式的利息费用比账户透支更低。

[4] Syndicators for investment such as real estate investment trusts (REITs) as well as domestic and foreign pension funds represent relatively new entries to the financial market for building mortgage money.

开发项目时，投资联合组织（如房地产投资信托 REITs 及国内外养老基金）代表了一种相对新型的建筑市场融资方式。

[5] As a result of these uncertainties, construction lending for unfinished facilities commands a premium interest charge of several percent compared to mortgage lending for completed facilities.

这些不确定性导致的结果就是，未完工程的贷款与竣工项目的抵押贷款相比需要支付百分之几的额外利息费。

Exercises

I. Translate the following phrases into English.

1. 项目融资
2. 借贷、拨款

3. 投资信托公司

4. 支付不可预见费

5. 最高贷款额度

II. Translate the following sentences into Chinese.

1. Investment in a constructed facility represents a cost in the short term that returns benefits only over the long term use of the facility.

2. In contrast, a contractor would receive periodic payments from the owner as construction proceeds. However, a contractor also may have a negative cash balance due to delays in payment and retainage of profits or cost reimbursements on the part of the owner.

3. In the short term, a wider variety of financing options exist, including borrowing, grants, corporate investment funds, payment delays and others.

4. A private corporation which plans to undertake large capital projects may use its retained earnings, seek equity partners in the project, issue bonds, offer new stocks in the financial markets, or seek borrowed funds in another fashion.

5. The cost of these reserve funds is the difference between the interest paid to bond holders and the interest received on the reserve funds plus any administrative costs.

Project versus Corporate Finance

We have focused so far on problems and concerns at the project level. While this is the appropriate viewpoint for project managers, it is always worth bearing in mind that projects must fit into **broader organizational decisions and structures**. This is particularly true for the problem of project finance, since it is often the case that financing is planned on a **corporate or agency level**, rather than a project level. Accordingly, project managers should be aware of the concerns at this level of decision making.

A construction project is only a portion of the general capital budgeting problem faced by an owner. Unless the project is very large in scope relative to the owner, a particular construction project is only a small portion of the capital budgeting problem. Numerous construction projects may be **lumped** together as a single category in the allocation of investment funds. Construction projects would compete for attention with equipment purchases or other investments in a private corporation.

Financing is usually performed at the corporate level using a mixture of long term corporate debt and retained earnings. A typical set of corporate debt instruments would include the different bonds and notes discussed in this chapter. Variations would typically include different **maturity dates**, different levels of security interests, different **currency denominations**, and, of course, different interest rates.

Grouping projects together for financing influences the type of financing that might be obtained. As noted earlier, small and large projects usually involve different institutional arrangements and financing arrangements. For small projects, the fixed costs of undertaking particular kinds of financing may be **prohibitively** expensive. For example, municipal bonds require fixed costs associated with printing and preparation that do not vary significantly with the size of the issue. By combining numerous small construction projects, different financing arrangements become more practical.

While individual projects may not be considered at the corporate finance level, the problems and analysis procedures described earlier are directly relevant to financial planning for groups of projects and other investments. Thus, the net present values of different financing arrangements can be computed and compared. Since the net present values of different sub-sets of either investments or financing alternatives are additive, each project or finance alternative can be disaggregated for closer attention or aggregated to provide information at a higher decision making level.

Example 14-2: Basic types of repayment schedules for loans.

Coupon bonds are used to obtain loans which involve no payment of principal until the maturity date. By combining loans of different maturities, however, it is possible to achieve almost any pattern of principal repayments. However, the interest rates charged on loans of different maturities will reflect market forces such as forecasts of how interest rates will vary over time. As an example, Table 14-2 illustrates the cash flows of debt service for a series of coupon bonds used to fund a municipal construction project; for simplicity not all years of payments are shown in the table.

Table 14-2 Illustration of a Twenty-five Year Maturity Schedule for Bonds

Date	Maturing Principal	Corresponding Interest Rate	Interest Due	Annual Debt Service
Dec. 1, 1987	$ 1 350 000	5.00%	$ 819 760	$ 819 760
June 1, 1988			894 429	
Dec. 1, 1988	1 450 000	5.25	860 540	3 104 969
June 1, 1989			860 540	
Dec. 1, 1989	1 550 000	5.50	822 480	3 133 020
June 1, 1990			822 480	
Dec. 1, 1990	1 600 000	5.80	779 850	3 152 330
June 1, 1991			779 850	
Dec. 1, 1991	1 700 000	6.00	733 450	3 113 300
June 1, 1992			733 450	
Dec. 1, 1992	1 800 000	6.20	682 450	3 115 900
June 1, 1993			682 450	
Dec. 1, 1993			626 650	3 109 100
⋮	⋮	⋮	⋮	⋮
June 1, 2011				
Dec. 1, 2011	880 000	8.00	68 000	984 000
June 1, 2012			36 000	
Dec. 1, 2012	96 000	8.00	36 000	996 000

In this financing plan, a series of coupon bonds were sold with maturity dates ranging from June 1988 to June 2012. Coupon interest payments on all outstanding bonds were to be paid every six months, on December 1 and June 1 of each year. The interest rate or "coupon rate" was larger on bonds with longer maturities, reflecting an assumption that inflation would increase during this period. The total principal obtained for construction was $ 26, 250, 000 from sale of these bonds. This amount represented the **gross sale** amount before subtracting issuing costs or any sales discounts; the amount available to support construction would be lower. The maturity dates for bonds were selected to require relative high repayment amounts until December 1995, with a declining repayment amount subsequently. By shifting the maturity dates and amounts of bonds, this pattern of repayments could be altered. The initial interest payment (of

$819,760 on December 1, 1987), reflected a payment for only a portion of a six month period since the bonds were issued in late June of 1987.

New Words and Phrases

lump   总共的
prohibitively   禁止的；过高的；过分的
broader organizational decision and structure   董事层和企业组织结构
corporate or agency level   公司层面或政府层面
maturity date   到期日；期满之日
currency denomination   货币种类
coupon bond   附息债券；无法各债券
gross sale   总销售额

Shifting Financial Burdens

The different participants in the construction process have quite distinct perspectives on financing. In the **realm** of project finance, the revenues to one participant represent an expenditure to some other participant. Payment delays from one participant result in a **financial burden** and a **cash flow problem** to other participants. It is common occurrence in construction to reduce financing costs by delaying payments in just this fashion. Shifting payment times does not eliminate financing costs, however, since the financial burden still exists.

Traditionally, many organizations have used payment delays both to shift financing expenses to others and to overcome momentary shortfalls in financial resources. From the owner's perspective, this policy may have short term benefits, but it certainly has long term costs. Since contractors do not have large **capital assets**, they typically do not have large amounts of credit available to cover payment delays. Contractors are also perceived as credit risks in many cases, so loans often require a **premium** interest charge. Contractors faced with large financing problems are likely to add premiums to bids or not bid at all on particular work. For example, A. Maevis noted:

... there were days in New York City when city agencies had trouble attracting bidders; yet contractors were beating on the door to get work from Consolidated Edison, the local utility. Why? First, the city was a **notoriously** slow payer, COs (change orders) years behind, decision process chaotic, and payments made 60 days after close of estimate. Consolidated Edison paid on the 20th of the month for work done to the first of the month. Change orders negotiated and paid within 30 days-60 days. If a decision was needed, it came in 10 days. The number of bids you receive on your projects are one measure of your administrative efficiency. Further, competition is bound to give you the lowest possible construction price.

Even after bids are received and contracts signed, delays in payments may form the basis for a successful claim against an agency on the part of the contractor.

The owner of a constructed facility usually has a better credit rating and can secure loans at a lower borrowing rate, but there are some notable exceptions to this rule, particularly for construction projects in developing countries. Under certain circumstances, it is advisable for the owner to advance periodic payments to the contractor in return for some **concession** in the contract price. This is particularly true for large-scale construction projects with long durations for which financing costs and capital requirements are high. If the owner is willing to advance these amounts to the contractor, the gain in lower financing costs can be shared by both parties through prior agreement.

Unfortunately, the choice of financing during the construction period is often left to the contractor who cannot take advantage of all available options alone. The owner is often shielded from participation through the traditional method of price **quotation for** construction contracts. This practice merely **exacerbates** the problem by excluding the owner from participating in decisions which may reduce the cost of the project.

Under conditions of economic uncertainty, a premium to **hedge the risk** must be added to the estimation of construction cost by both the owner and the contractor. The larger and longer the project is, the greater is the risk. For an **unsophisticated** owner who tries to avoid all risks and to place the financing burdens of construction on the contractor, the contract prices for construction facilities are likely to be increased to reflect the risk premium charged by the contractors. In dealing with small projects with short durations, this practice may be acceptable particularly when the owner lacks any expertise to evaluate the project financing alternatives or the financial stability to adopt innovative financing schemes. However, for large scale projects of long duration, the owner cannot escape the responsibility of participation if it wants to avoid **catastrophes** of run-away costs and expensive litigation. The construction of nuclear power plants in the private sector and the construction of transportation facilities in the public sector offer ample examples of such problems. If the responsibilities of risk sharing among various parties in a construction project can be clearly defined in the planning stage, all parties can be benefited to take advantage of cost saving and early use of the constructed facility.

New Words and Phrases

realm 领域；范围；王国
premium 额外费用
notoriously 臭名昭著地，声名狼藉地
concession 让步，退让；特许（权）；让予，授予
exacerbate 使……加剧（恶化）；使……气恼（发怒）
unsophisticated 不懂世故的；不精细的
catastrophe 大灾难；灾祸；祸患
financial burden 财务负担
cash flow problem 现金流问题
capital assets 固定资产；资本资产
quotation for 报价
hedge the risk 规避风险

Part II Speaking

Pre-Qualification

A: We read the announcement of the Parliament Centre project in yesterday's newspaper. Our company is very interested in this project and hopes to be qualified for tendering. May I get a set of your Pre-qualification Documents?

B: Sure, here you are. Please fill in all the forms in this Pre-qualification Document as required.

A: Let me skim through the document, for the "Company Name", should we fill in the name of our local registered company or our mother company in P. R. C. ?

B: On account of the huge scale and special complicity of this project, I think it would be better to use the name of your mother company instead of the local one.

A: Then, how should I fill in the blank for "Company Address"?

B: You should fill in the address of your mother company first, and write the registered address of your local company in the column of Remarks.

A: How should we deal with the forms regarding **Legal Litigation**?

B: You have to list all the legal cases your company may have been involved in over the last five years, if any.

A: Fortunately our company has not been involved in any legal cases during that time.

B: In that case, you should just fill "No" in the space provided. I'd like to remind you to prepare **certified true copies** of your Business License, Financial Report and **ISO Certificates** for submission.

A: Concerning the financial reports, are the "**Assets & Debts Report**" and "**Profit & Lost Report**" enough for our submission?

B: Yes. Please remember that the financial reports have to be audited by a **CPA**. And if you can provide a certificate from an honorable bank indicating your credit record with them, this will ensure identification of your financial position.

A: Thank you for your help and kind reminders.

New Words and Phrases

Legal Litigation　法律诉讼
certified true copy　经签字确认其真实性的复印件
ISO Certificate　国际标准组织质量认证证书
Assets & Debts Report　资产负债表
Profit & Loss Report　损益表
CPA（Certified Public Accountant）　注册会计师

Unit 15 International Business Negotiations

Part I Reading and Translating

Professional Knowledge Guidance

1. 国际工程商务谈判：在不同国家或地区的国际工程商务活动中，当事人为达成商务交易而进行的信息交流，磋商协议的行为过程。

各国工程建设企业积极在国际工程建设市场承包工程任务，无论是发包方（业主）主导的建设项目，还是承包商主导的分包工程、物资采购、咨询服务等，都要进行商务谈判。由于大型工程项目执行周期长、难度大，涵盖融资设计、设备采购、国外施工等各个环节，诸如 BT（Build-Transfer）建设—移交、BOT（Build-Operate-Transfer）建设—经营—转让或 PPP（Public Private Partnership）项目融资模式等方式还有较为复杂的运营还款阶段，因此在项目开发之初商务谈判处于十分重要地位，只有高度重视商务谈判工作，精心准备，才能达成共赢协议。

2. 国际工程承包：以招投标方式进行，以合同谈判为基础。谈判主要内容：材料，设备品种和规格，数量与价格，技术，劳务价格，工程条件，工期，工程质量和验收。

在国际招标项目中，发包方（业主）通常在签订合同之前将草拟的文本送达中标的承包商征询意见，并安排条款谈判。承包商利用签订合同前的谈判过程，尽最大努力争取符合自身利益的执行条件，既要适当应对业主直接或间接手段的压价，当业主拟修改设计、增加项目或提出更苛刻的设计标准时还要适当增加报价；同时必须争取改善不合理条款，澄清模糊的概念，增加保护自身利益的条款，维护己方的合法权益不受侵害，最大限度地消除合同条款的风险。

Negotiation

Introduction

Negotiation is an art, and negotiation in construction is a high form of that art, since requires the deliberate application of techniques and strategies aimed at a specific goal: the equitable adjustment of an impacted contract based on time and cost. [1] On small changes, the difference in an engineer's (owner's) estimate and those of the contractor are often resolved through the simple verification of prices and computations. Of course, if the engineer's estimate is higher than that of the contractor, the owner is likely to **settle for** the contractor's price without negotiation.

As the dollar or time magnitude of a contract change increases, the likelihood of negotiation is greater and **concurrently**, the gap between engineer's and contractor's estimates likely to widen. At this point the negotiating parties enter the picture, and politics, as well as engineering, **come into play**. In fact, negotiation is sometimes considered a relief from the normal administration of the contract, for it offers both parties the opportunity to **break away** from the daily administrative pressures of the contract. Innovation and personality now come into play.

Each side has particular advantages and disadvantages. The contractor knows his cost exactly, can adjust his prices for maximum revenue and can accept or reject a settlement as so chooses. The owner's representative, the engineer, has a strong advantage in that he **holds the purse strings**. Although there is an obligation to reach a settlement, the engineer is **bound** by procurement rules, regulations and approvals by superiors. He is often caught between trying to keep the contractor content and his superiors happy. Henry Kissinger said that each party has certain requirements and goals—and the art of negotiation is finding out what the other party's goals are and satisfying them. The successful contractor and negotiator is the one that knows how to achieve this goal quickly. Since the contractor has a larger degree of freedom in making his proposal and accepting a settlement, he has a tremendous **asset** in setting the pace and direction of the negotiations.

Preparation and Knowledge

Adequate preparation and familiarity with the job are the two most important items required of the successful negotiator. He can be more aggressive and is less likely to **end up floundering** for defensive comments when confronted with what would otherwise be unfamiliar questions. The contractor wants to **take the offensive** and be as aggressive as possible. Such an attitude, along with knowledge of the work, can be very persuasive and influential.

The successful negotiation of price demands careful and complete preparation. Negotiation without adequate preparation invites failure. Spending sufficient time and effort on analyzing the proposal, gathering pertinent pricing and other data, and formulating a definitive and defensible negotiation position will serve

Unit 15　International Business Negotiations

the negotiator better than any **repertoire** of bargaining table techniques. [2] Adequate preparation enables the negotiator to negotiate th with strength—to take and hold the initiative throughout the negotiation conference and to meet any contingency with confidence, self-respect, and integrity of position.

Preparation for the Negotiation Meeting

Before going into the negotiation meeting, it is important to establish a strategy, the framework from which the topics to be negotiated will be approached. The following points are stressed by the Construction Contract Negotiating guide:

1. Establish Objectives and How They Might Be Obtained
1) Which objectives cannot be **compromised** under any circumstances.
2) Which can be compromised and to which extent.
3) Which ones are expected to be compromised or dropped totally (pie-in-the-sky).

2. Anticipate Position of Your Opponent
1) Is there competition for forward priced changes (can another contractor be given he work)?
2) How bad is the need for the work?
3) Is there time pressure for an agreed price?
4) Are there any regulatory, legal, political and/or public pressure aspects that might affect an agreement?

3. Strategies Should Be Flexible (Plan alternate strategies in case the primary strategy has to be abandoned.)

Proper preparation also means assembling all necessary data and documents that may be required to support the contractor's position in the negotiation **sessions**. Most of this dada probably is already included in the claim document, but additional **substantiation** that might be of assistance—comparison charts, for example—should be brought along to the meeting.

Tactics—Control of the Meeting

The contractor wants to control the tone, pace and atmosphere of negotiations by choosing which items to discuss first, taking the heat off items that are not going well, accepting certain decisions and knowing when to compromise. Some claims are better negotiated by discussing the strongest sections first, to be reassured that no **flaws** or surprises will be **sprung** later to alter the rest of the claim. At other times, weaker portions should be discussed first to explore the attitude of the opposition. Keeping the opposition off balance is an active negotiation tactic that can be used to achieve optimum results. If the owner wants to begin discussions, he should be allowed to talk so long as his attitude is **conciliatory** and the contractor is comfortable with the direction pursued.

Remember, the owner is also trying to maintain control of negotiations. To control communication, the chief negotiator should avoid the defensive **stance**, and keep the negotiating team members quiet: "An **astute** contractor might trick the team members into contradicting each other, or a team member might say something that would upset the teams planned strategy." Control of communications can be maintained by diplomacy and tact. Be punctual, cordial, tolerant and patient. Use clear, simple language and keep

distractions to a minimum.

The contractor should try to maintain the pace of the meeting. The items within a claim can usually be arranged in any number of different logical sequences, so the contractor has a legitimate reason to request changes in topics. When negotiating large and difficult claims, it pays to be deliberate, and to plan and execute alternate strategies and tactics.

"Most contractors realize that, in negotiation, the less specific knowledge the government representatives possess, the more easily their judgment can be influenced. Consequently, during a negotiation the contractor will **pass over** a **vulnerable** point by presenting an abundance of information on the point, seemingly with good intentions, but actually with the aim of misdirecting the negotiator's thinking or by making sweeping generalizations that, in themselves are true, but which are not decisive for the point at hand."[3]

The government negotiator will consistently ask questions of the contractor and make requests for details in order to control the meeting, find **loopholes** and encourage the contractor to make concessions.

Tactics—Large Claims

In large claims, the amounts claimed will usually be negotiated item by item. Early in negotiations, the contractor should ascertain the owner's position on all items, without making commitments, to get an idea where he stands on an overall basis. He should then study the differences to see where more work can be accomplished, and how much work might be needed to get the settlement closer to an acceptable amount. After strengthening is position with additional data, the contractor is ready for a second negotiating session. This time the contractor should make an all-out effort to achieve his goal and begin to ke compromises on individual items. At the conclusion of the second session, the contractor should be approaching his goal and should attempt an overall settlement. If a satisfactory compromise cannot be reached, the negotiation sequence must be repeated until either an agreement or **impasse** is reached.

Even though all points are not won, a strong position is important and should be maintained.

Leave some bargaining room and expect some give and take. Initially, the contractor should request more than he expects to recover. No matter how justified his position, it is the naive contractor who is not prepared to bargain. What it ultimately **boils down to** is the strength of his position: "Within certain limits, at least, negotiation is a matter of 'horse trading'. The extent to which the negotiator or the contractor makes concessions without getting anything **in return** depends upon the relative bargaining positions of the parties."

Other Negotiation Tactics

Sometimes "bargaining table" tactics are necessary to change the pace of a meeting. Take the **adversary** out to lunch; create a less tense environment. As a last resort, use politics. That is go over the negotiator's head to his superiors who might be able to loosen things up, when justified.

If an item has to be **conceded**, do it **graciously** and with a sense of humor. Likewise, if a position is firm—don't back off. Never take a hard position from which you might retreat. If a lowest offer is tendered with the understanding that an appeal will be filed should that offer be rejected, then stick to that position.

There is a time and a place for bargaining tactics, and they should be used with care and discretion.

Other Negotiation Considerations

Getting the owner to the negotiation table can be a **chore** in itself. It is important not to give the owner any excuse to delay the negotiations. The proposal should be as complete as possible and submitted as early as possible. Meet with the owner and negotiate timetable for submission of the proposal and commencement of negotiations. Failure to negotiate can be a cause for breach of contract, so the contractor should stay on top of the owner to be sure he comes to the negotiation table with involved negotiations, the contractor should demand a schedule to insure that discussions remain continuous until a settlement is reached. Loss of **momentum** will do more harm than good when negotiating.

Authority to Negotiate

The contractor should seek the owner's assurance that his negotiator has full authority and will stick with the negotiation without unnecessary interruptions. The contractor should also confirm that the owner will participate or monitor the negotiations so that the whole effort will not be rejected or tossed back for renegotiation at a later date. [4]

Detailed records of the negotiations must be kept, including dates of all meetings cancelled or rescheduled. Meeting **minutes** should be dated, contain the names of all participants, the start-stop times, and as much detail as possible of the business that **transpired** in the meeting. Offers and counter-offers should be confirmed in writing by both parties. The method and schedule of payment should also be firmly established.

Conclusion

Negotiations should be fair and honest. In the long run, it behooves all concerned to attempt to negotiate equitable adjustments, for it keeps alive a spirit of cooperation and mutual respect. Sometimes it is difficult to reach agreements in the face of **valid** differences of opinion, the mass of government procurement rules and the maze of legal precedents that influence owners today. If, after earnest attempts, an agreement cannot be reached and the contractor believes his position is correct, he should implement the contract's "Disputes mechanism or take the matter to court", whichever procedure is appropriate under the contract in question. The government contractor, except in the case of a breach, must of course, exhaust his administrative remedies before seeking judicial to rely on.

New Words and Phrases

negotiation   谈判；转让；顺利的通过
concurrently   同时发生地，共存地，并存地
bind   使受法律（或合同，道义等）约束
asset   宝贵的人（或物），财产
flounder   挣扎，踉跄地走；错乱地做事（或说话）
repertoire   全部技能，所有组成部分
compromise   妥协，让步，互让解决；放弃（利益，原则等）

session 会议，会期，（从事某项活动的）一段时间
substantiation 证实，证明；使具体化，实现；充实，加强
tactic （一个）战术；（一个）策略
flaw 裂隙，裂缝；缺点，缺陷
spring 突然提出（或宣布）
conciliatory 抚慰的；调解的，调和的
stance 姿态，态度
astute 精明的，敏锐的；狡猾的
distraction 精神涣散，心神烦乱
vulnerable 易受伤的，易受攻击弱的
loophole （条文中的）漏洞，空子；逃避的手段
impasse 死路；绝境，僵局
adversary 对手，敌手
concede （退一步）承认，给予，让步
gracious 有礼貌的；宽厚的；谦和的
chore 困难的工作
momentum 势头，力量；要素，契机
minute 备忘录，笔记；[复] 会议记录
transpire 泄露，显露，被人知道；发生
valid 正当的，正确的，有根据的
settle for 无奈接受；勉强同意
come into play 开始活动（或起作用）
break away 逃脱，脱身，脱离
hold the purse strings 掌管金钱财务
end up 结束，告终
take the offensive 进攻，采取攻势
pass over 忽略，省略
boil down to 压缩；归结起来是
in return 作为报答；作为回报

Notes

[1] Negotiation is an art, and negotiation in construction is a high form of that art, since requires the deliberate application of techniques and strategies aimed at a specific goal: the equitable adjustment of an impacted contract based on time and cost.

谈判是一门艺术，而有关施工方面的谈判则是一门更高层次的艺术。因为它要求有目的地运用技巧和策略以达到某一具体的目的，即对一份以时间和费用为基础的谈判所涉及的合同进行合理的调整。

[2] Spending sufficient time and effort on analyzing the proposal, gathering pertinent pricing and other data, and formulating a definitive and defensible negotiation position will serve the negotiator better than any repertoire of bargaining table techniques.

以充足的时间和精力分析建议，收集相关的报价及其他数据，形成一个确定的并颇具防御性

的谈判立场,这些对谈判者来说要比在谈判桌上任何讨价还价的全部技巧更为重要。

[3] "Most contractors realize that, in negotiation, the less specific knowledge the government representatives possess, the more easily their judgment can be influenced. Consequently, during a negotiation the contractor will pass over a vulnerable point by presenting an abundance of information on the point, seemingly with good intentions, but actually with the aim of misdirecting the negotiator's thinking or by making sweeping generalizations that, in themselves are true, but which are not decisive for the point at hand."

"大多数承包商意识到,在谈判中政府代表掌握的专业知识越少,他们的判断便越容易受到影响,从而在谈判过程中,承包商通过列举大量资料来掩饰其弱点,看上去似乎有着良好的愿望,而事实上其目的是为了把谈判者的思路引入歧途,或通过大量的归纳总结来掩饰其弱点,虽然这些归纳本身是正确的,但它们并不对所讨论的问题产生决定性作用。"

[4] The contractor should seek the owner's assurance that his negotiator has full authority and will stick with the negotiation without unnecessary interruptions. The contractor should also confirm that the owner will participate or monitor the negotiations so that the whole effort will not be rejected or tossed back for renegotiation at a later date.

承包商应要求业主确保给予谈判代表以充分的权利,并坚持谈判,而不要无故中止谈判。承包商还应确保业主将参加或监督谈判的进行,从而使所有的努力不会在后期被拒绝或重新谈判。

Exercises

I. Translate the following phrases into English.
1. 有关施工方面的谈判
2. 策略应灵活机动
3. 谈判的控制权
4. 谈判的授权
5. 合同的"争端"机制

II. Translate the following sentences into Chinese.
1. The owner's representative, the engineer, has a strong advantage in that he holds the purse strings.
2. He can be more aggressive and is less likely to end up floundering for defensive comments when confronted with what would otherwise be unfamiliar questions.
3. If a lowest offer is tendered with the understanding that an appeal will be filed should that offer be rejected, then stick to that position.
4. Sometimes it is difficult to reach agreement in the face of valid differences of opinion, the mass of government procurement rules and the maze of legal precedents that influence owners today.

Construction Negotiation Strategies and Skills

Introduction

With high competitiveness of construction environment, construction projects have become increasingly complex, where the parties involved often have conflicting objectives. Therefore negotiation can be complicated but often present important opportunities and risks for the various parties involved. First, negotiation is a very important mechanism for arranging construction contracts. Second, as a general rule, **exogenous** factors such as the history of a contractor and the general economic climate in the construction industry will determine the results of negotiations. However, the skill of a negotiator can affect the possibility of reaching an agreement, the profitability of the project, the scope of any eventual disputes, and the possibility for additional work among the participants. Even after a contract is awarded on the basis of competitive bidding, there are many occasions in which subsequent negotiations are required as conditions chang over time. Thus, negotiations are an extremely important task for many project managers.

Negotiation in Construction Management

The successful delivery of a project requires the full **collaboration** of all concerned parties, so that the time, costs, resources, and objectives of a project can be **coordinated**. Therefore, negotiation has been a daily routine for construction project managers. Construction project managers seem to learn negotiating skills only through experience and observation Therefore, practical negotiation **methodologies** may be useful for the construction industry in enabling project managers to handle negotiations more productively. For example, negotiation on work contracts can involve issues such as completion date, arbitration procedures, special work item compensation, **contingency** allowances as well as the overall price.

Construction material procurement is a key business where negotiation is commonly required to reach final contractual agreement. The cost and time involved in negotiation mean that contractors must limit the number of prospective suppliers they negotiate with, and also the number of options included in negotiations. A cheap and efficient negotiation method would allow the exploration of more prospective suppliers and options.

Among many alternative dispute resolution tactics, such as negotiation and mediation, negotiation has gained popularity as a method to **remedy** the shortcomings of litigation. Not only are the costs and times of court claims avoided but also the involved parties have more control over the negotiation outcomes in a less hostile environment.

Negotiation strategies

Negotiations involve each party using the strategy of predicting the **bottom line** of the other presenting an offer that maximizes their own benefit. Negotiation consists of discussions between two or more parties around specific issues for the purpose of reaching a mutually satisfactory agreement. Traditionally, negotiation has been seen as **adversarial** or **confrontational**, e. g. , talk tough and see how much you can get this negative attitude to negotiation is deeply **embedded** in many cultures. Most books and courses on negotiation focus on the adversarial relationship modeled after project's commencement and hostile competitions of awarding.

The best strategy for negotiation is obtaining a **win-win** outcome. Successful negotiators do try to "win at all costs". Win-win negotiating is an approach to negotiating that stresses common interests and goals. By working together, parties can seek creative solutions and reach decisions in which all parties can win.

Because each negotiator has different preferences regarding each negotiable issue and option, the strategy is to make **tradeoffs** accordingly and eve a higher satisfaction level. Most smart negotiators, such as excellent leaders and decision makers believe that the key to negotiation success is quite straightforward: Obtain the trust and confidence of partners and collaborators. However, we must keep in mind that sometimes negotiations are actually commercial battles or wars, opponents usually play win or lose games. The general rules should be complied with as follows:

Confidence

Negotiation is interactive and involves relationships, confidence is the value showed to be axis for a long term business relationship. It is important when we need the consent of others to achieve our ends, when we can meet our ends better by involving others, our confidence will our credits. Do a body check to make sure your words match your nonverbal **gestures**. Otherwise, you won't be taken seriously.

Gratitude

The action of appreciating others' help, suggestions and contributions showed to be important for the willingness of collaborators to want to keep contributing in future projects. It is critical to consider the impact of the spiritual values and reference practices for long term business relationships and their consequence in the economic performance of the organizations. Atmosphere of trust reduces the time required to create win-win outcomes. Cooperativeness attitude eliminates ill feelings and creates good will and outcome.

Fairness

The win-win attitude among those working in the same project demonstrated to have a positive impact even when projects were not successful in the end. On the other hand, the attitude of trying to take the credit for the work of others had a very negative impact to the outcome of the negotiation.

Transparency

To act transparently in a negotiation process regarding the positions of the parties had a positive impact on building confidence. A negotiator of well prepared and knowledgeable in the relevant field of negotiation **in question** will be much helpful to advance progress. The possibility of negotiating failures highlights the importance of strategy with respect to revealing information. Strategic information is something you should only give away **parsimoniously** and then when you some information back.

Integrity

The act of trying to circumvent had a very negative impact in the negotiation process and it was not accepted by the decision makers. Attitudes like being friendly and empathic will be demonstrated through high integrity and socially intelligent, although we indeed need to do it sometime when opponent change his credit. However, being kept up to date via copies of e-mails, or actualized about the process of the negotiation by partners or collaborators, had a very positive pact in inspiring trust.

Negotiation skills

Understanding yourself

Probably the most important skill for an effective negotiator is a clear understanding of oneself with a particular conflict in mind, answer the following questions about yourself as honestly as you can and prepare a brief paragraph describing yourself in a negotiation. Select a partner and tell him.

- What are my strengths limitations?
- Am I a good listener?
- Where am I psychologically vulnerable? Emotionally vulnerable?
- What are my prejudices and biases?
- What kind of climate do I create in negotiations?
- What are my needs during negotiation?

Defining outcomes

A second key skill for effective negotiating is to define your own "bottom line", i. e., least acceptable outcome for you. Using your sample conflict (or another example), if determine your best outcome and your least acceptable outcome. You may wish to speculate on the same questions from the other party's point of view. In conducting negotiations between two parties, each side will have a series of objectives and constraints. The overall objective of each party is to obtain the most favorable, acceptable agreement.

In light of these **tactical** problems, it is often beneficial to all parties to adopt objective standards in determining appropriate contract provisions. These standards would prescribe a particular agreement or a method to arrive at appropriate values in a negotiation. Objective standards can be derived from numerous sources, including market values, precedent, professional standards, what a court would decide, etc. By using objective criteria of this sort, personalities and disruptive negotiating tactics do not become impediments to reaching mutual, beneficial agreements.

As for two parties, one issue negotiation illustrates this fundamental point. With different constraints, it might be impossible to reach an agreement. Of course, the two parties typically do not know at the beginning of negotiations if agreements will be possible. But it is quite important for each party to the negotiation to have a sense of their own reservation price, such as the owner's minimum selling price or the buyers maximum purchase price within both parties acceptable range. This reservation price is equal to the value of the best alternative to a negotiated agreement.

Understanding positions and interests

A key technique in negotiation is to understand the difference between positions and interests, thus going beyond position to determine the underlying interests. A position is an option that one party is committed to as a solution to the conflict. An interest is the concerns, needs, and/or desires underlying the conflict, i. e., why the conflict is being raised. It is especially important to understand your best alternative to a negotiated agreement.

Silence is Golden

When the other person is a talker and you want to learn as much as you can without making any type of commitment, saying nothing and letting the other person do the talking may be the best tactic. This is also a good choice when someone says something angry, attacking or **outrageous**. If you say nothing, there isn't anything for the other person to counter. Silence can work wonders in a negotiation session. It effectively keeps you from talking too much, and may offer the other party the opportunity to express feelings on a particular problems or issue.

Unit 15 International Business Negotiations

Higher Authority

The tactic of higher authority works for either person in a negotiation. Sometimes you cannot get a situation resolved by working with a particular person. Perhaps that person has decided not to comply with your request or they may not have the authority to do so. So, you go to a higher authority to obtain a satisfactory outcome on the other hand, lacking a final say in a situation can create a very powerful position for the other person, since it provides him an opportunity to take your request to someone at a higher level in the organization.

Perspective on Negotiation Outcome

With additional issues, negotiations become more complex both in procedure and in result. With respect to procedure, the sequence in which issues are defined or considered can be very important. For example, negotiations may proceed on an issue-by-issue basis, and the outcome may depend upon the exact sequence of issues considered. Alternatively, the parties may proceed by proposing complete agreement packages and then proceed to compare packages. With respect to outcomes, the possibility of the parties having different valuations or weights on particular issues arises. In this circumstance, it is possible to trade off the outcomes on different issues to the benefit of both parties. By yielding on an issue of low value to himself but high value to the other party, concessions on other issues may be obtained. Poor negotiating strategies adopted by one or the other party may also preclude an agreement even with the existence of a feasible agreement range.

New Words and Phrases

exogenous   外成的，外因的
collaboration   合作，协作；通敌，勾结
coordinate   使协调，使调和
methodology   （从事某一活动的）一套方法；方法学；方法论
contingency   意外事故，偶发事件；可能性，偶然性
remedy   治疗法；补救办法；纠正办法；改正，纠正，改进；补救；治疗
adversarial   敌手的，对手的，对抗（性）的
confrontational   挑衅的；对抗的
embedded   植入的，深入的，内含的
win-win   双赢的，互惠互利的
tradeoff   （公平）交易，折中，权衡
gratitude   感激，感谢；感激的样子
gesture   手势，姿态；做手势，做姿态
parsimoniously   极度俭省地，吝啬地
tactical   战术的；策略上的；巧妙设计的；有谋略的
outrageous   粗暴的；无法容忍的；反常的；令人惊讶的
bottom line   概要，账本底线
in question   正被谈论的，正在考虑的；有关的
in light of   鉴于；根据；考虑到

Passage B

Negotiation Simulation: An Example

This construction negotiation game simulates a contract negotiation between a utility, "CMG Gas" and a design/construct firm, "Pipeline Constructors, inc." . The negotiation involves only two parties but multiple issues. Participants in the game are assigned to represent one party or the other and to negotiate with a designated partner. In a class setting, numerous negotiating partners are created. The following overview from the CMG Gas participants' instructions describes the setting for the game:

CMG Gas has the opportunity to provide natural gas to an automobile factory under construction. Service will require a new sixteen mile pipeline through farms and light forest. The **terrain** is hilly with moderate slopes, and equipment access is relatively good. The pipeline is be buried three feet deep. Construction of the pipeline itself will be contracted to a qualified design/construction firm, while required compression stations and **ancillary work** will be done by CMG Gas. As project manager for CMG Gas, you are about to enter negotiations with a local contractor, "Pipeline Constructors, inc." This firm is the only local contractor qualified to handle such a large project. If a suitable contract agreement cannot be reached, then you will have to break off negotiations soon and turn to another company.

The Pipeline Constructors, Inc, instructions offers a similar overview.

To focus the negotiations, the issues to be decided in the contract are already defined:

- **Duration.** The final contract must specify a required completion date.
- **Penalty for late completion.** The final contract may include a daily penalty for late project completion on the part of the contractor.
- **Bonus for Early Completion.** The final contract may include a daily bonus for early project completion.
- **Report format.** Contractor progress reports will either conform to the traditional CMG Gas format or to a new format proposed by the state.
- **Frequency of progress reports.** Progress reports can be required daily, weekly, bi-weekly or monthly.
- **Conform to pending legislation regarding pipeline marking.** State legislation is pending to require special markings and drawings for pipelines. The parties have to decide whether to conform to this pending legislation.
- **Contract type.** The construction contract may be a flat fee, a cost plus a percentage profit, or a guaranteed maximum with cost plus a percentage profit below the maximum.
- **Amount of flat fee.** If the contract is a flat fee, the dollar amount must be specified.
- **Percentage of profit.** If the contract involves a percentage profit, then the percentage must be agreed upon.
- **CMG Gas Clerk on Site.** The contract may specify that a CMG Gas Clerk may be on site and have access to all accounts or that only progress reports are made by Pipeline Constructors, Inc.
- **Penalty for late starting date.** CMG Gas is responsible for obtaining right-of-way agreements for the

new pipeline. The parties may agree to a daily penalty if CMG Gas cannot obtain these agreements.

A final contract requires an agreement on each of these issues, represented on a form signed by both negotiators.

As a further aid, each participant is provided with additional information and a scoring system to indicate the relative desirability of different contract agreements. Additional information includes items such as estimated construction cost and expected duration as well as company policies such as desired reporting formats or work arrangements. This information may be revealed or withheld from the other party depending upon an individual's negotiating strategy. The numerical scoring system includes point totals for different agreements on specific issues, including interactions among the various issues. For example, the amount of points received by Pipeline Constructors, Inc. for a bonus for early completion increases as the completion date become later. An earlier completion becomes more likely with a later completion date, and hence the probability of receiving a bonus increases, so the resulting point total likewise increases.

The two firms have differing perceptions of the desirability of different agreements. In some cases, their views will be directly conflicting. For example, increases in a flat fee imply greater profits for Pipeline Constructors, Inc. and greater costs for CMG Gas. In some cases, one party may feel strongly about a particular issue, whereas the other is not particularly concerned. For example, CMG Gas may want a clerk on site, while Pipeline Constructors, Inc. may not care. As described in the previous section, these differences in the evaluation of an issue provide opportunities for negotiators. By conceding an unimportant issue to the other party, a negotiator may trade for progress on an issue that is more important to his or her firm. Examples of instructions to the negotiators appear below.

Instructions to the Pipelines Constructors, Inc. Representative

After examining the project site, your company's estimators are convinced that the project can be completed in thirty-six weeks. In bargaining for the duration, keep two things in mind; the longer past thirty-six weeks the contract duration is, the more money that can be made off, the bonuses for being early and the chances of being late are reduced. That reduces the risk of paying a "penalty for lateness".

Throughout the project the gas company will want progress reports. These reports take time to compile and therefore the fewer you need to submit, the better. In addition, State law dictates that the required standard report be used unless the contractor and the owner agree otherwise. These standard reports are even more time consuming to produce than more traditional reports.

The state legislature is considering a law that requires accurate drawings and markers of all pipelines by all utilities. You would prefer not to conform to this uncertain set of requirements, but this is negotiable.

What type of contract and the amount your company will be paid are two of the most important issues in negotiations. In the flat Fee contract, your company will receive an agreed amount from CMG Gas. Therefore, when there are any delay or cost overruns, it will be the full responsibility of your company, with this type of contract, your company assumes all the risk and will in turn want a higher price. Your estimators believe a cost and contingency amount of 4,500,000 dollars. You would like a higher fee, of course.

With the cost plus contract, the risk is shared by the gas company and your company. With this type of contract, your company will bill CMG Gas for all of its costs, plus a specified percentage of those costs. In this case, cost overruns will be paid by the gas company. Not only does the percentage above cost have to be decided upon but also whether or not your company will allow a field clerk from the gas company to be at the job site to monitor reported costs. Whether or not he is around is of no concern to your company since its policy is not to inflate costs, this point can be used as a bargaining weapon.

Finally, your company is worried whether the gas company wills obtain the land rights to lay the pipe. Therefore, you should demand a penalty for the potential delay of the project starting date.

Instructions to the CMG Gas Company Representative

In order to satisfy the auto manufacturer, the pipeline must be completed in forty weeks. An earlier completion date will not result in receiving revenue any earlier. Thus, the only reason to bargain for shorter duration is to feel safer about having the project done on time. If the project does exceed the forty week maximum, a penalty will have to be paid to the auto manufacturer. Consequently, if the project exceeds the agreed upon duration, the contractor should pay you a penalty. The penalty for late completion might be related to the project duration. For example, if the duration is agreed to be thirty-six weeks, then the penalty for being late need not be so severe. Also, it is normal that the contractor get a bonus for early completion. Of course, completion before forty weeks doesn't yield any benefit other than your own peace of mind. Try to keep the early bonus as low as possible.

Throughout the project you will want progress reports. The more often these reports are received, the better to monitor the progress. State law dictates that the required standard report be used unless the contractor and the owner agree otherwise. These reports are very detailed and time consuming to review. You would prefer to use the traditional CMG Gas reports.

The state legislature is considering a law that requires accurate drawings and markers of all pipelines by all utilities. For this project it will cost an additional \$250,000 to do this now, or \$750,000 to do this when the law is passed.

One of the most important issues is the type of contract, and the amount of be paid. The flat fee contract means that CMG Gas will pay the contractor a set amount. Therefore, when there are delays and cost overruns, the contractor assumes full responsibility for the individual costs. However, this **evasion** of risk has to be paid for and results in a higher price. If flat fee is chosen, only the contract price is to be determined. Your company's estimators have determined that the project should cost about \$5,000,000.

The cost plus percent contract may be cheaper, but the risk is shared. With this type of contract, the contractor will bill the gas company for all costs, plus a specified percentage of those costs. In this case, cost overruns will be paid by the gas company. If this type of contract is chosen, not only must the profit percentage be chosen, but also whether or not a gas company representative will be allowed on site all of the time acting as a field clerk, to ensure that a proper amount of material and labor is billed. The usual percentage agreed upon is about ten percent.

Contractors also have a concern whether or not they will receive a penalty if the gas right-of-way is not obtained in time to start the project. In this case, CMG Gas has already secured the right-of-ways. But, if the penalty is too high, this is a dangerous precedent for future negotiations. However, you might try to use this as a bargaining tool.

Example 15-1: An example of a negotiated contract

A typical contract resulting from a simulation of the negotiation between CMG Gas and Pipeline

Constructors, Inc. appears in Table 15-1. An agreement with respect to each pre-defined issue is included, and the resulting contract signed by both negotiators.

Table 15-1 Example of a Negotiated Contract between CMG Gas and Pipeline Constructors, Inc

Duration	38 weeks
Penalty for Late Completion	$ 6,800 per day
Bonus for Early Completion	$ 0 per day
Report Format	traditional CMG form
Frequency of Progress Reports	weekly
Conform to Pending Pipeline Marking Legislation	yes
Contract Type	flat fee
Amount of Flat Fee	$ 5,050,000
Percentage of Profit	Not applicable
CMG Gas Clerk on Site	yes
Penalty for Late Starting Date	$ 3,000 per day

Signed:

    CMG Gas
    Representative

    Pipeline Constructors
    Inc

New Words and Phrases

terrain 地形；地势；领域
evasion 逃避；回避；借口
ancillary work 辅助作业；辅助工作
frequency of progress reports 工期延误赔偿
penalty for late completion 提前完工奖
percentage of profit 利润率
amount of flat fee 固定费用额度
penalty for late starting date 开工日拖延罚款

Part II Speaking

Negotiation on a Joint Venture Agreement

(After getting confirmation from the head office, Mr. Bian invites Mr. Daly again for a specific discussion on a joint venture agreement.)

Bian: Now, Mr. Daly, we were talking last time about your idea on forming a joint venture for the Morpan Project. Our head office agrees to your proposal and I am authorized to discuss it.

Daly: That's very good news, Mr. Bian. Do you have something specific in mind?

Bian: First, we have to make clear our purpose in this cooperation. That is, both sides agree to jointly prepare and submit a bid for the Morpan Project.

Daly: How much fund would you be prepared to provide for this purpose?

Bian: Are there any regulations regarding the foreign party's share in a joint venture in this country?

Daly: No, not really, but as a general practice, the leading company shall be the one which provides the most fund.

Bian: We'd like to act as the leader of the joint venture and lay out more than half of all the required fund for it, say, 55%.

Daly: That includes cash, construction equipment and other temporary facilities, if I understand correctly, Mr. Bian?

Bian: Of course.

Daly: I suppose you will provide the equipment and facilities used on your Morpan Project. How do we arrive at the true value of them?

Bian: That's a very good question. We could ascertain such values through joint assessment. In order to have an **impartial assessment**, we might also invite a third party to attend, if necessary.

Daly: That's good. So, we will provide 45% of the fund. I think I should be frank with you. We can provide the fund in local currency only, as we don't have **foreign currencies**.

Bian: Accordingly, you will share the profit, if any, in local currency only, too. The **exchange rate** for **currency conversion** will be the same as stated in the Owner's bidding documents.

Daly: I agree. All the profits, losses and liabilities arising out of the contract shall be shared out between us in the same proportion as our respective fund contributions.

Bian: That's the basis of our agreement.

Daly: How about the management of the joint venture?

Bian: I am thinking of establishing the **Joint Venture Executive Committee** as the highest authority to decide on the general policy and to deal with such important matters as the appointment of the general site manager and approval of the financial statements.

Daly: What about the appointment of the chairman of the committee?

Bian: It's sensible to say that the chairman shall be appointed by the leading company.

Daly: What are the general responsibilities of each party during the execution of the project if we win the contract?

Bian: I haven't thought of that. Considering you are a local company with good connections, I would suggest that you are responsible for recruiting and administering the local labour and dealing with the relevant departments in **external affairs**.

Daly: Not only that, if we are in charge of purchasing the materials and equipment, I am sure we will do a good job, too. We know the market well.

Bian: Why not leave this to our next talk, Mr. Daly?

Daly: All right. I do say that we've had **an extremely fruitful discussion** today.

Bian: Yes, we know each other's position and have **agreed on** a number of points. Could we meet again, Mr. Daly, to discuss other aspects for our joint venture agreement next week? I'd like to have a visit to your company, if possible.

Daly: That's what I am thinking. Let's have our next discussion in my company so that you could gain a

better understanding of it at the same time. I will call you to confirm the date for our discussion.
Bian: A good idea. Thank you.

New Words and Phrases

impartial assessment   公正的估价
foreign currency   外币
exchange rate   汇率，兑换率
currency conversion   货币兑换
Joint Venture Executive Committee   联营体执行委员会
extern affair   对外事务
an extremely fruitful discussion   极富有成果的商谈
agree on   就……达成一致意见

参 考 文 献

[1] Project Management Institute. A guide to the project management body of knowledge (PMBOK®Guide) [M]. 6th ed. New York：Project Management Institute, 2017.

[2] Richard H Clough, Glenn A Sears, KeokiSears S. Construction project management [M]. 5th ed. New York：John Wiley & Sons, Inc., 2008.

[3] 翰觉克森. 建设项目管理 [M]. 徐勇戈, 曹吉鸣, 等译. 北京：高等教育出版社, 2005.

[4] OGC. Managing Successful Projects with PRINCE2 [M]. Londan：Stationery Office Books (TSO), 2009.

[5] Chris T Hendrickson, Tung Au. Project management for construction [M]. New Jersey：Prentice Hall College Division, 1989.

[6] Michael E Staten, Anthony Yezer. Project management [M]. Dordrecht：Kluwer Academic Publishers, 2004.

[7] 徐勇戈. 工程管理专业英语 [M]. 北京：中国建筑工业出版社, 2013.

[8] B W. Totterdill FIDIC users' guide：A practical guide to the 1999 red book [M]. London：Thomas Telford Publishing, 2001.

[9] 杨云会. 建筑工程管理专业英语 [M]. 北京：北京大学出版社, 2013.

[10] 柳立生. 工程管理专业英语 [M]. 武汉：武汉理工大学出版社, 2015.

[11] 周可荣. 国际工程管理专业英语阅读选编 [M]. 北京：中国建筑工业出版社, 2005.

[12] Hacket M, Robinson I. Pre-contract practice and contract administration for the building team [M]. Oxford：Blackwell Publishing, 2003.

[13] Frederick E Gould. Construction project management [M]. Beijing：China Architecture & Building Press, 2008.

[14] McNeil Stokes. Construction law in contractor's language [M]. New York：McGraw Hill Book Company, 1990.

[15] Brad Hardin. BIM and construction management [M]. New York：Wiley, 2009.

[16] Bill Scott, Bertil Billing. Negotiating skills in engineering and construction [M]. London：Thomas Telford, 1990.

[17] 张水波. 工程管理专业 [M]. 北京：中国建筑工业出版社, 2007.

[18] Paul Levin. Claims and Changes [M]. Cambridge：WPL Associate, 1978.

[19] 韩英爱, 刘茉. 工程项目管理 [M]. 北京：机械工业出版社, 2014.

[20] 全国一级建造师执业资格考试用书编写委员会. 建设工程项目管理 [M]. 北京：中国建筑工业出版社, 2017.

[21] 吴之昕, 张珺. 工程承包实用英语会话 [M]. 北京：中国建筑工业出版社, 2003.

[22] 张水波, 刘英. 国际工程管理实用英语口语——承包工程在国外 [M]. 北京：中国建筑工业出版社, 1997.